BUREAU FOR PARANORMAL RESEARCH AND DEFENSE

The Dead

Created by Mike Mignola

ABE SAPIEN

An amphibious man discovered in a long-forgotten subbasement beneath a Washington, D.C. hospital sealed inside a primitive stasis chamber. All indications suggest a previous life, dating back to the Civil War—an unfolding mystery for Abe.

LIZ SHERMAN

A fire-starter since the age of 11, when she accidentally burned her entire family to death. She has been a ward of the B.P.R.D. since then, learning to control her pyrokinetic abilities and cope with the trauma those abilities have wrought.

ROGER

A homunculus made from human blood and herbs. Discovered in Romania, Roger was first brought to life by Liz's pyrokinetic touch. Whether or not he is actually alive may be up for debate, but his child-like love of that life is not.

JOHANN KRAUS

A medium whose physical form was destroyed while his ectoplasmic projection was out-of-body. That essence now resides in a containment suit. A psychic empath, Johann can create temporary forms for the dead to speak to the living.

DR. KATE CORRIGAN

A former professor at New York University, an authority on folklore and occult history. Dr. Corrigan has been a B.P.R.D. consultant for over 10 years, now serving as special liaison to the a

MIKE MIGNOLA'S

B.P.R.D.™

THE DEAD

Story by
MIKE MIGNOLA and JOHN ARCUDI

Art by
GUY DAVIS

Colors by
DAVE STEWART

Letters by
CLEM ROBINS

Editor
SCOTT ALLIE

Assistant Editors
MATT DRYER and DAVE MARSHALL

Collection Designer
AMY ARENDTS

Publisher
MIKE RICHARDSON

DARK HORSE BOOKS™

NEIL HANKERSON ♦ *executive vice president*

TOM WEDDLE ♦ *vice president of finance*

RANDY STRADLEY ♦ *vice president of publishing*

CHRIS WARNER ♦ *senior books editor*

ANITA NELSON ♦ *vice president of sales & marketing*

MICHAEL MARTENS ♦ *vice president of business development*

DAVID SCROGGY ♦ *vice president of product development*

LIA RIBACCHI ♦ *art director*

DALE LaFOUNTAIN ♦ *vice president of information technology*

DARLENE VOGEL ♦ *director of purchasing*

KEN LIZZI ♦ *general counsel*

*Special thanks to Jason Hvam, John Nortz,
and Andreas Mergenthaler*

www.hellboy.com

Published by Dark Horse Books
A division of Dark Horse Comics, Inc.
10956 SE Main Street
Milwaukie, OR 97222

First edition September 2005
ISBN: 1-59307-380-1

1 3 5 7 9 10 8 6 4 2

Printed in China

This book collects the *B.P.R.D. The Dead* comic-book series, issues 1-5, published by Dark Horse Comics, and the story "B.P.R.D. Born Again" from the *Hellboy Premiere Edition* published by Dark Horse Comics and Gareb Shamus Enterprises.

lking about working together, I was very excited. Who wouldn't be, right? A chance to work with one of the most fertile, creative minds—and easily the best storyteller—in the business? Hell, I wasn't just excited. I was flattered. Of course, as with all freelancers in comics who are used to false starts and premature finishes, there was a little voice in the back of my head saying, "Don't get your hopes up, buddy." At the time, Mike was working hard, drawing and writing *Hellboy* stories, and doing production work for Disney's *Atlantis*. Not to mention, he had a few other projects he wanted to do on his own, so realistically I had to wonder when he was going to find the time to do anything else.

Still, it was fun to talk about it. At worst, our conversations would leave me laughing as hard as I've ever laughed in my life (Mike's a funny guy, in case nobody's told you), or at best, we would end up with an agreement to do this or that project, and over the years there were a few of them. For instance, we talked extensively about creating a comics series starring a science-fiction/adventure/space-opera character. For a brief time, we bandied about the notion of doing a WW II-era superhero epic for one of the "Big Two." Then there was the horror-themed animated series we wanted to do. That one actually went so far as putting together a pitch for the Cartoon Network, but somehow none of these ever came to fruition. Eventually Mike started flying out to L.A. and Prague to do production work first on *Blade II* and then

seemed a much more realistic proposition. For reasons I'll never understand, his creative genius has yet to be fully appreciated, but everyone else's oversight was to be my gain. At least, that was my thinking. For years we tried to find something to collaborate on: a new book for Vertigo, reworking an existing character for Marvel, etc., but much to our mutual disappointment, we couldn't make any of it happen, and my little voice was needling me with a nasty, "Dude, you cannot catch a break."

Now this is where the introduction starts to look a little bit like an episode of *Seinfeld*, as these two parallel plotlines dovetail. See, Mike had been trying to work with Guy for a long time as well, and he was certainly in a better position to make that happen than I was. In fact, if you've read *Plague of Frogs*, you know that he *did* make it happen, and that they made a hell of a team. Fortunately for me, Mike wanted to keep the B.P.R.D. series going, and he wanted me to help him do that, and thank you very much for that, Mike!

To think, there was a time not too long ago when the prospects of working with either one of these huge talents seemed utterly hopeless, and now I get to sit around with *both* of them and dream out loud. They give me all their best ideas so that I look good as a writer, and then they turn out amazing artwork to make me look just about great. For once, Fate's plan for me turned out to be better than my own.

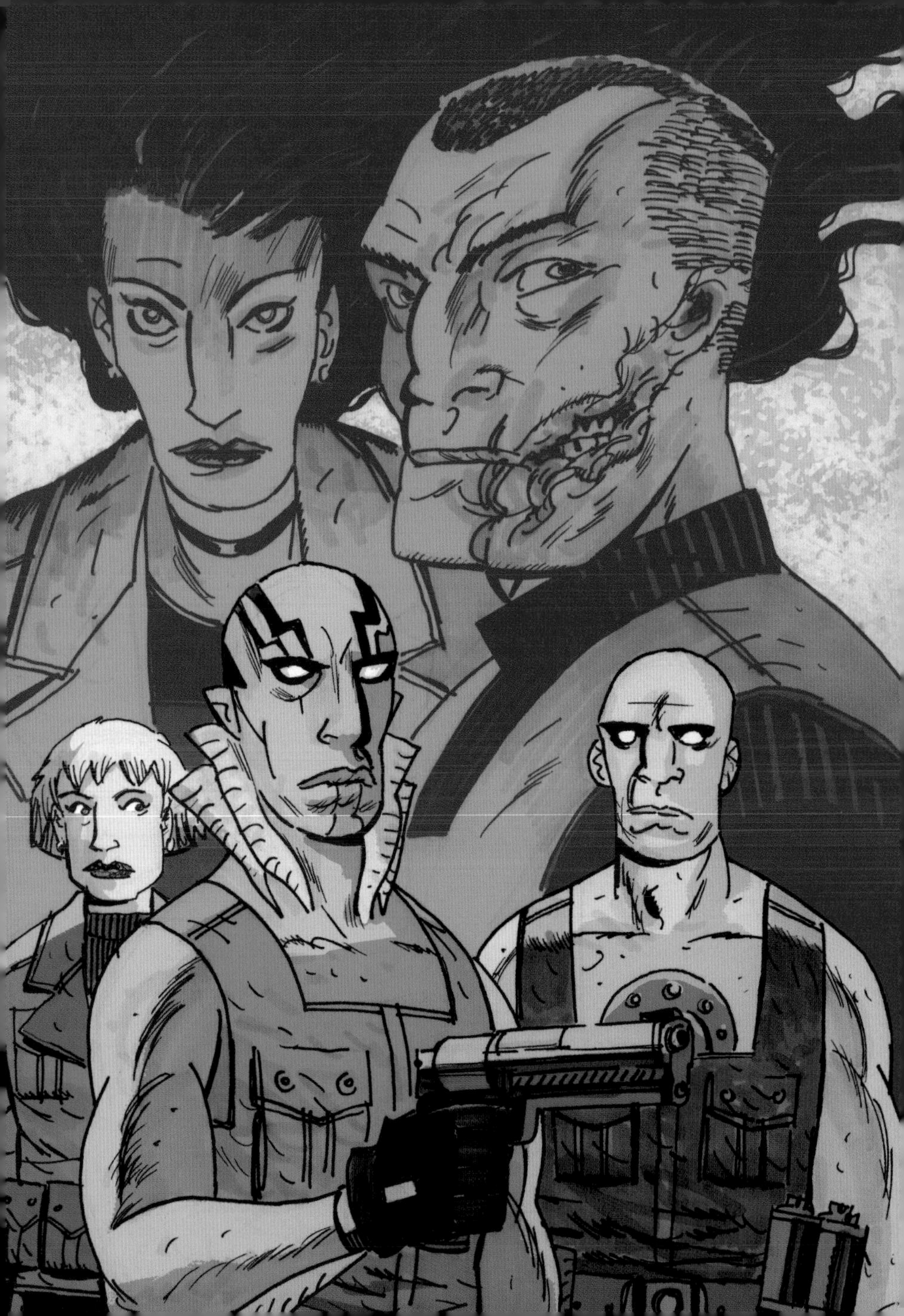

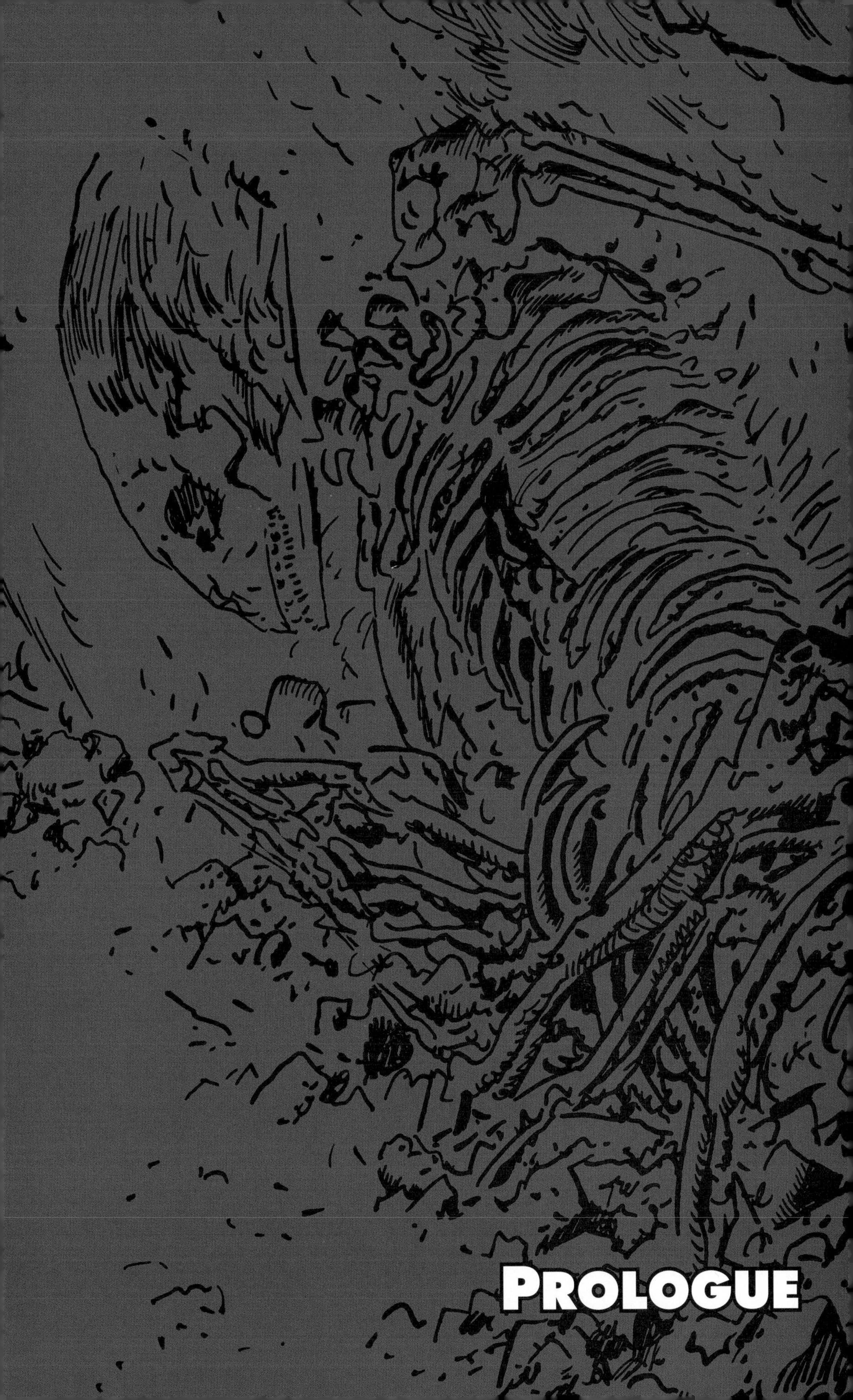

PROLOGUE

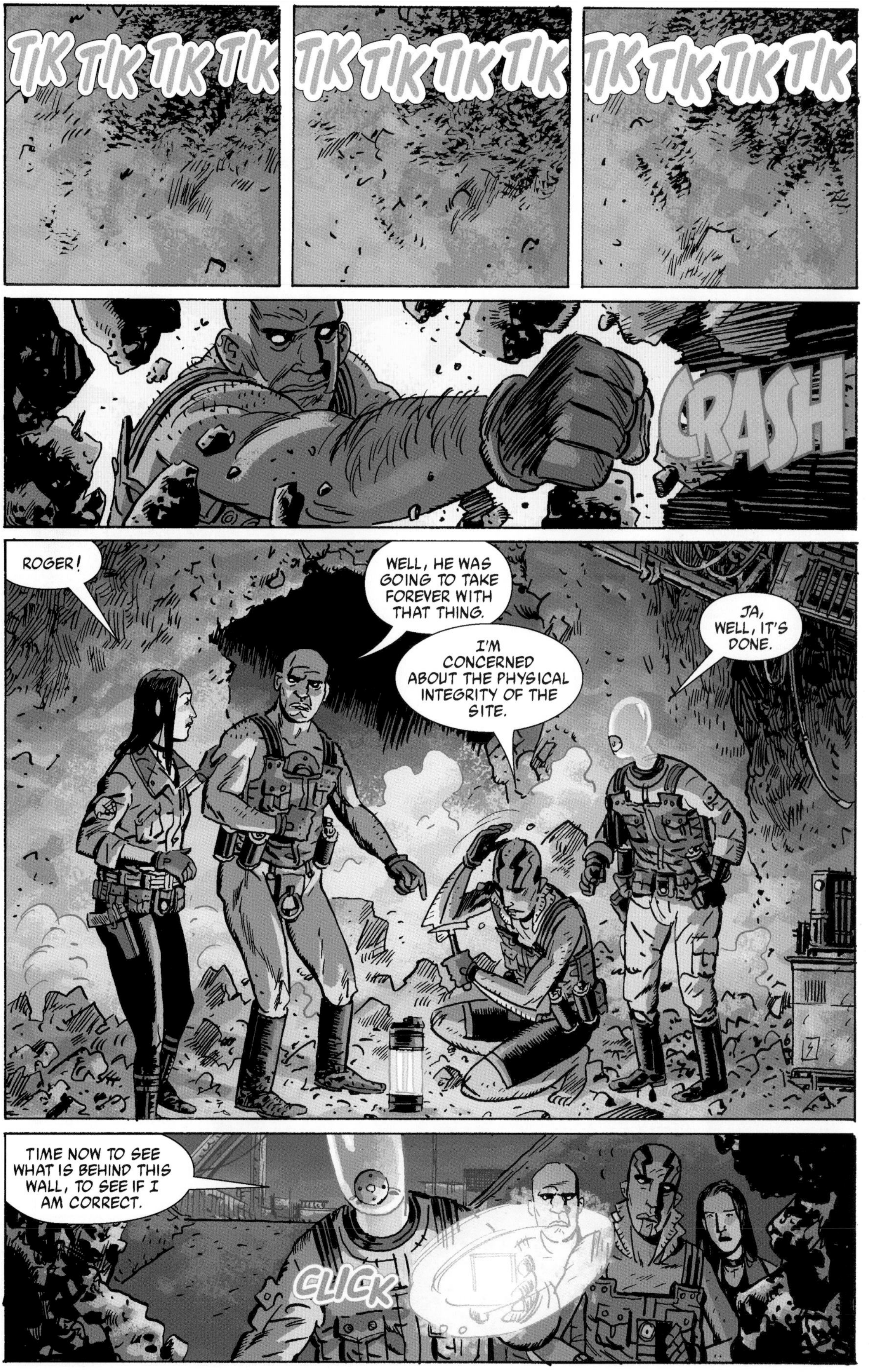
TIK TIK TIK TIK
TIK TIK TIK TIK
TIK TIK TIK TIK
CRASH
ROGER!
WELL, HE WAS GOING TO TAKE FOREVER WITH THAT THING.
I'M CONCERNED ABOUT THE PHYSICAL INTEGRITY OF THE SITE.
JA, WELL, IT'S DONE.
TIME NOW TO SEE WHAT IS BEHIND THIS WALL, TO SEE IF I AM CORRECT.
CLICK

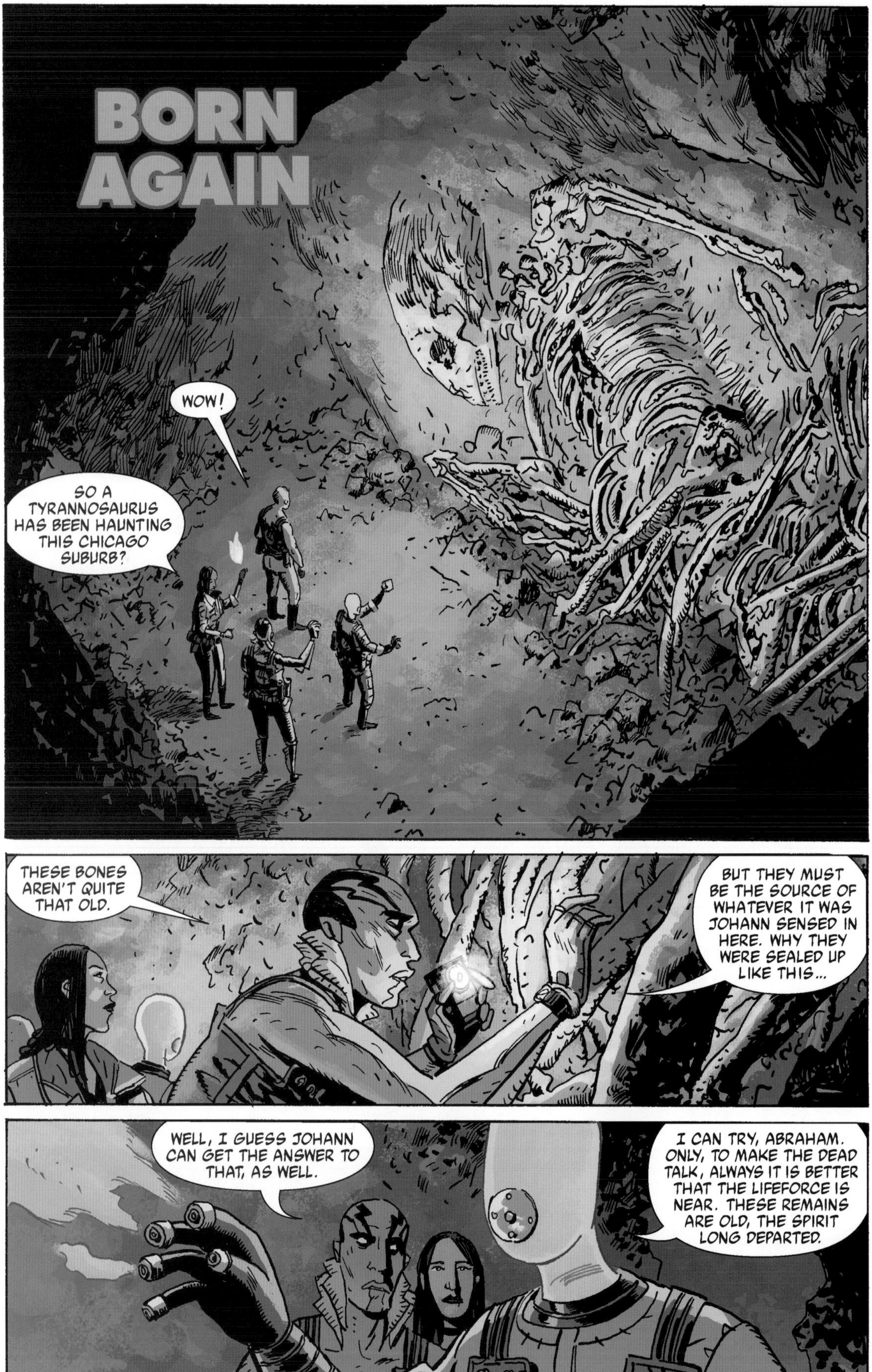
BORN AGAIN
WOW!
SO A TYRANNOSAURUS HAS BEEN HAUNTING THIS CHICAGO SUBURB?
THESE BONES AREN'T QUITE THAT OLD.
BUT THEY MUST BE THE SOURCE OF WHATEVER IT WAS JOHANN SENSED IN HERE. WHY THEY WERE SEALED UP LIKE THIS...
WELL, I GUESS JOHANN CAN GET THE ANSWER TO THAT, AS WELL.
I CAN TRY, ABRAHAM. ONLY, TO MAKE THE DEAD TALK, ALWAYS IT IS BETTER THAT THE LIFEFORCE IS NEAR. THESE REMAINS ARE OLD, THE SPIRIT LONG DEPARTED.

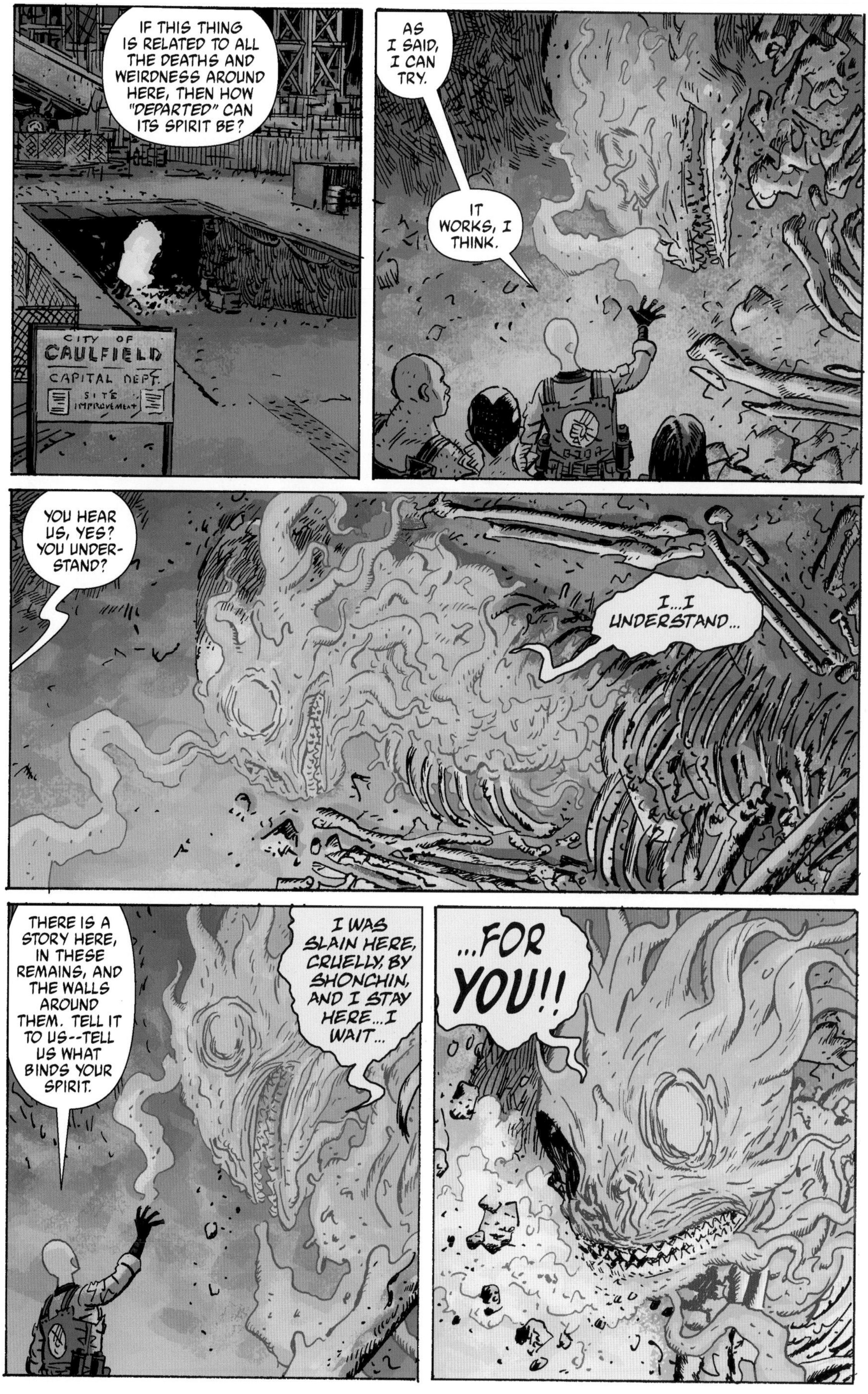
IF THIS THING IS RELATED TO ALL THE DEATHS AND WEIRDNESS AROUND HERE, THEN HOW "DEPARTED" CAN ITS SPIRIT BE?
CITY OF CAULFIELD
CAPITAL DEPT.
SITE IMPROVEMENT
AS I SAID, I CAN TRY.
IT WORKS, I THINK.
YOU HEAR US, YES? YOU UNDERSTAND?
I...I UNDERSTAND...
THERE IS A STORY HERE, IN THESE REMAINS, AND THE WALLS AROUND THEM. TELL IT TO US--TELL US WHAT BINDS YOUR SPIRIT.
I WAS SLAIN HERE, CRUELLY, BY SHONCHIN, AND I STAY HERE...I WAIT...
...FOR YOU!!

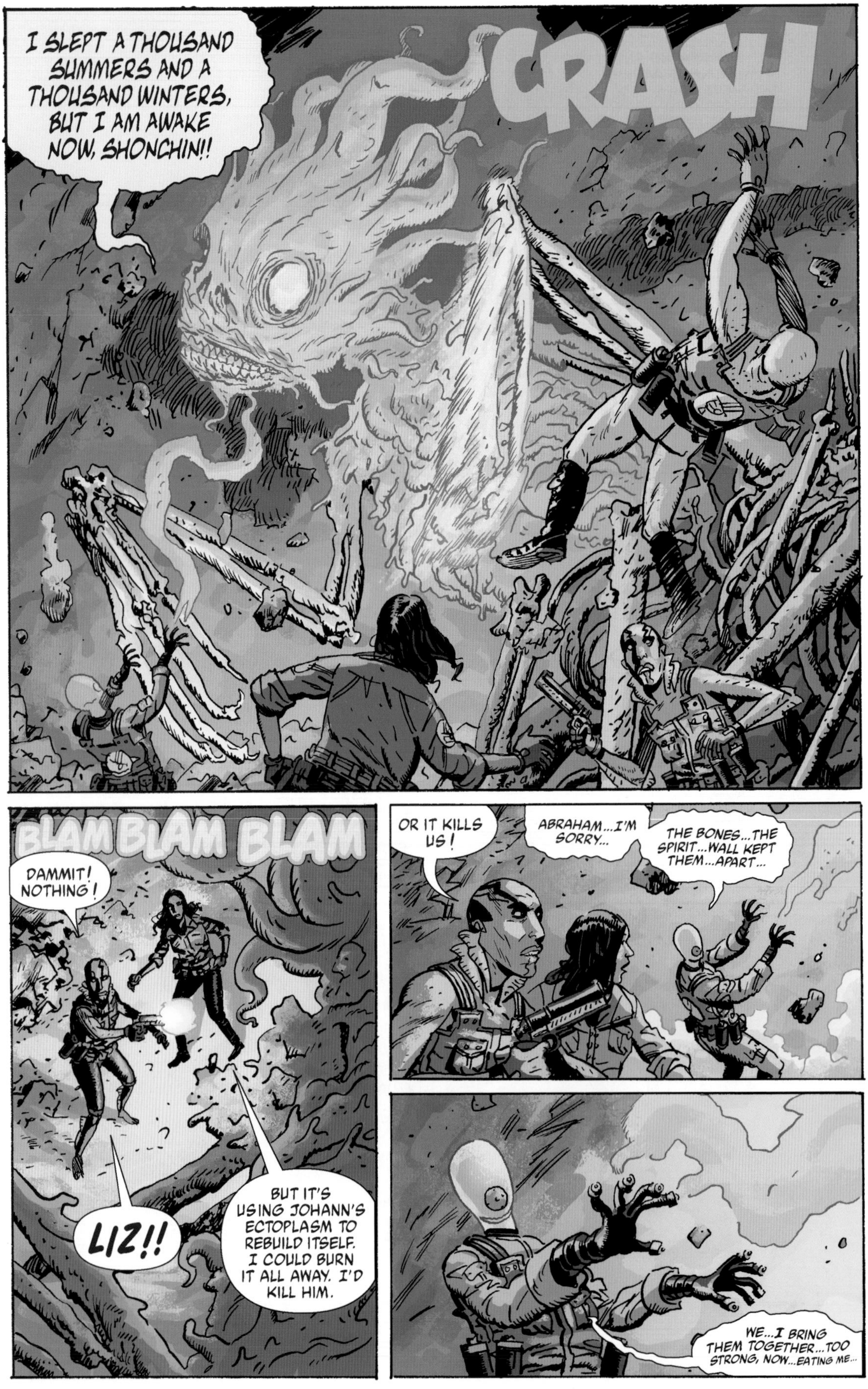
I SLEPT A THOUSAND SUMMERS AND A THOUSAND WINTERS, BUT I AM AWAKE NOW, SHONCHIN!!
CRASH
BLAM BLAM BLAM
DAMMIT! NOTHING!
LIZ!!
BUT IT'S USING JOHANN'S ECTOPLASM TO REBUILD ITSELF. I COULD BURN IT ALL AWAY. I'D KILL HIM.
OR IT KILLS US!
ABRAHAM...I'M SORRY...
THE BONES...THE SPIRIT...WALL KEPT THEM...APART...
WE...I BRING THEM TOGETHER...TOO STRONG, NOW...EATING ME...

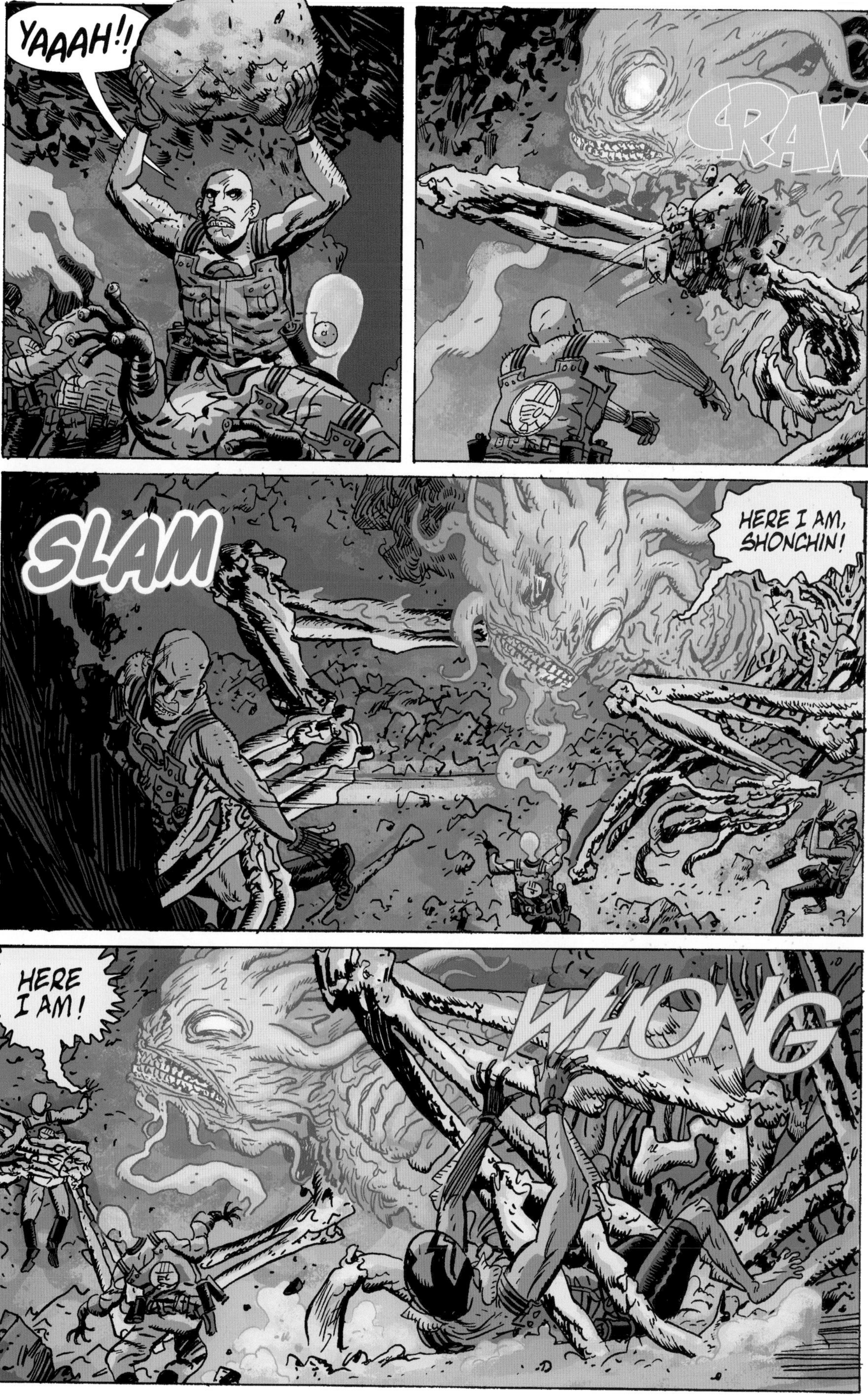
YAAAH!!
CRAK
SLAM
HERE I AM, SHONCHIN!
HERE I AM!
WHONG

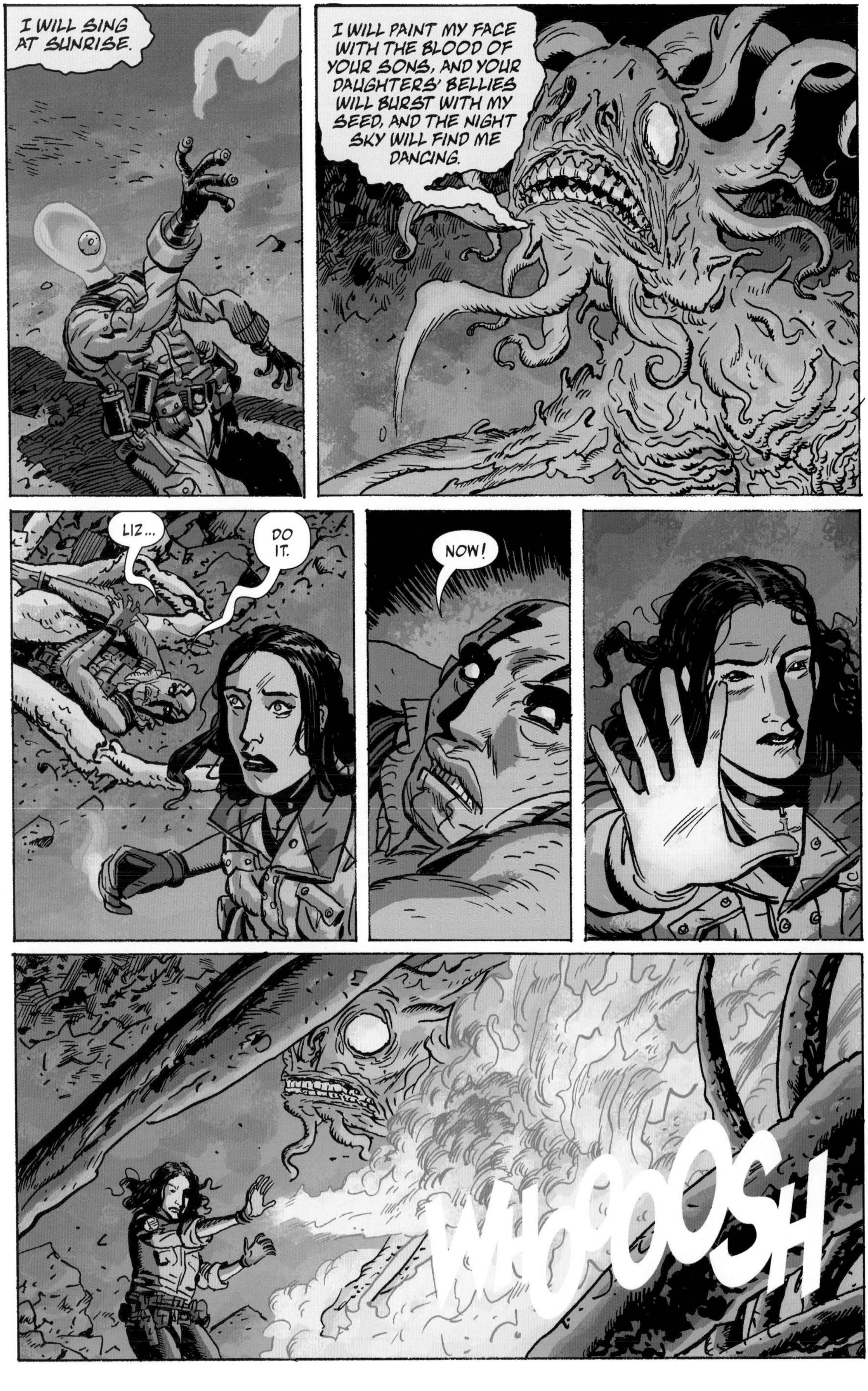
I WILL SING AT SUNRISE.
I WILL PAINT MY FACE WITH THE BLOOD OF YOUR SONS, AND YOUR DAUGHTERS' BELLIES WILL BURST WITH MY SEED, AND THE NIGHT SKY WILL FIND ME DANCING.
LIZ...
DO IT.
NOW!
WHOOOOSH

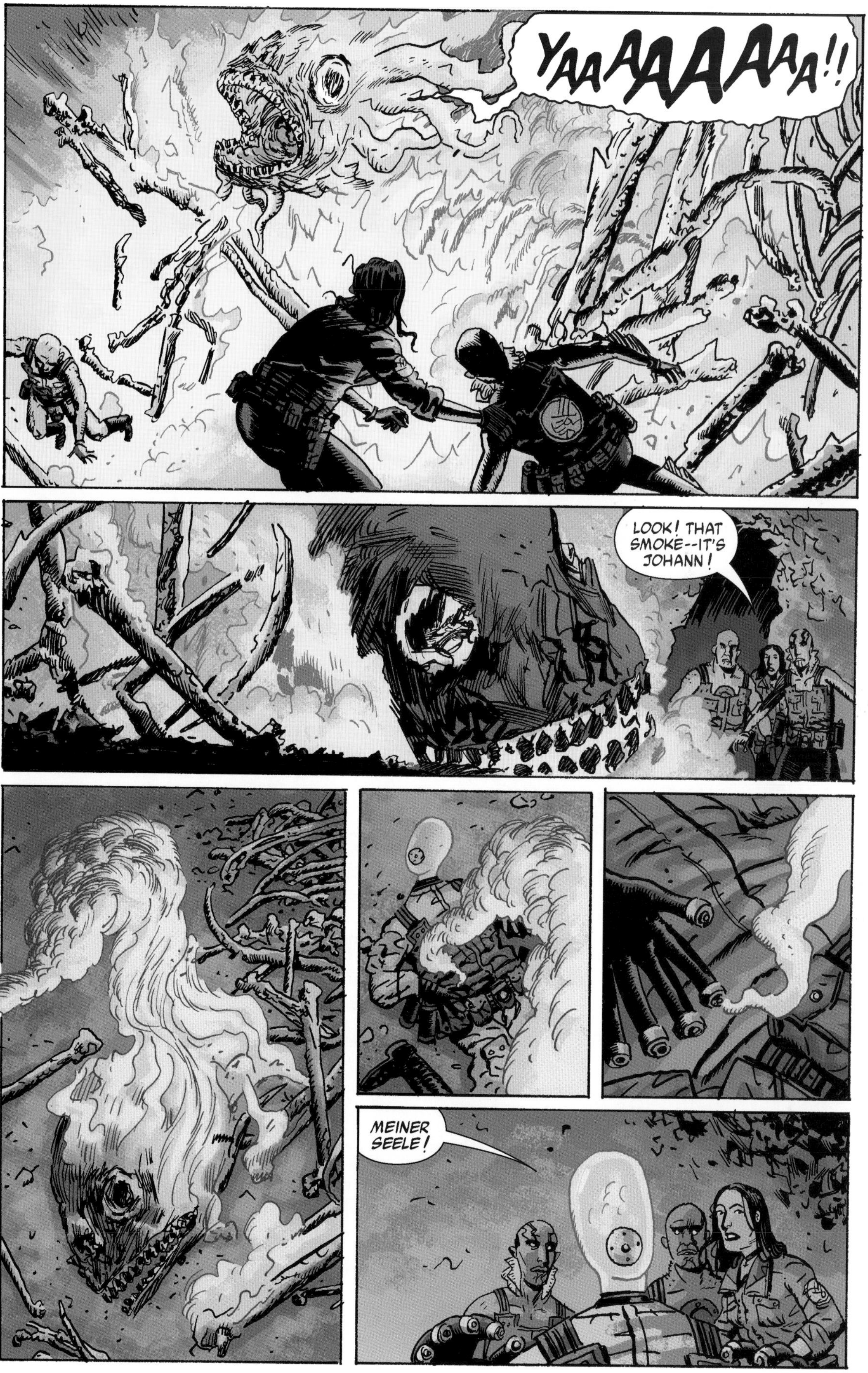
YAAAAAAAAA!!
LOOK! THAT SMOKE--IT'S JOHANN!
MEINER SEELE!

NOT SO HELPFUL, THAT CREATURE.

BUT I THINK THIS SHONCHIN WAS ONE OF YOUR NORTH AMERICAN ABORIGINAL SHAMANS.

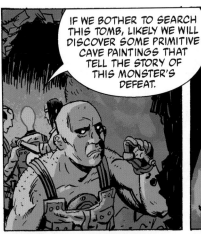

IF WE BOTHER TO SEARCH THIS TOMB, LIKELY WE WILL DISCOVER SOME PRIMITIVE CAVE PAINTINGS THAT TELL THE STORY OF THIS MONSTER'S DEFEAT.

?

COLONEL. YOUR MEN WILL FIND SOME BURNT REMAINS UNDER THE SITE. JUST BAG IT UP. THE BUREAU WILL SEND THE RECOVERY CREW TOMORROW.

YOU GOT IT.

ARE YOU SURE YOU'RE OKAY, JOHANN?

YES, GOOD. ONLY I HAVE THIS SENSATION, A FEELING I NEVER THOUGHT I'D HAVE AGAIN.

WHAT'S THAT?

I'M VERY WARM.

CHAPTER ONE

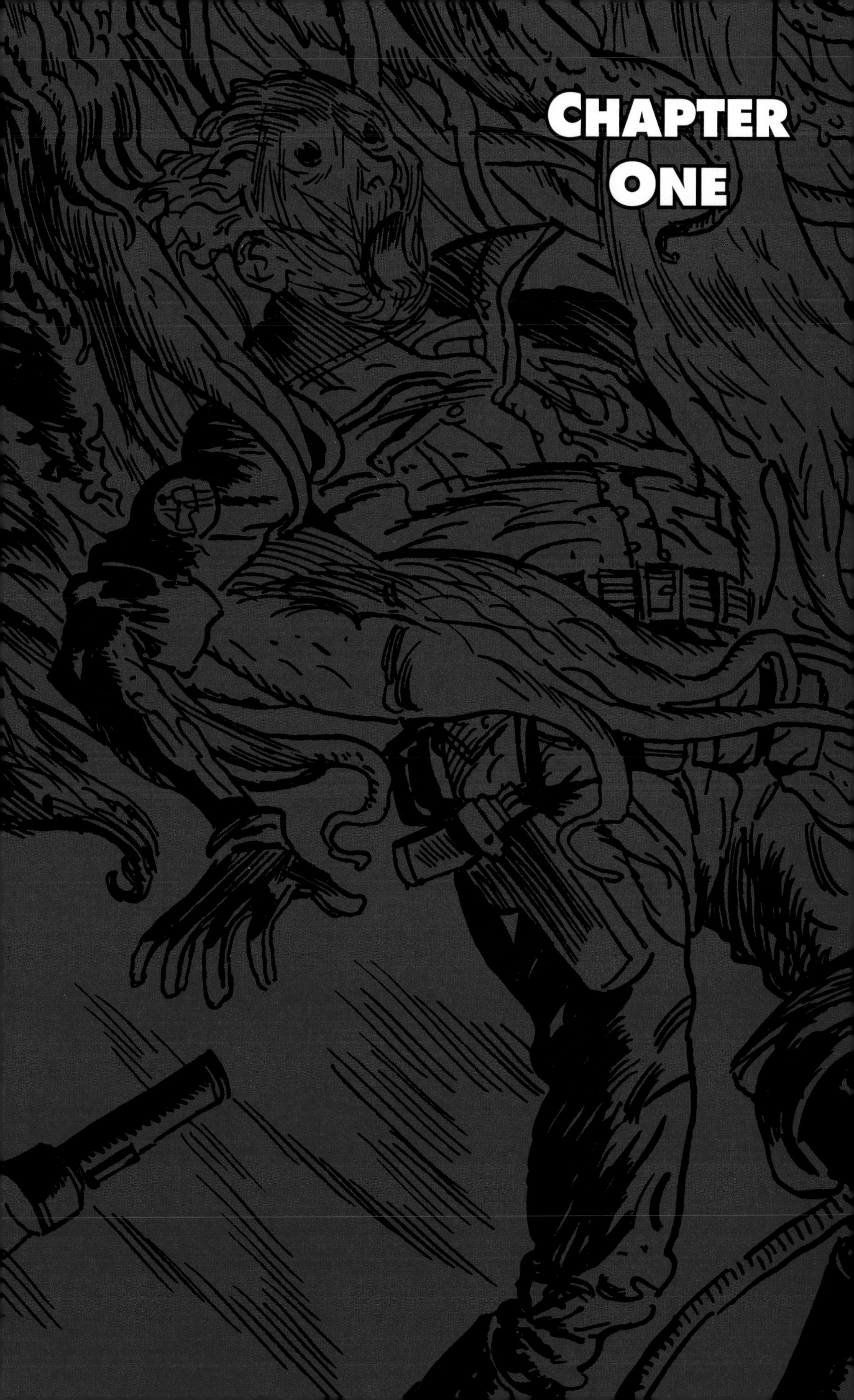

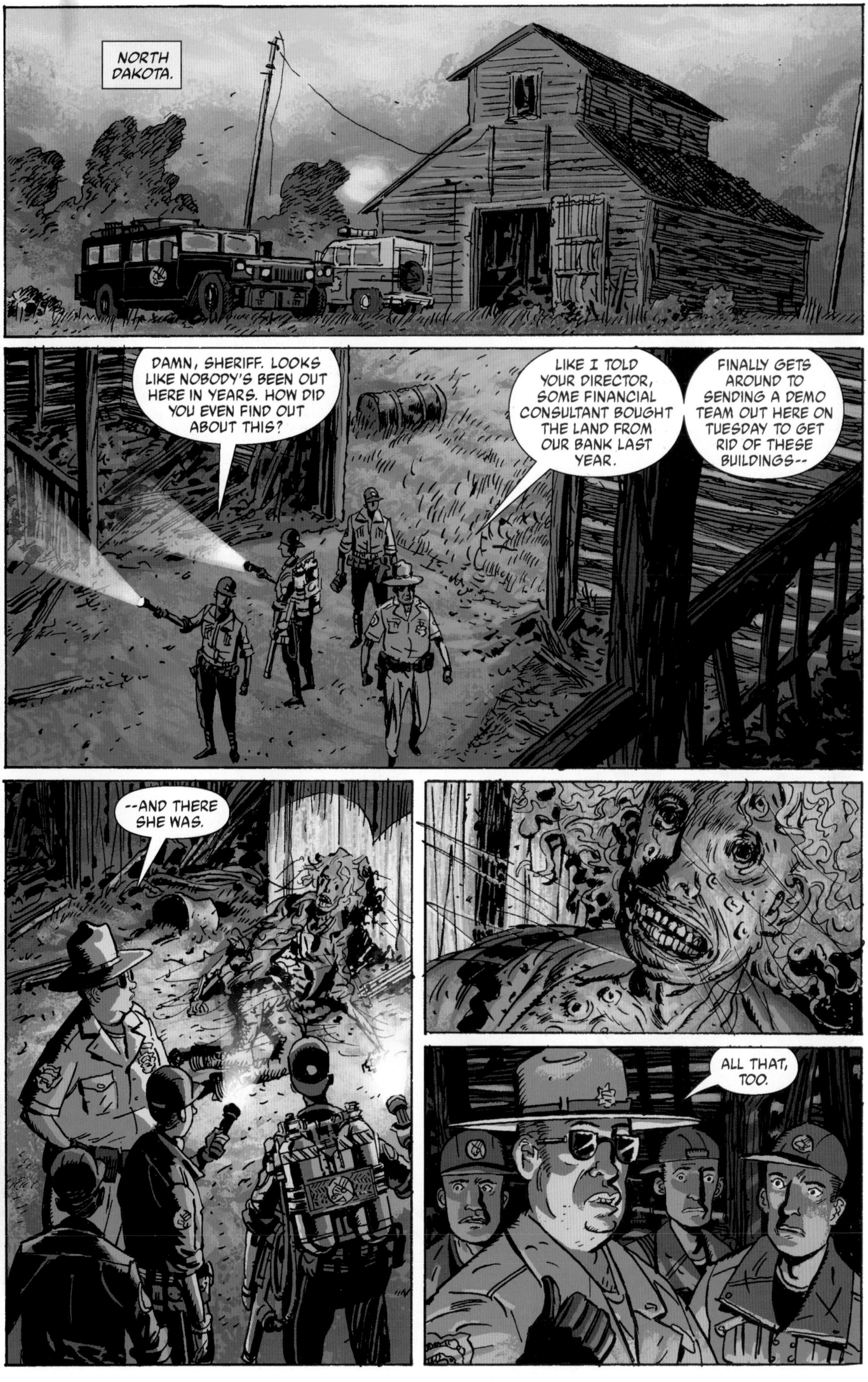
NORTH DAKOTA.
DAMN, SHERIFF. LOOKS LIKE NOBODY'S BEEN OUT HERE IN YEARS. HOW DID YOU EVEN FIND OUT ABOUT THIS?
LIKE I TOLD YOUR DIRECTOR, SOME FINANCIAL CONSULTANT BOUGHT THE LAND FROM OUR BANK LAST YEAR.
FINALLY GETS AROUND TO SENDING A DEMO TEAM OUT HERE ON TUESDAY TO GET RID OF THESE BUILDINGS--
--AND THERE SHE WAS.
ALL THAT, TOO.

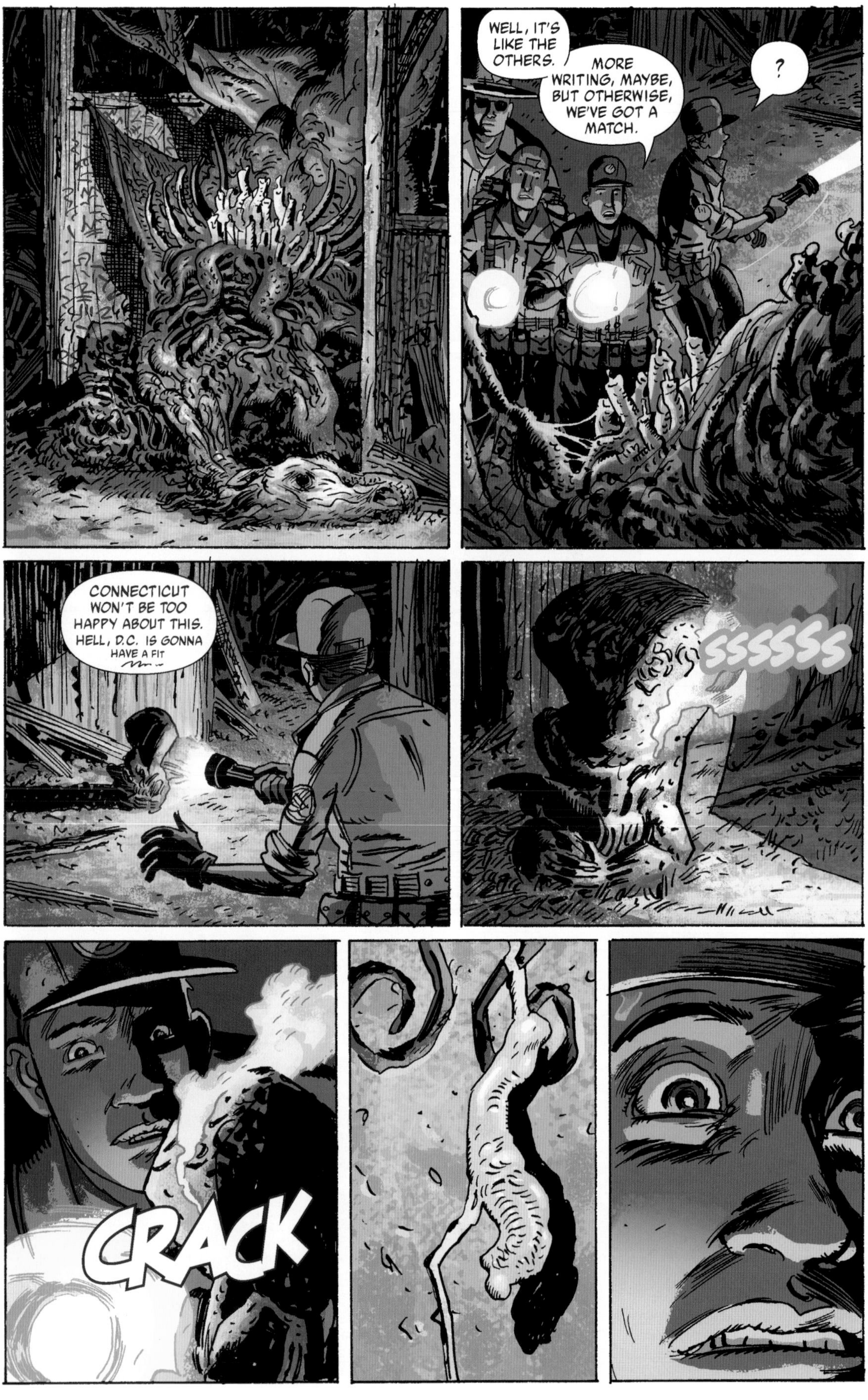
WELL, IT'S LIKE THE OTHERS.
MORE WRITING, MAYBE, BUT OTHERWISE, WE'VE GOT A MATCH.
?
CONNECTICUT WON'T BE TOO HAPPY ABOUT THIS. HELL, D.C. IS GONNA HAVE A FIT
SSSSSS
CRACK

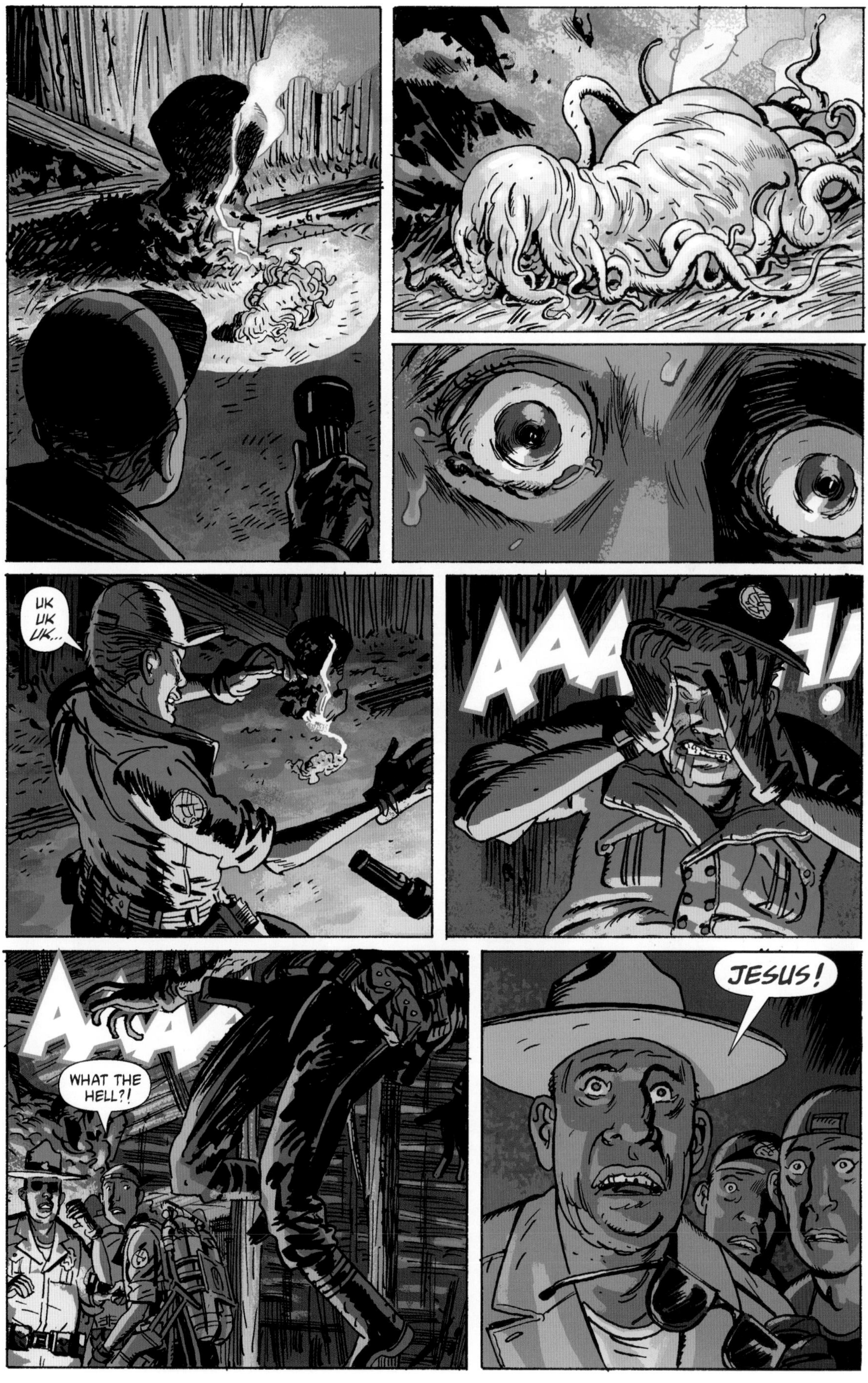
UK
UK
UK...
AAAAAAH!
AAAA
WHAT THE HELL?!
JESUS!

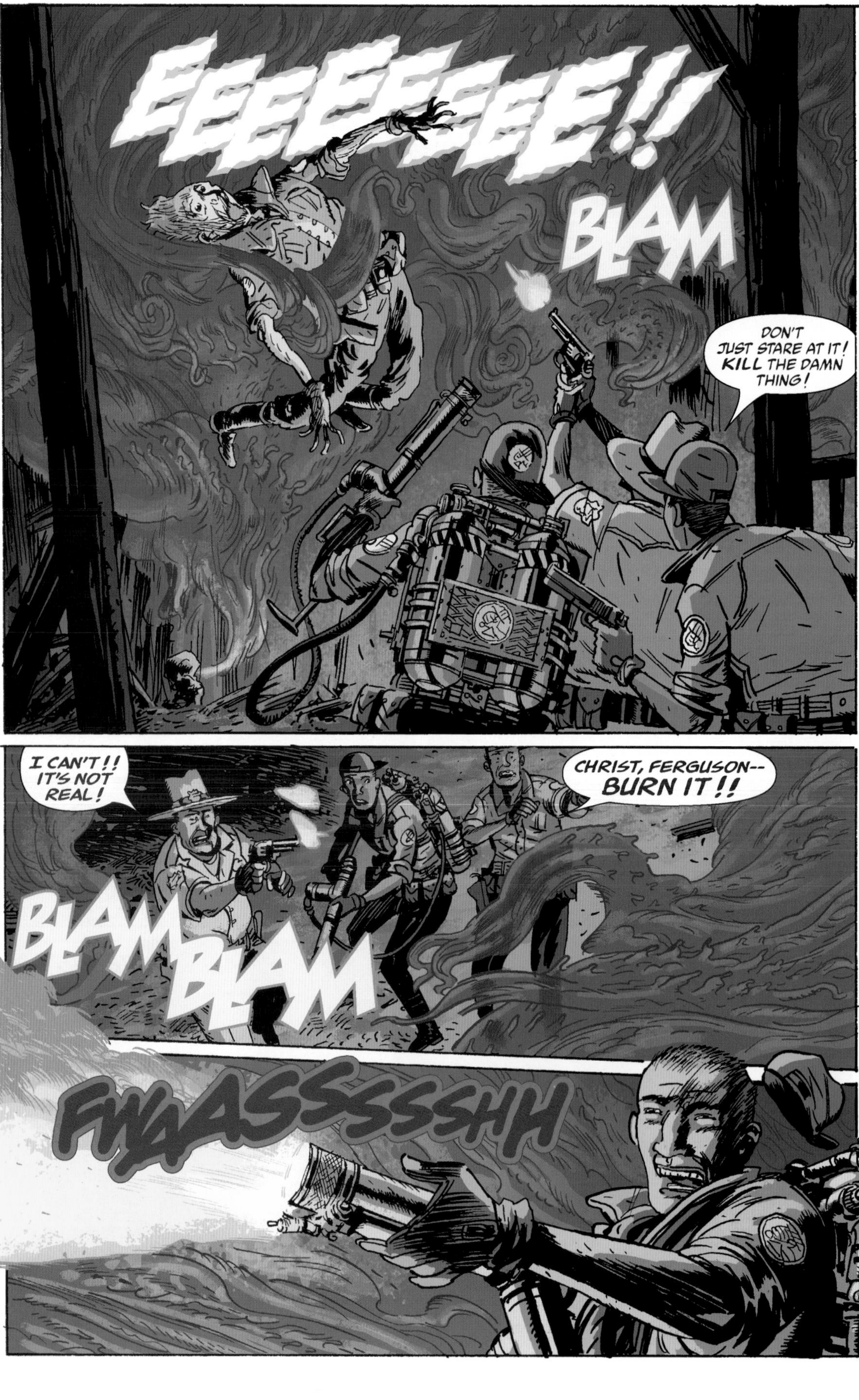
EEEEEEEEE!!
BLAM
DON'T JUST STARE AT IT! KILL THE DAMN THING!
I CAN'T!! IT'S NOT REAL!
CHRIST, FERGUSON-- BURN IT!!
BLAM BLAM
FWASSSSSSHH

B.P.R.D HEADQUARTERS, FAIRFIELD, CONNECTICUT.

--LEAVING EVERYONE BUT THE SHERIFF DEAD.

NOW, THIS IS THE SEVENTH SUCH INCIDENT, AND THE FURTHEST WEST SO FAR.

THIS FROG CULT IS SPREADING QUICKLY, AND SOMEHOW, THEY MANAGE TO STAY AHEAD OF US EVERY STEP OF THE WAY.

WE HAVE INTERNATIONAL CO-OPERATION FROM THE CANADIANS, BUT IT'S NOT ENOUGH. WE'RE LOSING MEN, THEY'RE LOSING MEN, AND THE FROGS, JUDGING FROM THE EVIDENCE, ARE GROWING IN NUMBERS.

ROGER, YOU DON'T HAVE TO RAISE YOUR HAND. WHAT IS IT?

SO, ARE WE STILL FIGHTING THOSE FROG MEN?

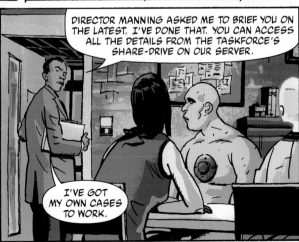

DIRECTOR MANNING ASKED ME TO BRIEF YOU ON THE LATEST. I'VE DONE THAT. YOU CAN ACCESS ALL THE DETAILS FROM THE TASKFORCE'S SHARE-DRIVE ON OUR SERVER.

I'VE GOT MY OWN CASES TO WORK.

LIKE WE NEED THE DETAILS.

THOSE FROG-MONSTERS WILL ESTABLISH POPULATIONS AS FAR AS VANCOUVER BEFORE THE END OF THE YEAR. ONCE THAT HAPPENS...

I WOULD LIKE TO SEE THOSE FILES, ACTUALLY.

I KNOW EACH INCIDENT IS A LITTLE DIFFERENT--

MORE THAN ONLY A LITTLE, ELIZABETH.

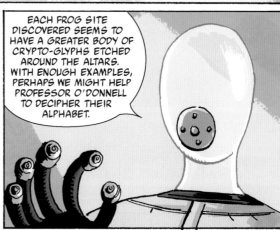

EACH FROG SITE DISCOVERED SEEMS TO HAVE A GREATER BODY OF CRYPTO-GLYPHS ETCHED AROUND THE ALTARS. WITH ENOUGH EXAMPLES, PERHAPS WE MIGHT HELP PROFESSOR O'DONNELL TO DECIPHER THEIR ALPHABET.

CODE-CRACKING? THAT'S WHAT THE BUREAU'S BEEN REDUCED TO?

THE MIGRATION IS IN THE NATION'S MID-WEST, THE BUREAU HERE IN CONNECTICUT--NOT IDEALLY PLACED TO DO MORE.

FOR NOW.

THAT MEETING WE'RE HAVING WITH OUR ESTEEMED DIRECTOR? I HEARD IT'S ABOUT A POSSIBLE RELOCATION.

IS THAT WHERE KATE AND ABE WENT?

DID THEY ALREADY RELOCATE?

NO, ROGER. NOT EXACTLY.

DON'T WORRY. THEY'LL BE BACK SOON.

THEY BETTER BE.

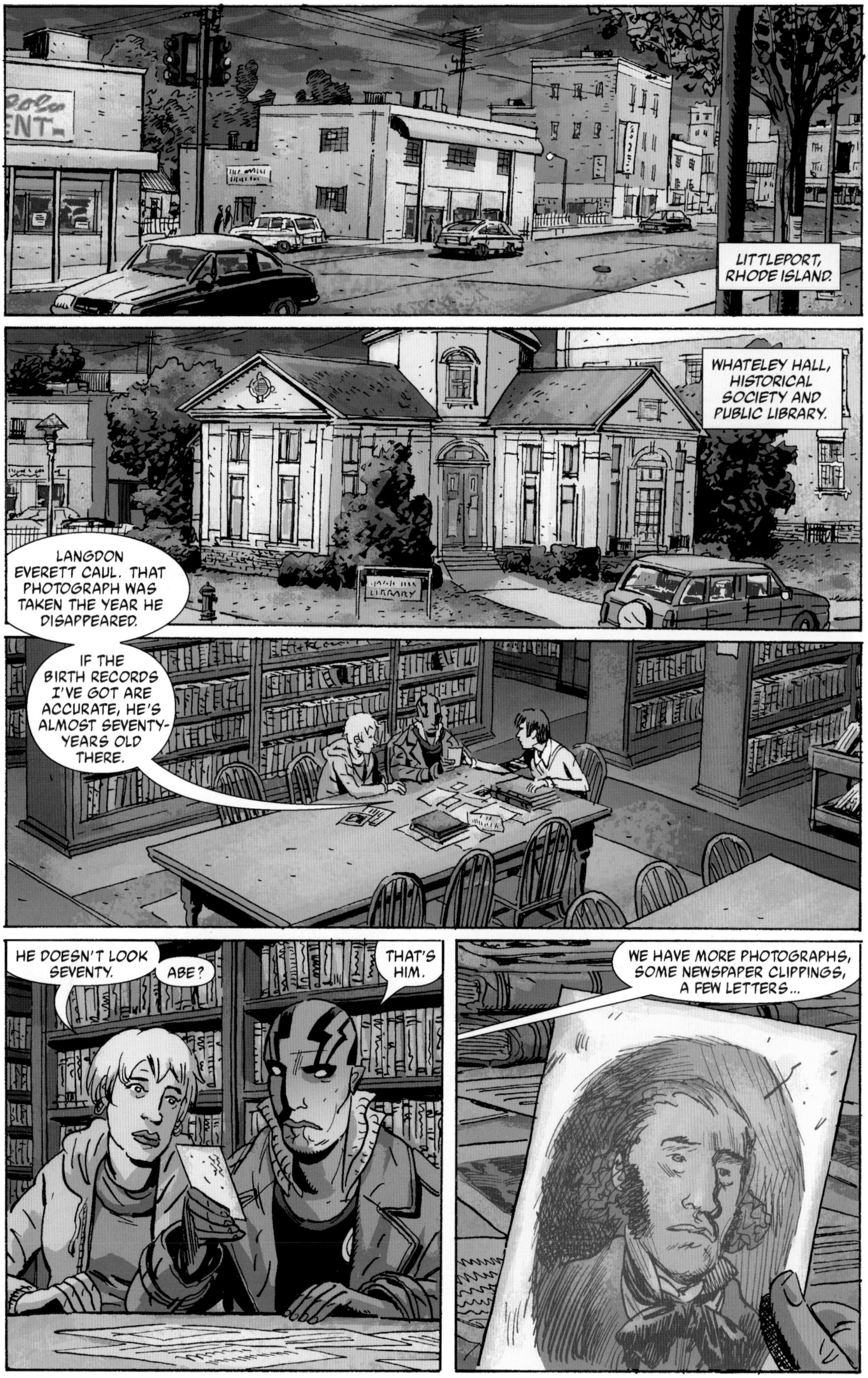
LITTLEPORT, RHODE ISLAND.
WHATELEY HALL, HISTORICAL SOCIETY AND PUBLIC LIBRARY.
LANGDON EVERETT CAUL. THAT PHOTOGRAPH WAS TAKEN THE YEAR HE DISAPPEARED.
IF THE BIRTH RECORDS I'VE GOT ARE ACCURATE, HE'S ALMOST SEVENTY-YEARS OLD THERE.
HE DOESN'T LOOK SEVENTY.
ABE?
THAT'S HIM.
WE HAVE MORE PHOTOGRAPHS, SOME NEWSPAPER CLIPPINGS, A FEW LETTERS...

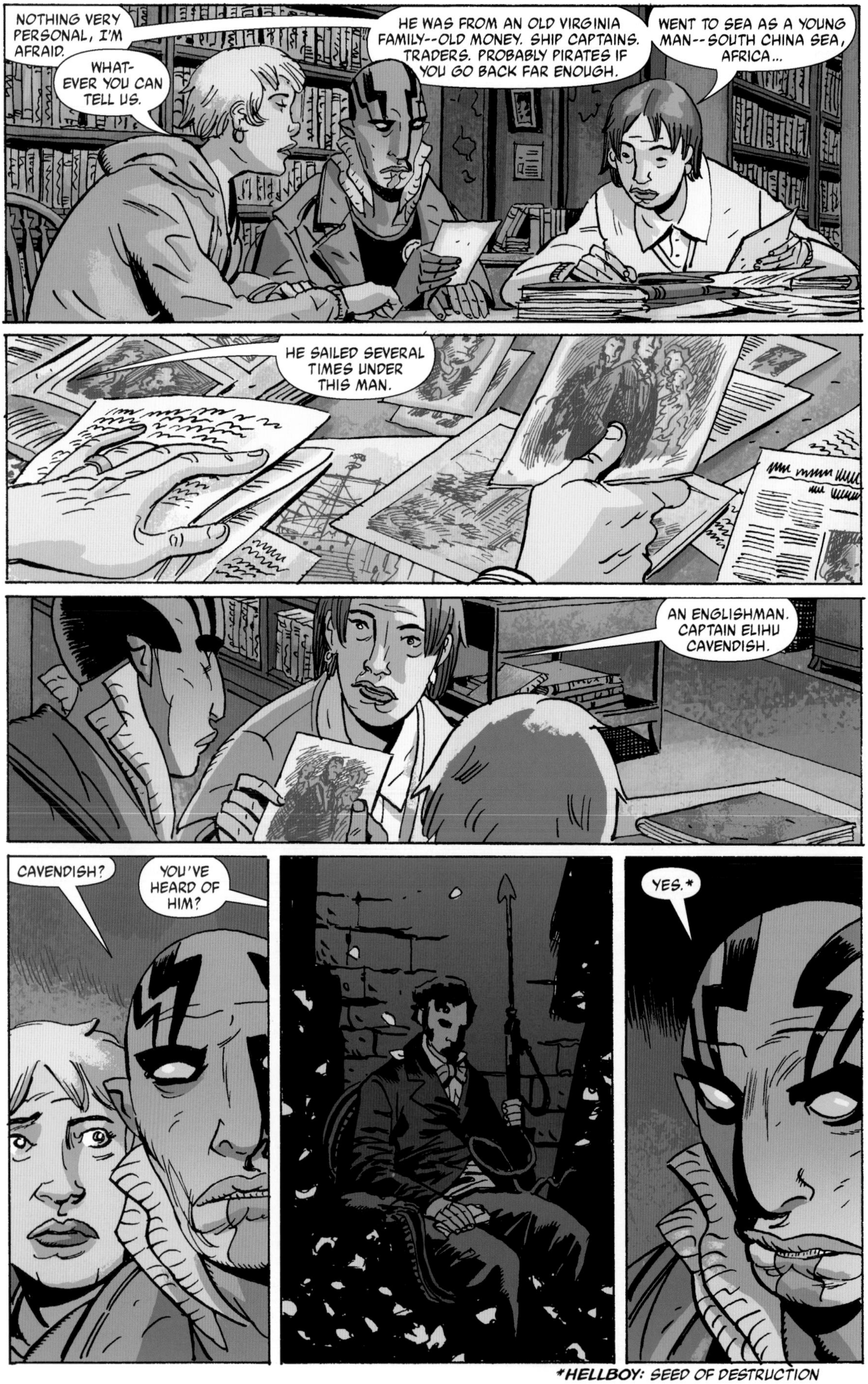
NOTHING VERY PERSONAL, I'M AFRAID.
WHAT-EVER YOU CAN TELL US.
HE WAS FROM AN OLD VIRGINIA FAMILY--OLD MONEY. SHIP CAPTAINS. TRADERS. PROBABLY PIRATES IF YOU GO BACK FAR ENOUGH.
WENT TO SEA AS A YOUNG MAN--SOUTH CHINA SEA, AFRICA...
HE SAILED SEVERAL TIMES UNDER THIS MAN.
AN ENGLISHMAN. CAPTAIN ELIHU CAVENDISH.
CAVENDISH?
YOU'VE HEARD OF HIM?
YES.*

*HELLBOY: SEED OF DESTRUCTION

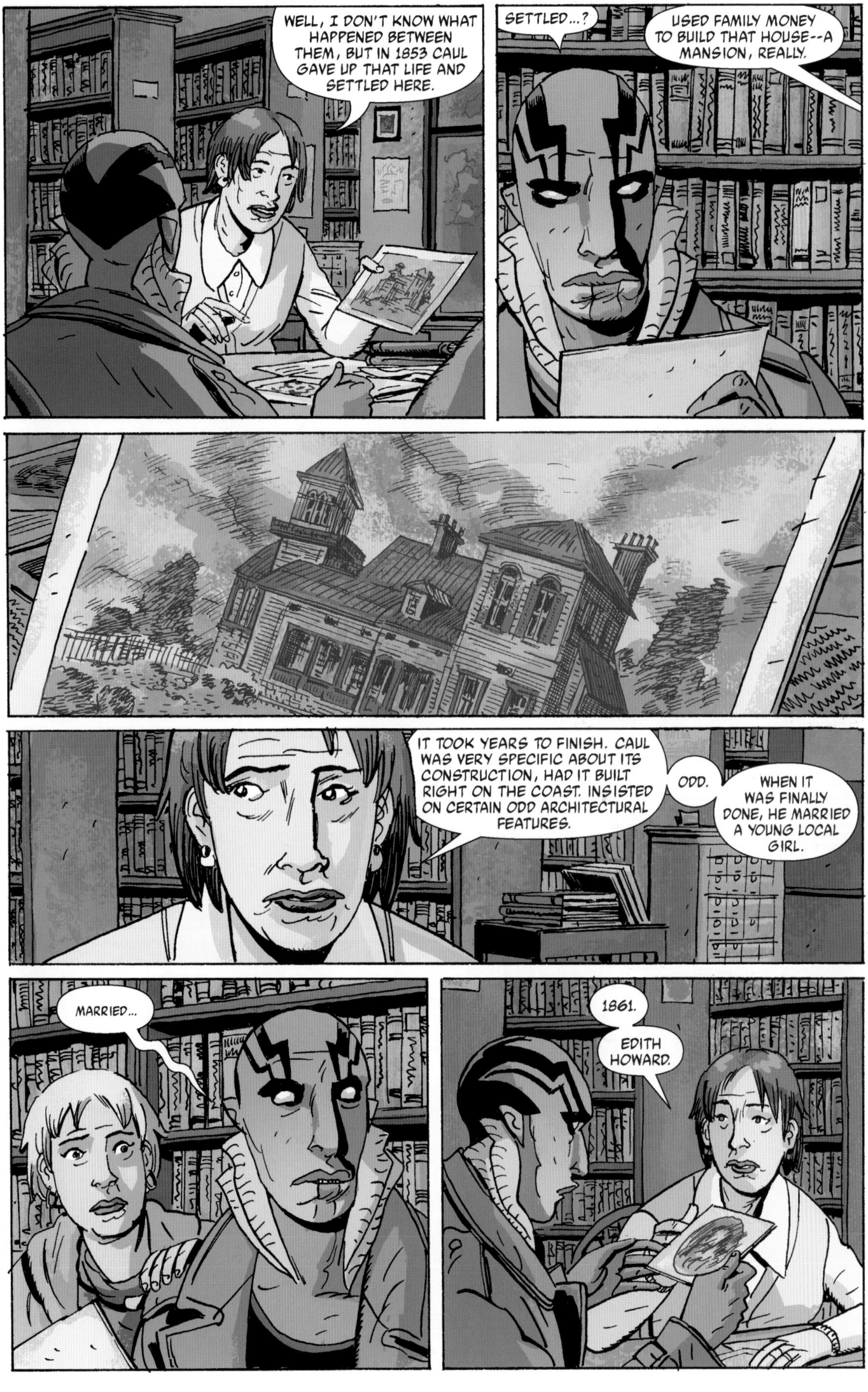
WELL, I DON'T KNOW WHAT HAPPENED BETWEEN THEM, BUT IN 1853 CAUL GAVE UP THAT LIFE AND SETTLED HERE.
SETTLED...?
USED FAMILY MONEY TO BUILD THAT HOUSE--A MANSION, REALLY.
IT TOOK YEARS TO FINISH. CAUL WAS VERY SPECIFIC ABOUT ITS CONSTRUCTION, HAD IT BUILT RIGHT ON THE COAST. INSISTED ON CERTAIN ODD ARCHITECTURAL FEATURES.
ODD.
WHEN IT WAS FINALLY DONE, HE MARRIED A YOUNG LOCAL GIRL.
MARRIED...
1861.
EDITH HOWARD.

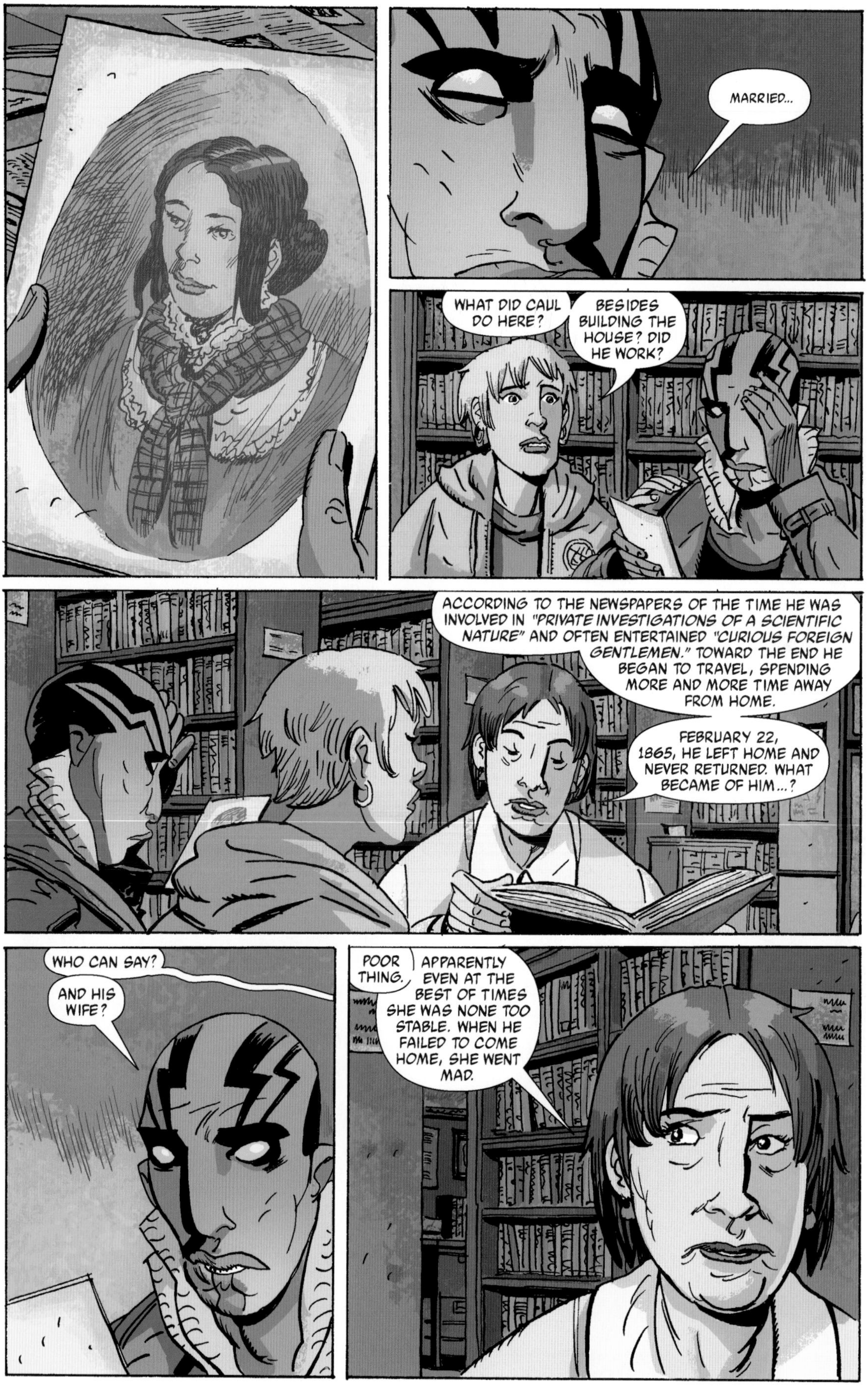
MARRIED...
WHAT DID CAUL DO HERE?
BESIDES BUILDING THE HOUSE? DID HE WORK?
ACCORDING TO THE NEWSPAPERS OF THE TIME HE WAS INVOLVED IN *"PRIVATE INVESTIGATIONS OF A SCIENTIFIC NATURE"* AND OFTEN ENTERTAINED *"CURIOUS FOREIGN GENTLEMEN."* TOWARD THE END HE BEGAN TO TRAVEL, SPENDING MORE AND MORE TIME AWAY FROM HOME.
FEBRUARY 22, 1865, HE LEFT HOME AND NEVER RETURNED. WHAT BECAME OF HIM...?
WHO CAN SAY?
AND HIS WIFE?
POOR THING.
APPARENTLY EVEN AT THE BEST OF TIMES SHE WAS NONE TOO STABLE. WHEN HE FAILED TO COME HOME, SHE WENT MAD.

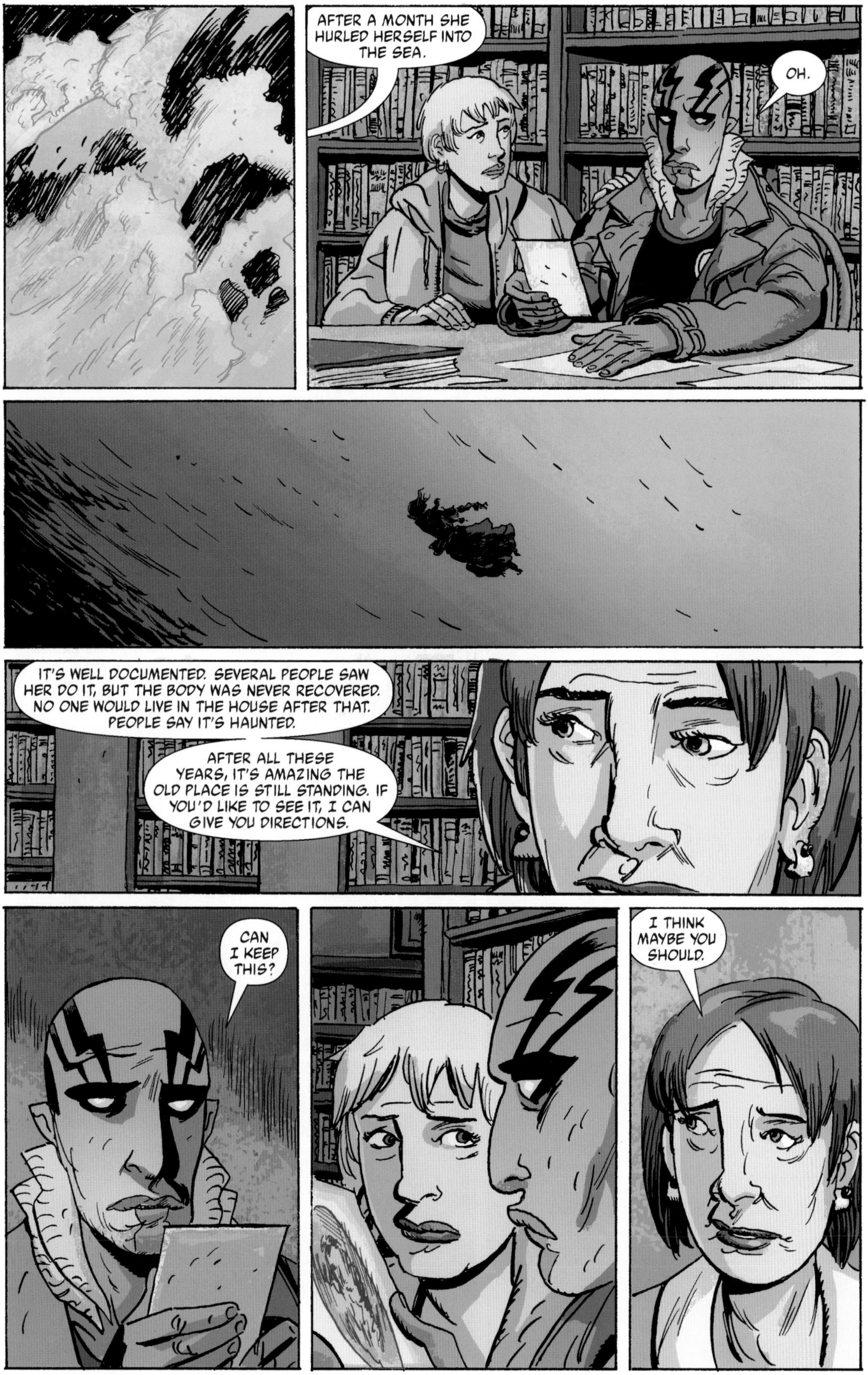
AFTER A MONTH SHE HURLED HERSELF INTO THE SEA.
OH.
IT'S WELL DOCUMENTED. SEVERAL PEOPLE SAW HER DO IT, BUT THE BODY WAS NEVER RECOVERED. NO ONE WOULD LIVE IN THE HOUSE AFTER THAT. PEOPLE SAY IT'S HAUNTED.
AFTER ALL THESE YEARS, IT'S AMAZING THE OLD PLACE IS STILL STANDING. IF YOU'D LIKE TO SEE IT, I CAN GIVE YOU DIRECTIONS.
CAN I KEEP THIS?
I THINK MAYBE YOU SHOULD.

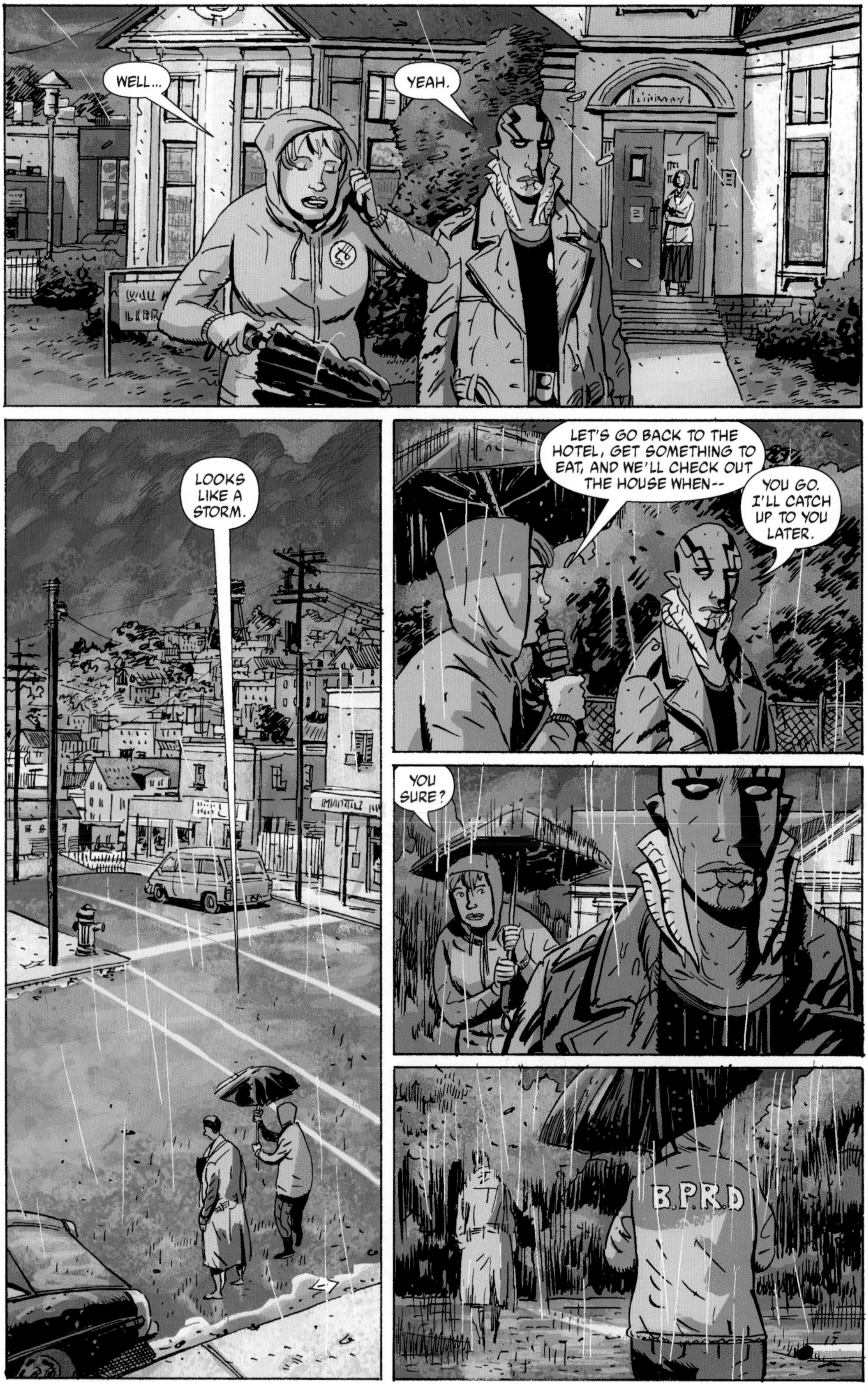
WELL...
YEAH.
LOOKS LIKE A STORM.
LET'S GO BACK TO THE HOTEL, GET SOMETHING TO EAT, AND WE'LL CHECK OUT THE HOUSE WHEN--
YOU GO. I'LL CATCH UP TO YOU LATER.
YOU SURE?
B.P.R.D

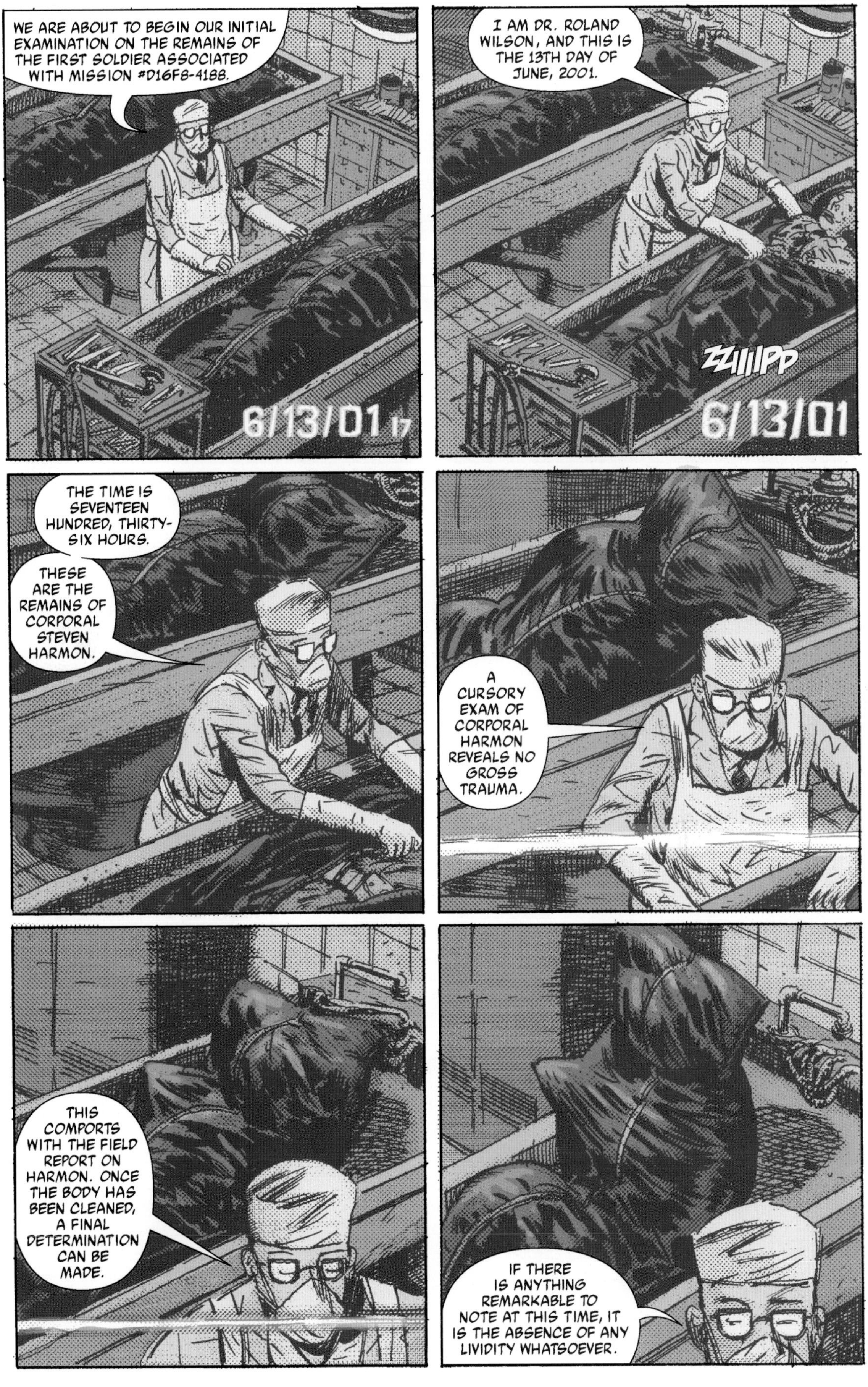
WE ARE ABOUT TO BEGIN OUR INITIAL EXAMINATION ON THE REMAINS OF THE FIRST SOLDIER ASSOCIATED WITH MISSION #D16F8-4188.
6/13/01 17
I AM DR. ROLAND WILSON, AND THIS IS THE 13TH DAY OF JUNE, 2001.
ZZIIIIPP
6/13/01
THE TIME IS SEVENTEEN HUNDRED, THIRTY-SIX HOURS.
THESE ARE THE REMAINS OF CORPORAL STEVEN HARMON.
A CURSORY EXAM OF CORPORAL HARMON REVEALS NO GROSS TRAUMA.
THIS COMPORTS WITH THE FIELD REPORT ON HARMON. ONCE THE BODY HAS BEEN CLEANED, A FINAL DETERMINATION CAN BE MADE.
IF THERE IS ANYTHING REMARKABLE TO NOTE AT THIS TIME, IT IS THE ABSENCE OF ANY LIVIDITY WHATSOEVER.

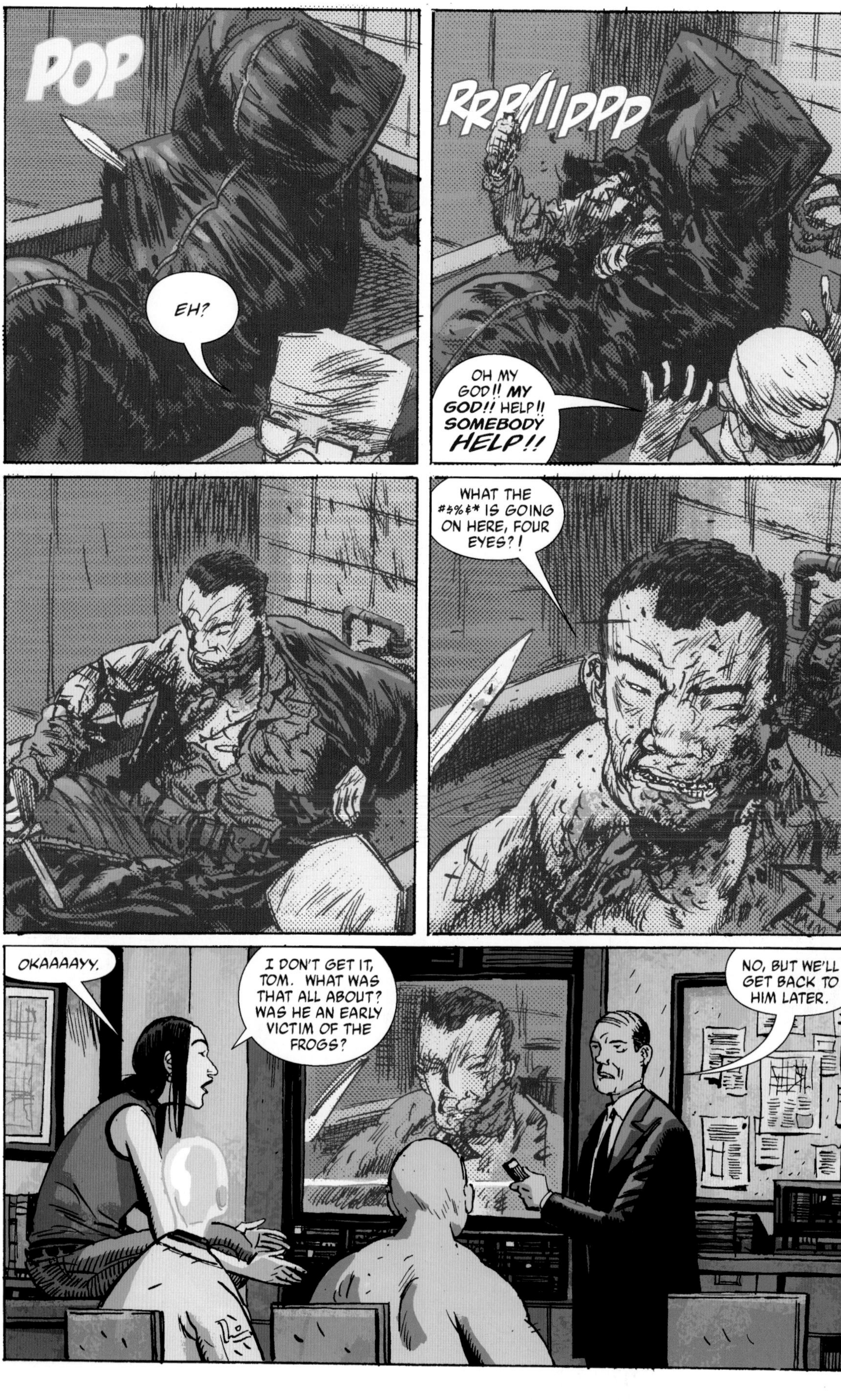
POP
EH?
RRRIIIPPP
OH MY GOD!! MY GOD!! HELP!! SOMEBODY HELP!!
WHAT THE #$%&* IS GOING ON HERE, FOUR EYES?!
OKAAAAYY.
I DON'T GET IT, TOM. WHAT WAS THAT ALL ABOUT? WAS HE AN EARLY VICTIM OF THE FROGS?
NO, BUT WE'LL GET BACK TO HIM LATER.

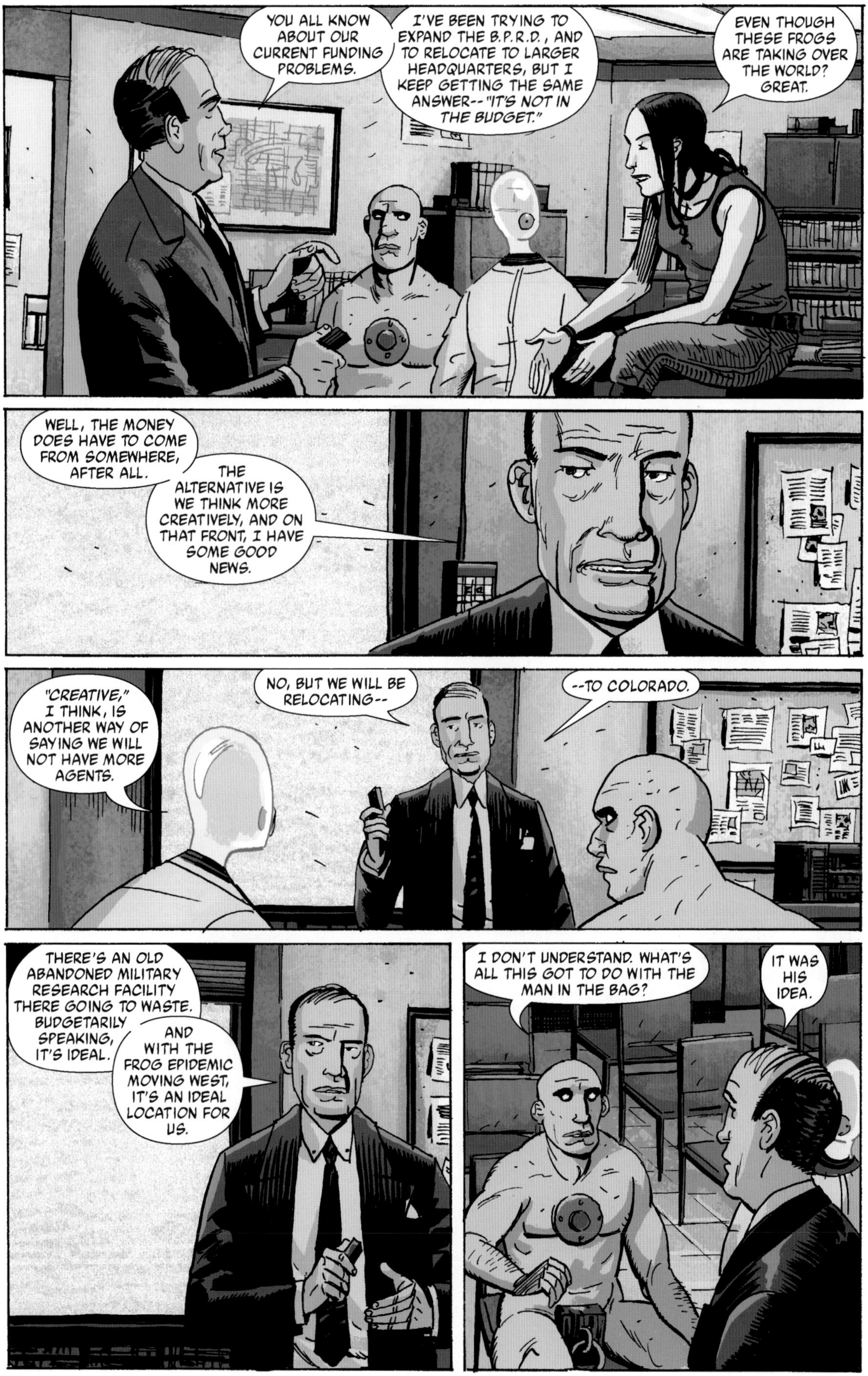
YOU ALL KNOW ABOUT OUR CURRENT FUNDING PROBLEMS.
I'VE BEEN TRYING TO EXPAND THE B.P.R.D., AND TO RELOCATE TO LARGER HEADQUARTERS, BUT I KEEP GETTING THE SAME ANSWER-- "IT'S NOT IN THE BUDGET."
EVEN THOUGH THESE FROGS ARE TAKING OVER THE WORLD? GREAT.
WELL, THE MONEY DOES HAVE TO COME FROM SOMEWHERE, AFTER ALL.
THE ALTERNATIVE IS WE THINK MORE CREATIVELY, AND ON THAT FRONT, I HAVE SOME GOOD NEWS.
"CREATIVE," I THINK, IS ANOTHER WAY OF SAYING WE WILL NOT HAVE MORE AGENTS.
NO, BUT WE WILL BE RELOCATING--
--TO COLORADO.
THERE'S AN OLD ABANDONED MILITARY RESEARCH FACILITY THERE GOING TO WASTE. BUDGETARILY SPEAKING, IT'S IDEAL.
AND WITH THE FROG EPIDEMIC MOVING WEST, IT'S AN IDEAL LOCATION FOR US.
I DON'T UNDERSTAND. WHAT'S ALL THIS GOT TO DO WITH THE MAN IN THE BAG?
IT WAS HIS IDEA.

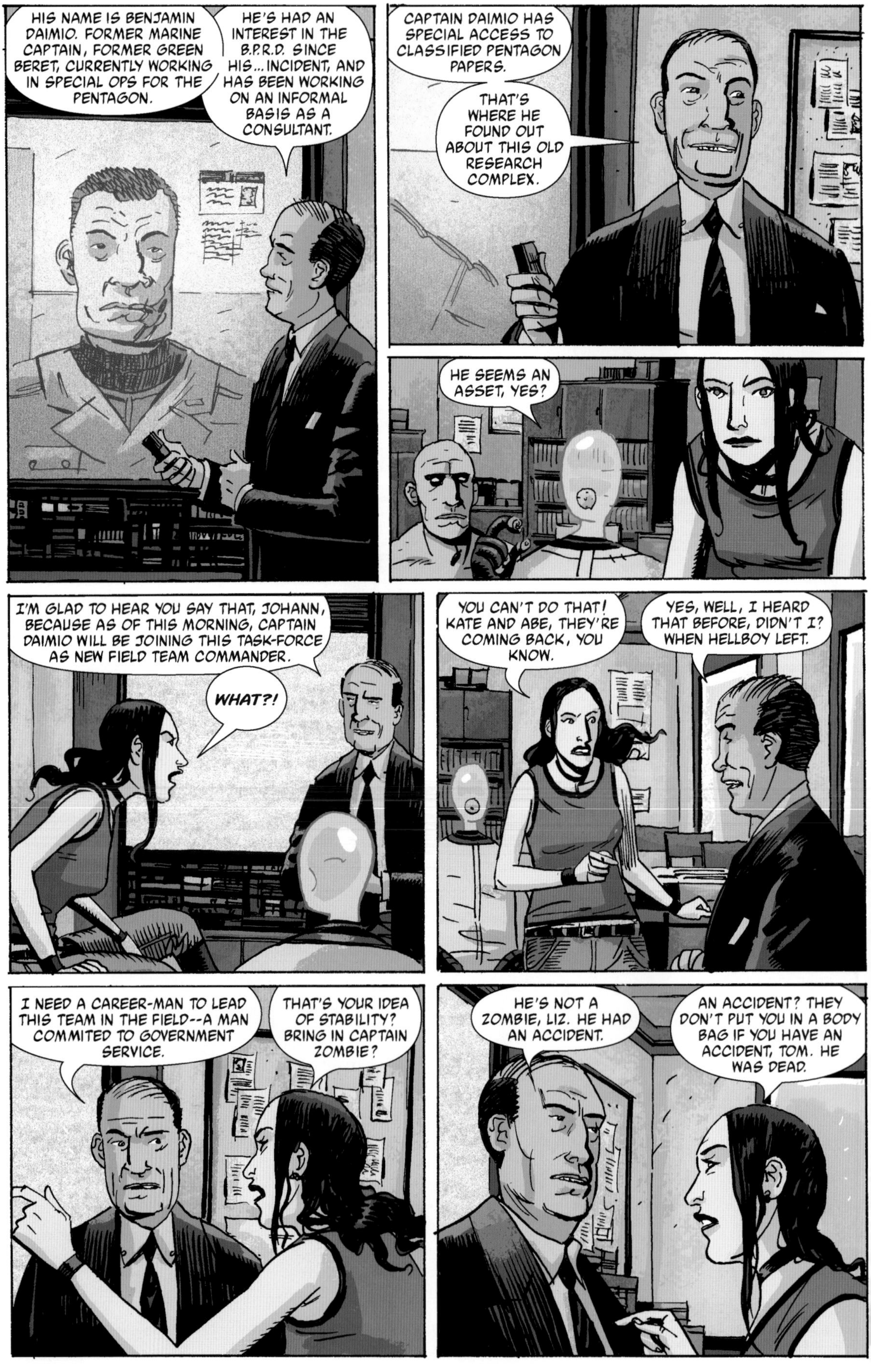
HIS NAME IS BENJAMIN DAIMIO. FORMER MARINE CAPTAIN, FORMER GREEN BERET, CURRENTLY WORKING IN SPECIAL OPS FOR THE PENTAGON.
HE'S HAD AN INTEREST IN THE B.P.R.D. SINCE HIS... INCIDENT, AND HAS BEEN WORKING ON AN INFORMAL BASIS AS A CONSULTANT.
CAPTAIN DAIMIO HAS SPECIAL ACCESS TO CLASSIFIED PENTAGON PAPERS.
THAT'S WHERE HE FOUND OUT ABOUT THIS OLD RESEARCH COMPLEX.
HE SEEMS AN ASSET, YES?
I'M GLAD TO HEAR YOU SAY THAT, JOHANN, BECAUSE AS OF THIS MORNING, CAPTAIN DAIMIO WILL BE JOINING THIS TASK-FORCE AS NEW FIELD TEAM COMMANDER.
WHAT?!
YOU CAN'T DO THAT! KATE AND ABE, THEY'RE COMING BACK, YOU KNOW.
YES, WELL, I HEARD THAT BEFORE, DIDN'T I? WHEN HELLBOY LEFT.
I NEED A CAREER-MAN TO LEAD THIS TEAM IN THE FIELD--A MAN COMMITED TO GOVERNMENT SERVICE.
THAT'S YOUR IDEA OF STABILITY? BRING IN CAPTAIN ZOMBIE?
HE'S NOT A ZOMBIE, LIZ. HE HAD AN ACCIDENT.
AN ACCIDENT? THEY DON'T PUT YOU IN A BODY BAG IF YOU HAVE AN ACCIDENT, TOM. HE WAS DEAD.

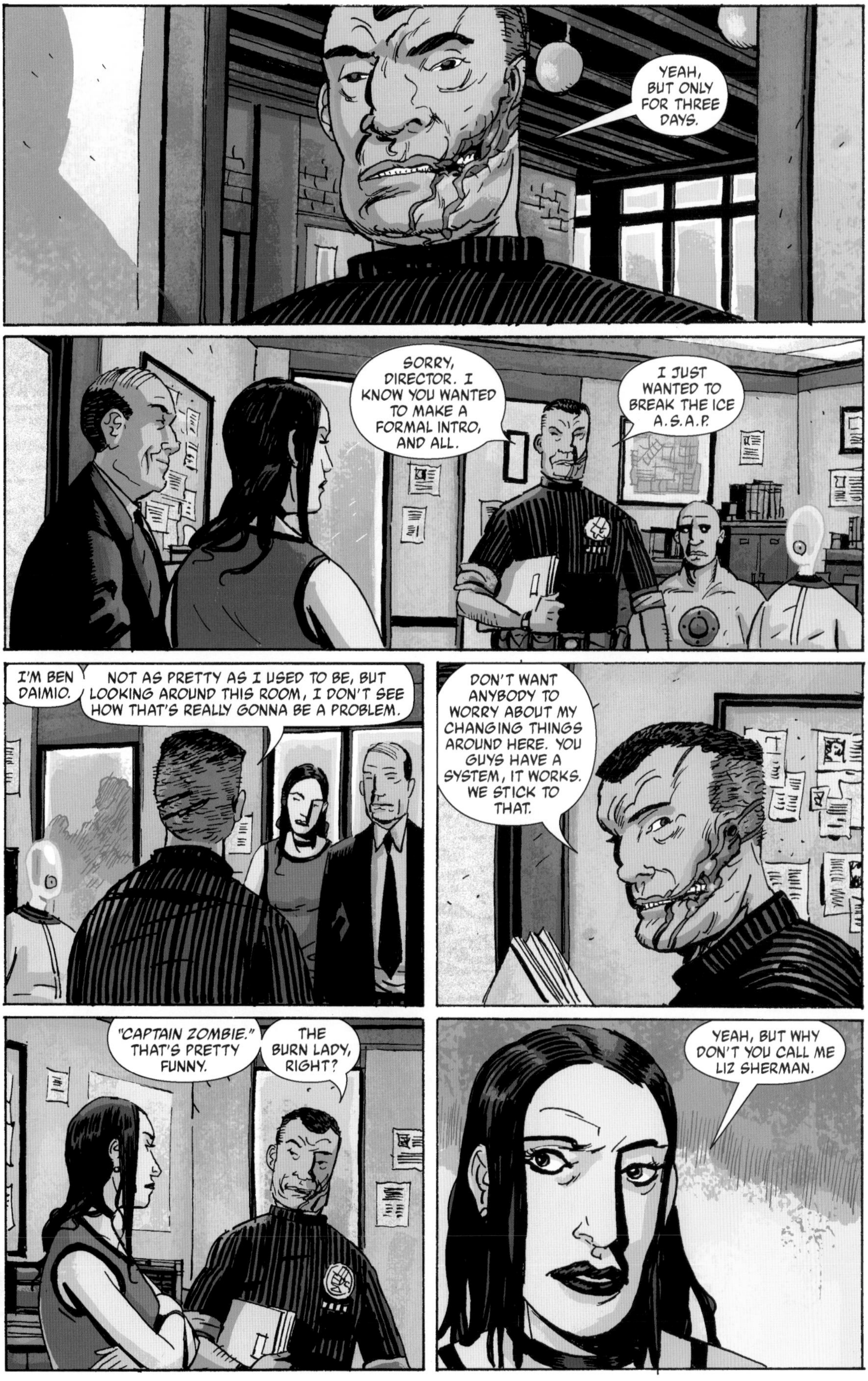
YEAH, BUT ONLY FOR THREE DAYS.
SORRY, DIRECTOR. I KNOW YOU WANTED TO MAKE A FORMAL INTRO, AND ALL.
I JUST WANTED TO BREAK THE ICE A.S.A.P.
I'M BEN DAIMIO.
NOT AS PRETTY AS I USED TO BE, BUT LOOKING AROUND THIS ROOM, I DON'T SEE HOW THAT'S REALLY GONNA BE A PROBLEM.
DON'T WANT ANYBODY TO WORRY ABOUT MY CHANGING THINGS AROUND HERE. YOU GUYS HAVE A SYSTEM, IT WORKS. WE STICK TO THAT.
"CAPTAIN ZOMBIE." THAT'S PRETTY FUNNY.
THE BURN LADY, RIGHT?
YEAH, BUT WHY DON'T YOU CALL ME LIZ SHERMAN.

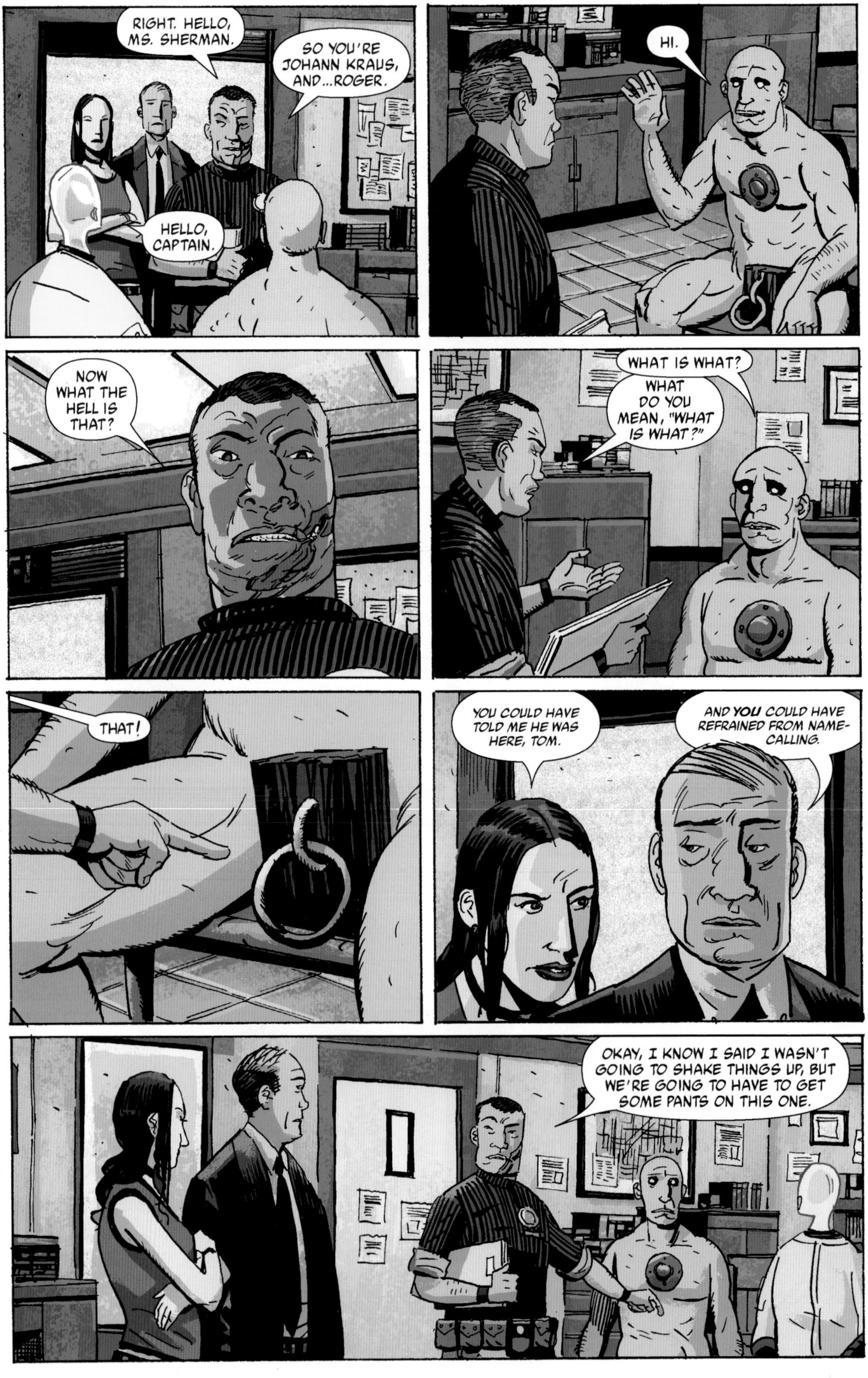
RIGHT. HELLO, MS. SHERMAN.
SO YOU'RE JOHANN KRAUS, AND...ROGER.
HELLO, CAPTAIN.
HI.
NOW WHAT THE HELL IS THAT?
WHAT IS WHAT?
WHAT DO YOU MEAN, "WHAT IS WHAT?"
THAT!
YOU COULD HAVE TOLD ME HE WAS HERE, TOM.
AND YOU COULD HAVE REFRAINED FROM NAME-CALLING.
OKAY, I KNOW I SAID I WASN'T GOING TO SHAKE THINGS UP, BUT WE'RE GOING TO HAVE TO GET SOME PANTS ON THIS ONE.

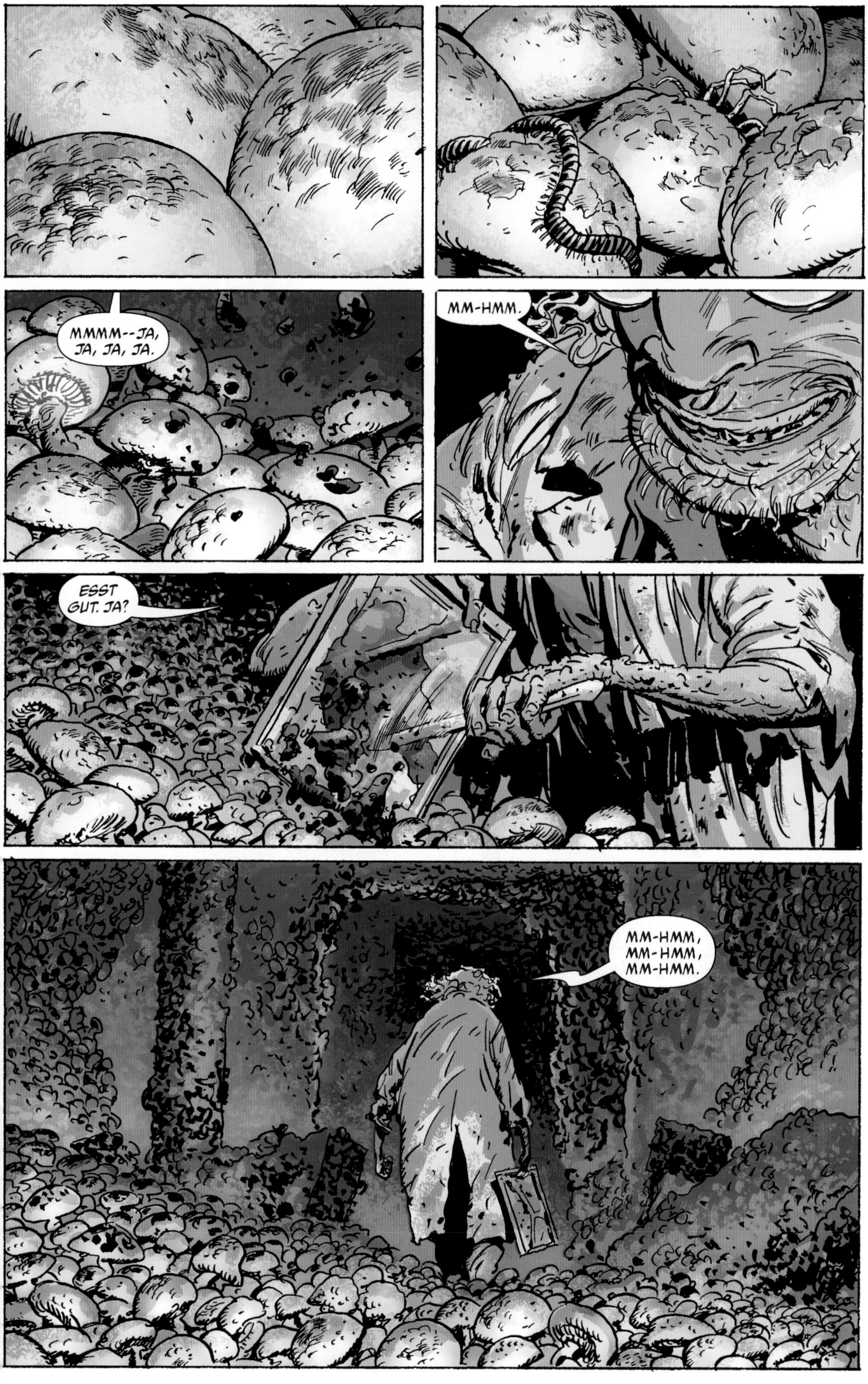
MMMM--JA, JA, JA, JA.
MM-HMM.
ESST GUT. JA?
MM-HMM, MM-HMM, MM-HMM.

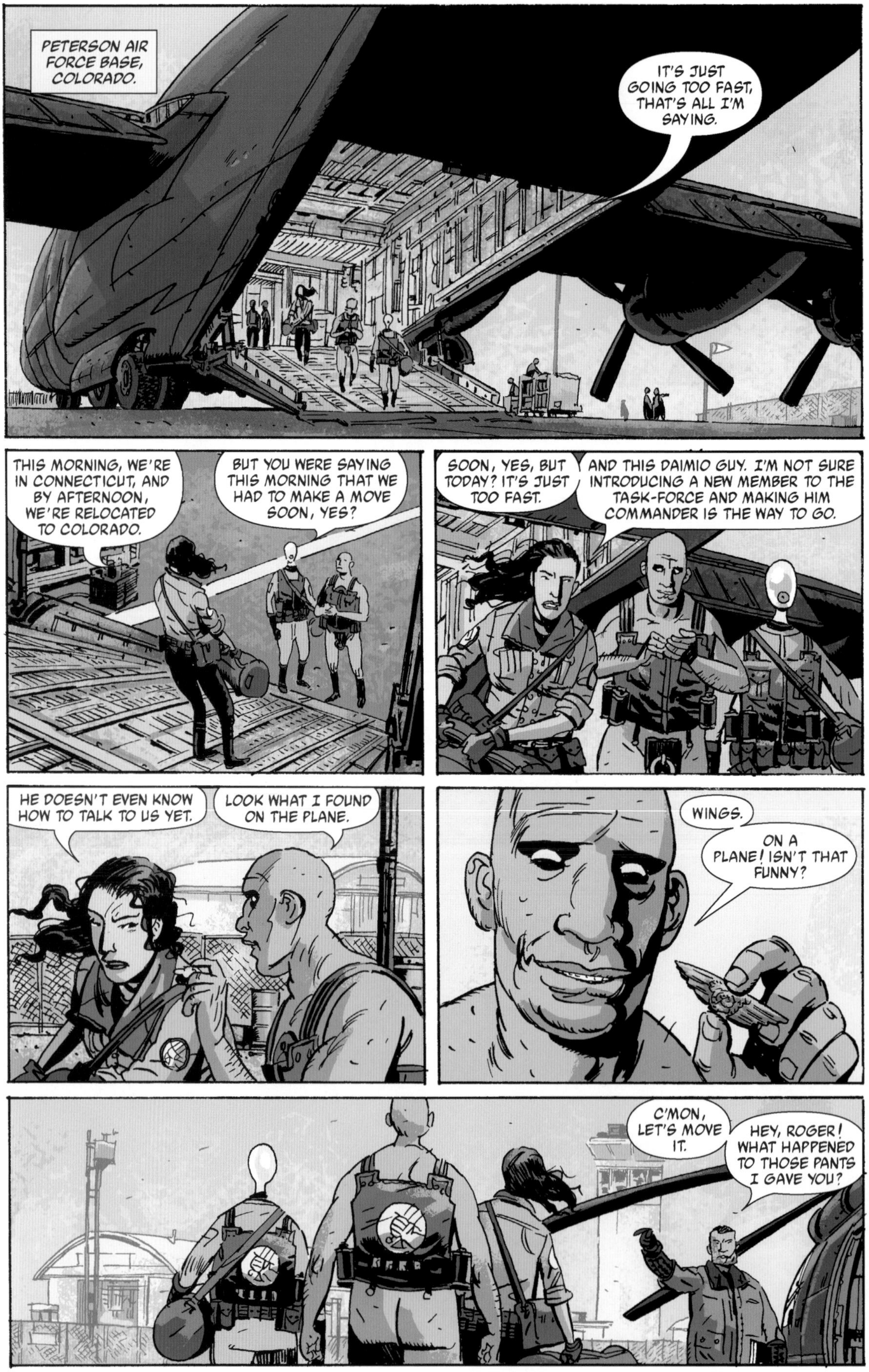
PETERSON AIR FORCE BASE, COLORADO.
IT'S JUST GOING TOO FAST, THAT'S ALL I'M SAYING.
THIS MORNING, WE'RE IN CONNECTICUT, AND BY AFTERNOON, WE'RE RELOCATED TO COLORADO.
BUT YOU WERE SAYING THIS MORNING THAT WE HAD TO MAKE A MOVE SOON, YES?
SOON, YES, BUT TODAY? IT'S JUST TOO FAST.
AND THIS DAIMIO GUY. I'M NOT SURE INTRODUCING A NEW MEMBER TO THE TASK-FORCE AND MAKING HIM COMMANDER IS THE WAY TO GO.
HE DOESN'T EVEN KNOW HOW TO TALK TO US YET.
LOOK WHAT I FOUND ON THE PLANE.
WINGS.
ON A PLANE! ISN'T THAT FUNNY?
C'MON, LET'S MOVE IT.
HEY, ROGER! WHAT HAPPENED TO THOSE PANTS I GAVE YOU?

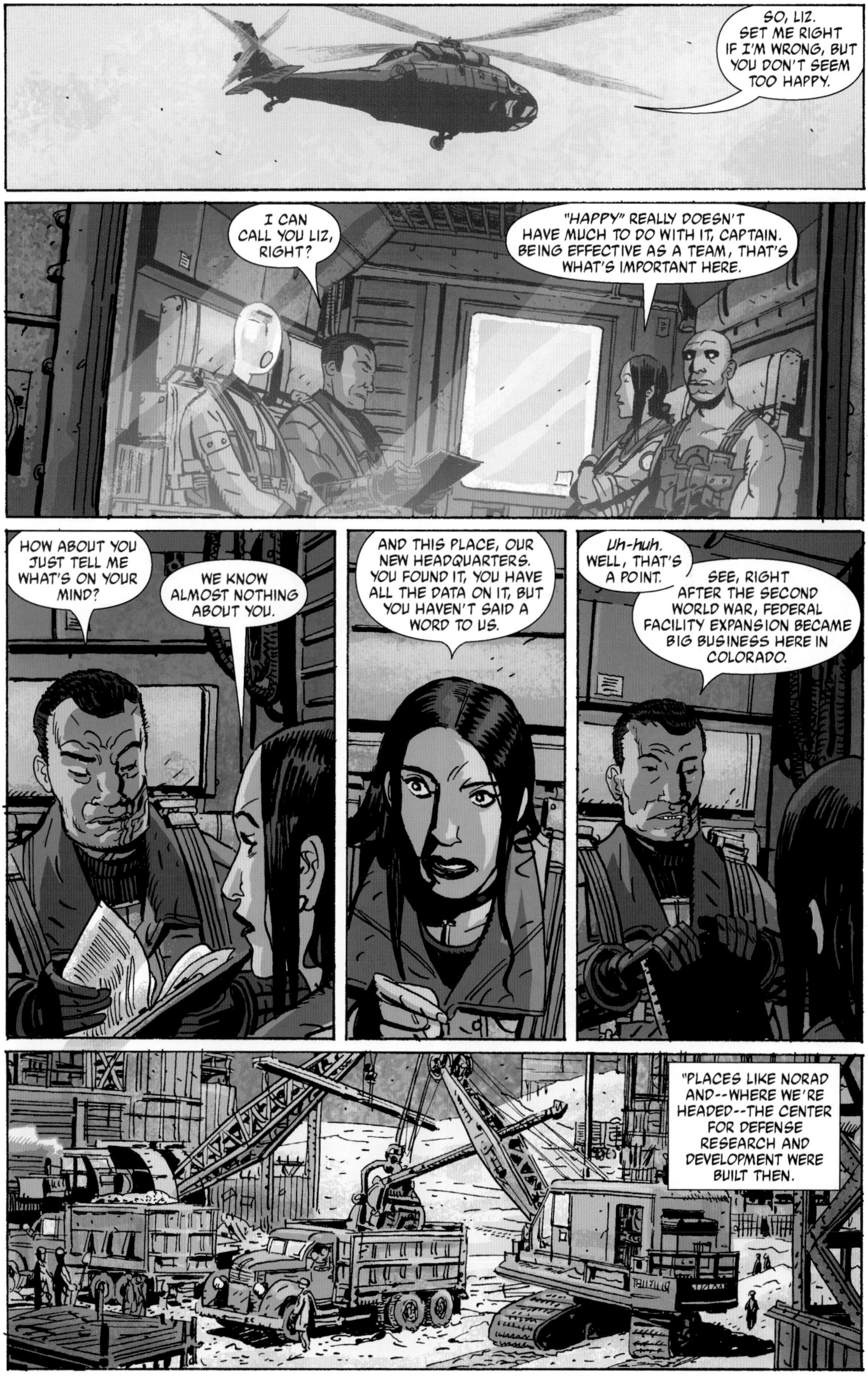
SO, LIZ. SET ME RIGHT IF I'M WRONG, BUT YOU DON'T SEEM TOO HAPPY.
I CAN CALL YOU LIZ, RIGHT?
"HAPPY" REALLY DOESN'T HAVE MUCH TO DO WITH IT, CAPTAIN. BEING EFFECTIVE AS A TEAM, THAT'S WHAT'S IMPORTANT HERE.
HOW ABOUT YOU JUST TELL ME WHAT'S ON YOUR MIND?
WE KNOW ALMOST NOTHING ABOUT YOU.
AND THIS PLACE, OUR NEW HEADQUARTERS. YOU FOUND IT, YOU HAVE ALL THE DATA ON IT, BUT YOU HAVEN'T SAID A WORD TO US.
Uh-huh. WELL, THAT'S A POINT.
SEE, RIGHT AFTER THE SECOND WORLD WAR, FEDERAL FACILITY EXPANSION BECAME BIG BUSINESS HERE IN COLORADO.
"PLACES LIKE NORAD AND--WHERE WE'RE HEADED--THE CENTER FOR DEFENSE RESEARCH AND DEVELOPMENT WERE BUILT THEN.

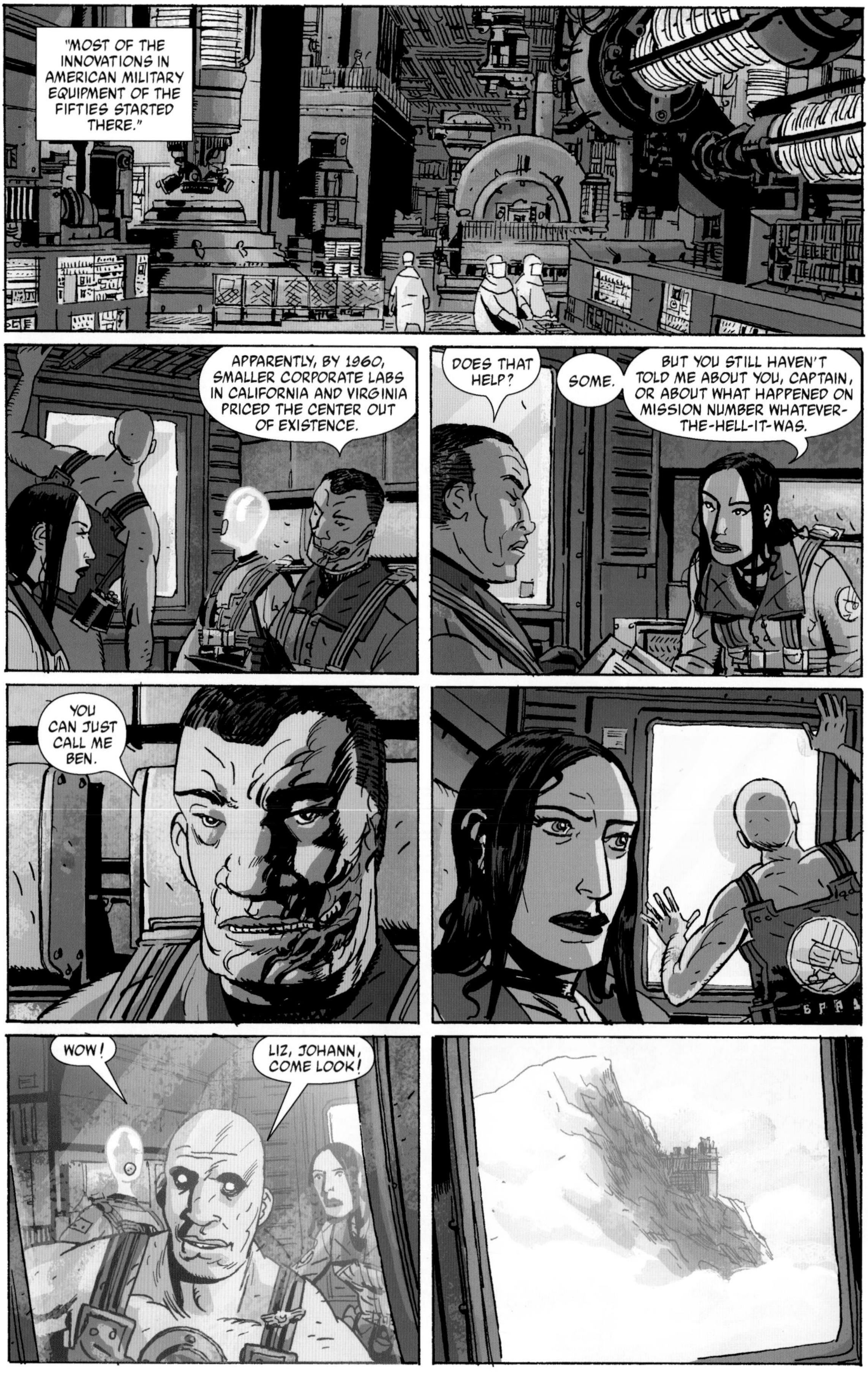
"MOST OF THE INNOVATIONS IN AMERICAN MILITARY EQUIPMENT OF THE FIFTIES STARTED THERE."
APPARENTLY, BY 1960, SMALLER CORPORATE LABS IN CALIFORNIA AND VIRGINIA PRICED THE CENTER OUT OF EXISTENCE.
DOES THAT HELP?
SOME.
BUT YOU STILL HAVEN'T TOLD ME ABOUT YOU, CAPTAIN, OR ABOUT WHAT HAPPENED ON MISSION NUMBER WHATEVER-THE-HELL-IT-WAS.
YOU CAN JUST CALL ME BEN.
WOW!
LIZ, JOHANN, COME LOOK!

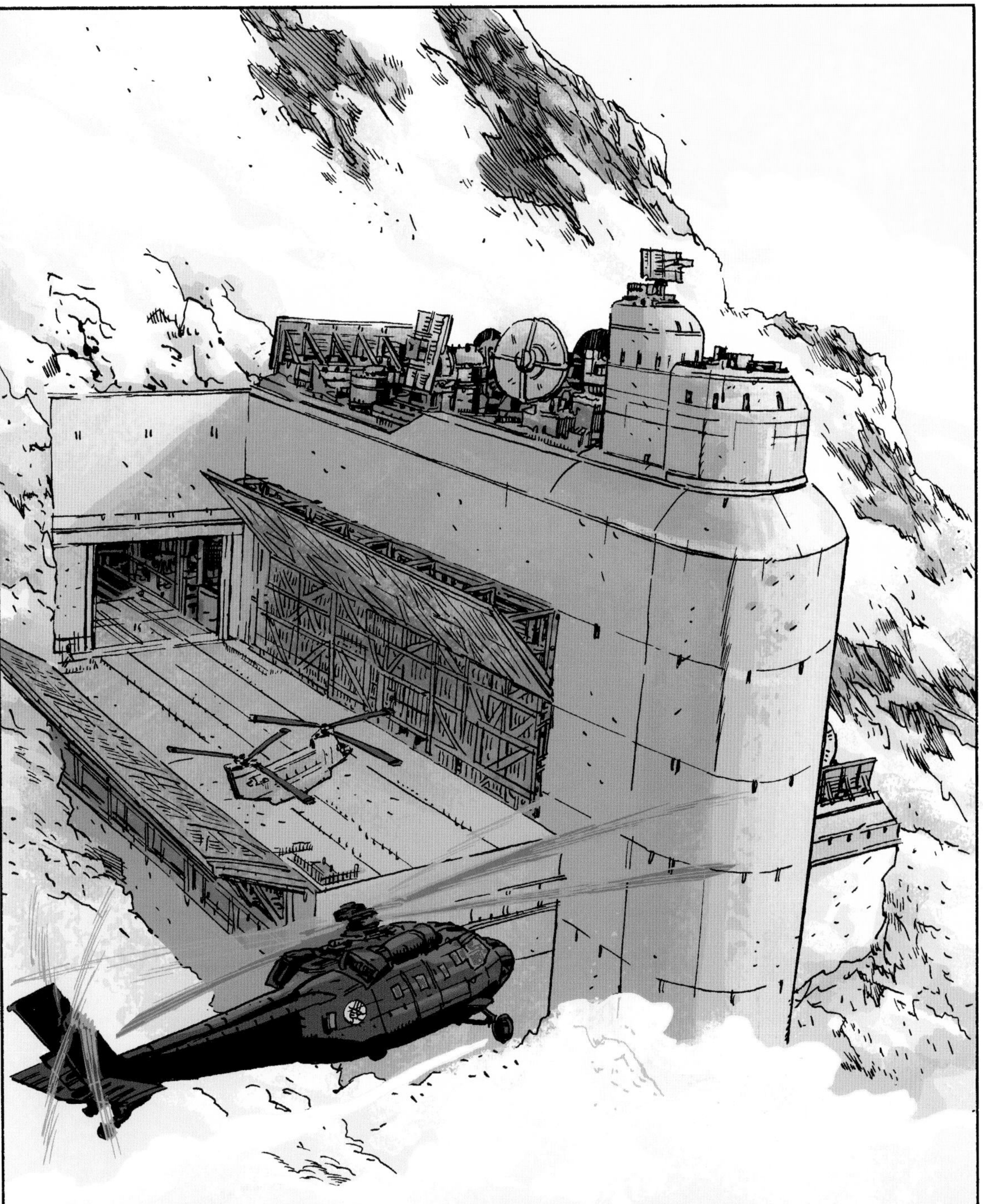

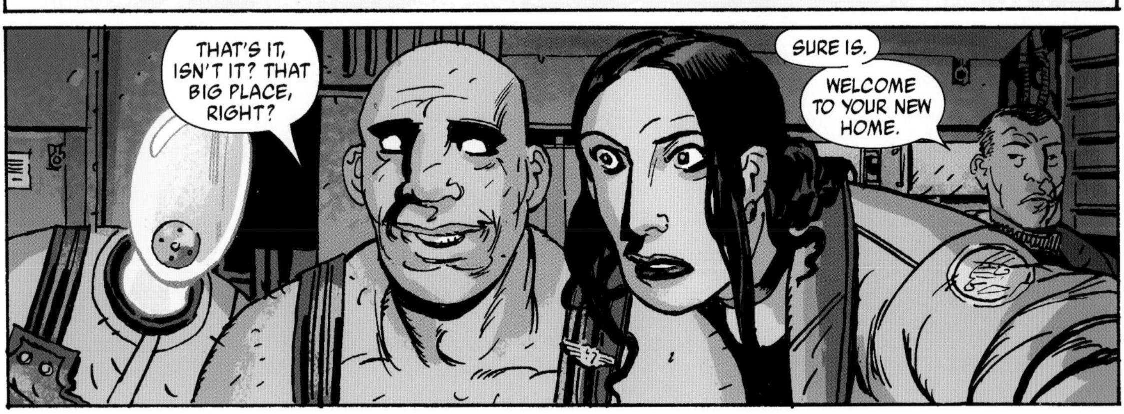
THAT'S IT, ISN'T IT? THAT BIG PLACE, RIGHT?
SURE IS.
WELCOME TO YOUR NEW HOME.

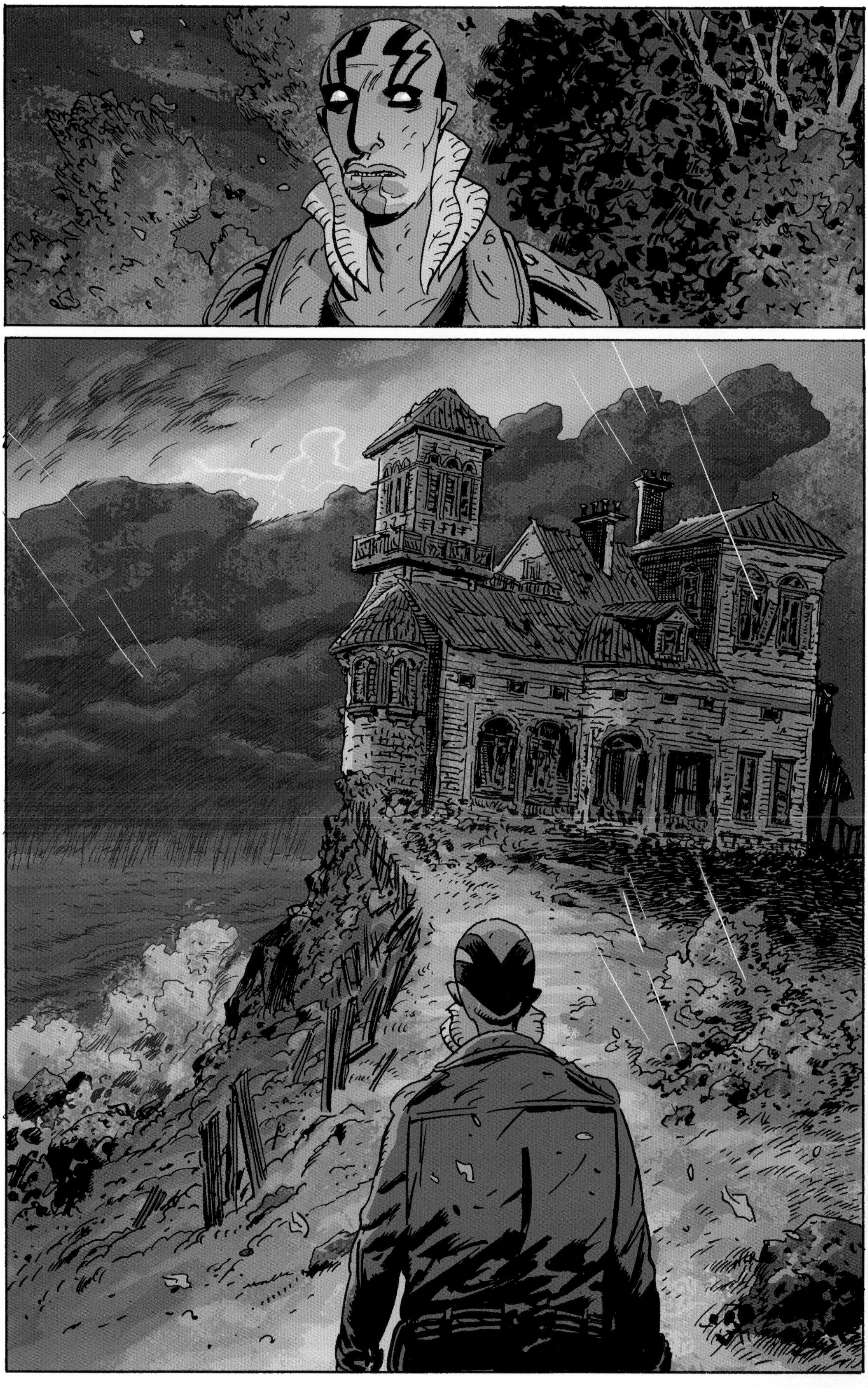

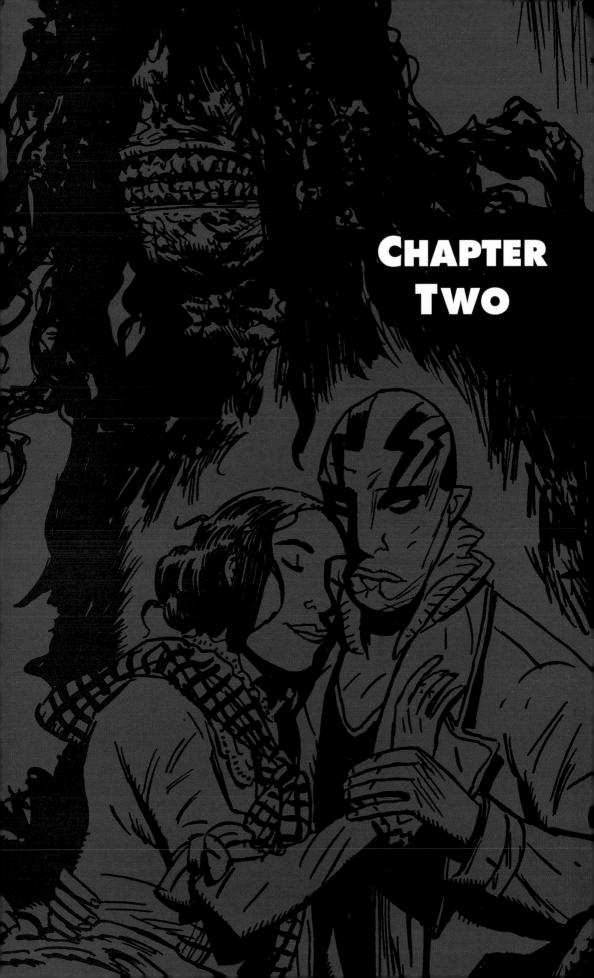

CHAPTER TWO

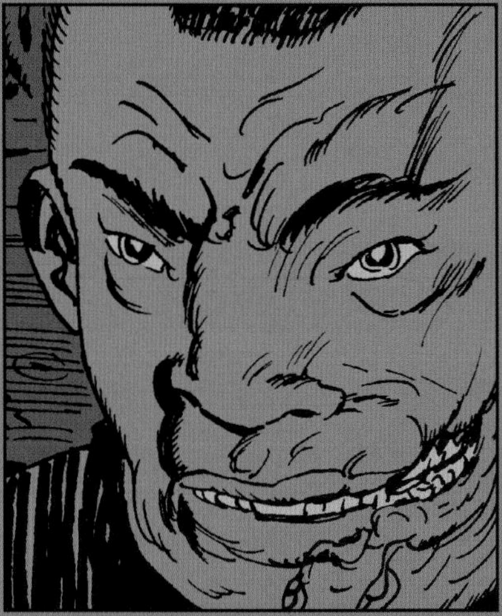

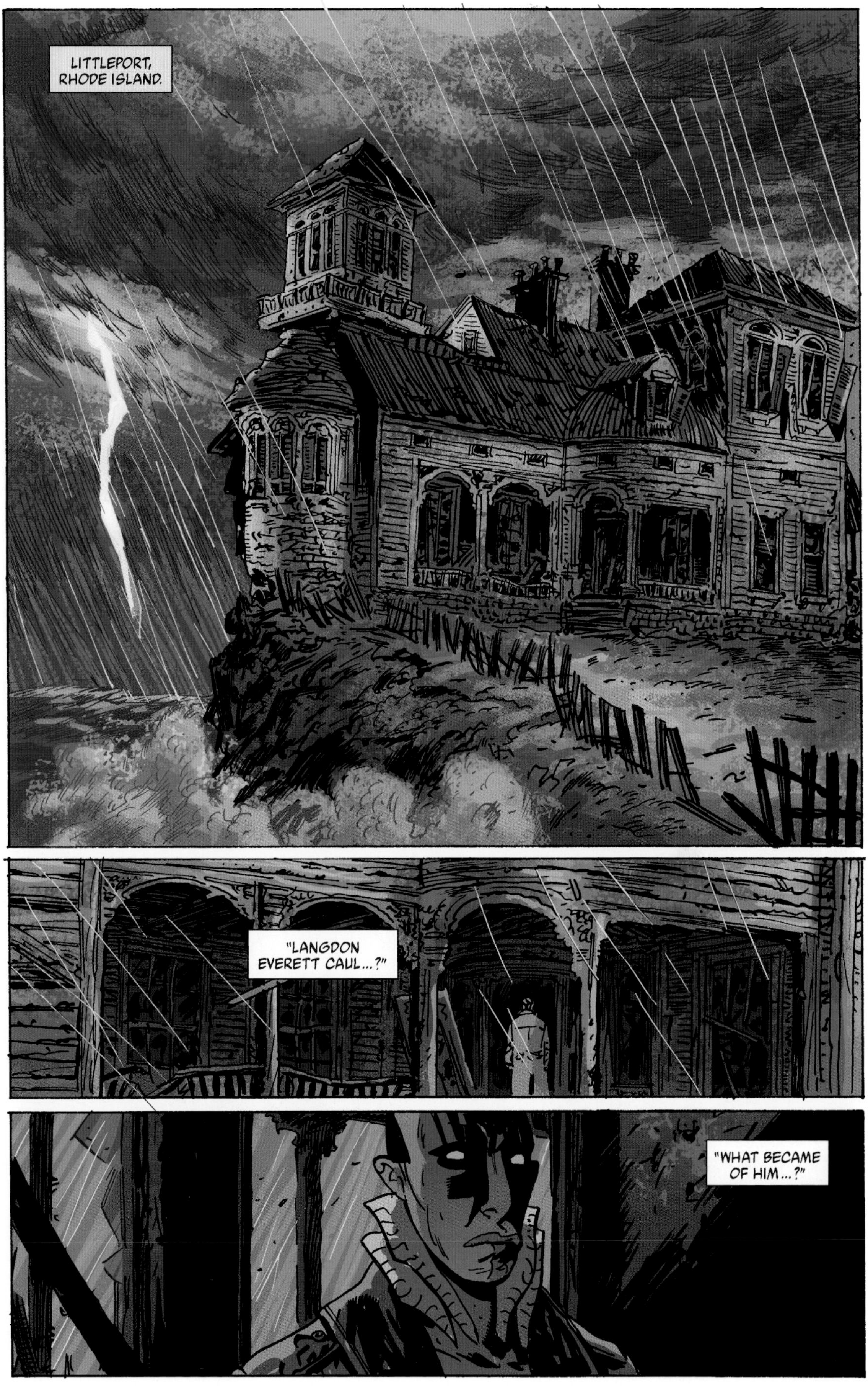
LITTLEPORT, RHODE ISLAND.
"LANGDON EVERETT CAUL...?"
"WHAT BECAME OF HIM...?"

"HE WAS INVOLVED IN PRIVATE INVESTIGATIONS OF A SCIENTIFIC NATURE..."

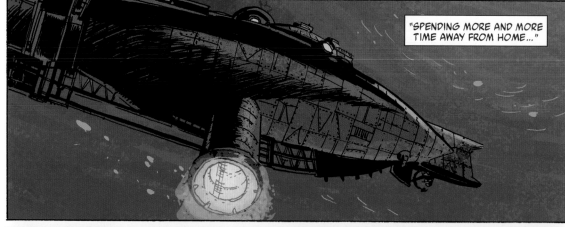

"SPENDING MORE AND MORE TIME AWAY FROM HOME..."

"ENTERTAINING CURIOUS FOREIGN GENTLEMEN..."

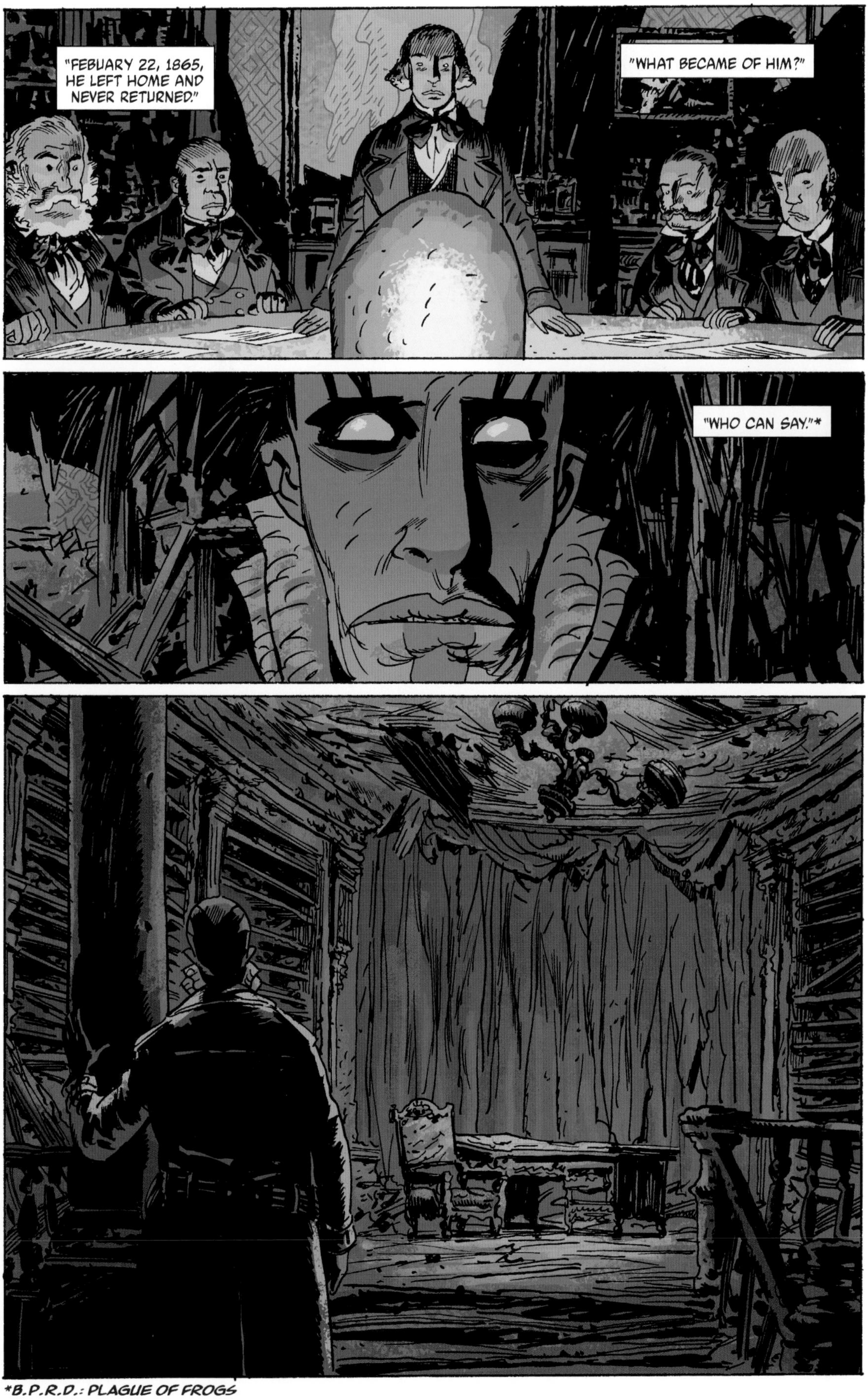
"FEBUARY 22, 1865, HE LEFT HOME AND NEVER RETURNED."
"WHAT BECAME OF HIM?"
"WHO CAN SAY."*

*B.P.R.D.: PLAGUE OF FROGS

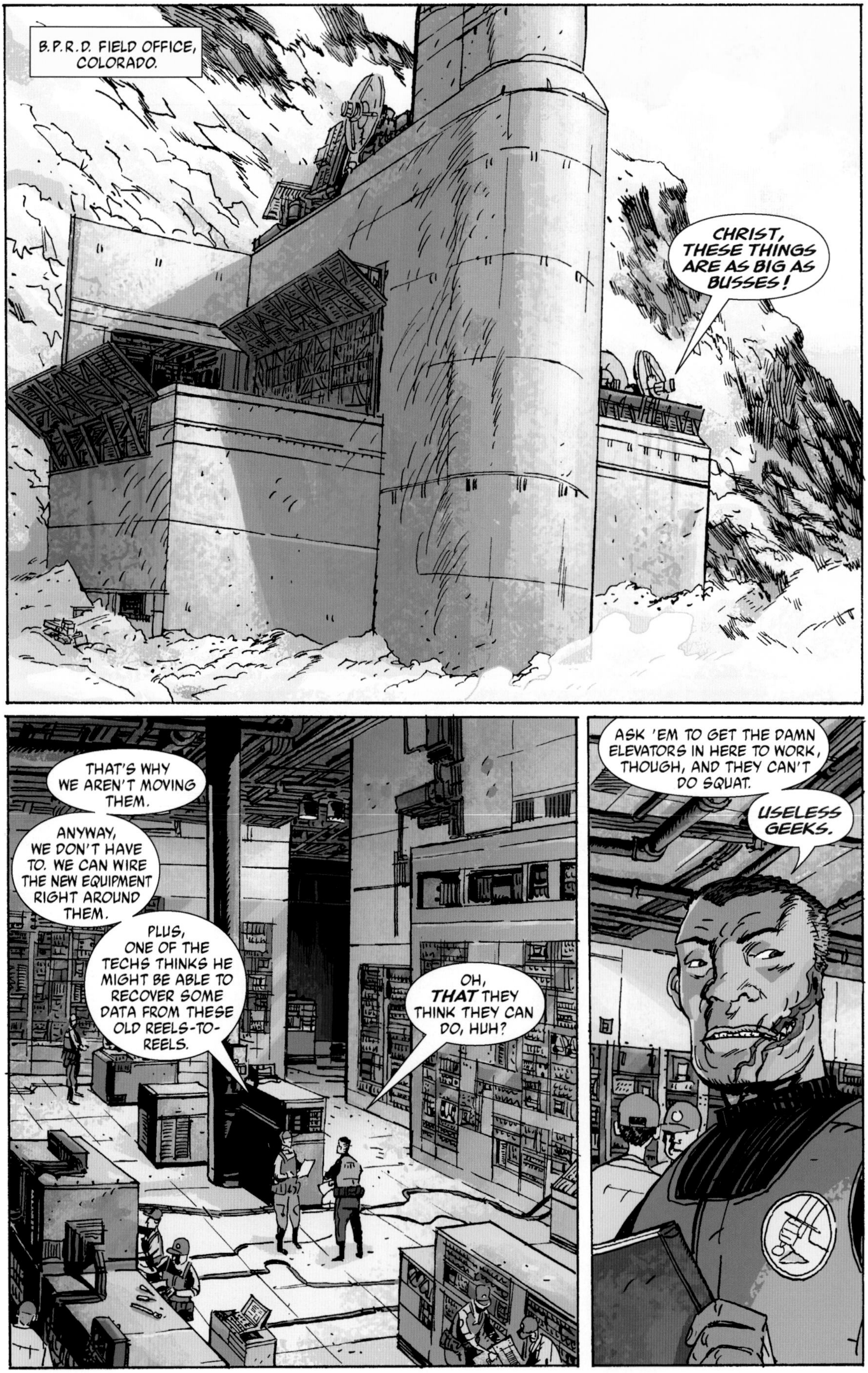
B.P.R.D. FIELD OFFICE, COLORADO.
CHRIST, THESE THINGS ARE AS BIG AS BUSSES!
THAT'S WHY WE AREN'T MOVING THEM.
ANYWAY, WE DON'T HAVE TO. WE CAN WIRE THE NEW EQUIPMENT RIGHT AROUND THEM.
PLUS, ONE OF THE TECHS THINKS HE MIGHT BE ABLE TO RECOVER SOME DATA FROM THESE OLD REELS-TO-REELS.
OH, THAT THEY THINK THEY CAN DO, HUH?
ASK 'EM TO GET THE DAMN ELEVATORS IN HERE TO WORK, THOUGH, AND THEY CAN'T DO SQUAT.
USELESS GEEKS.

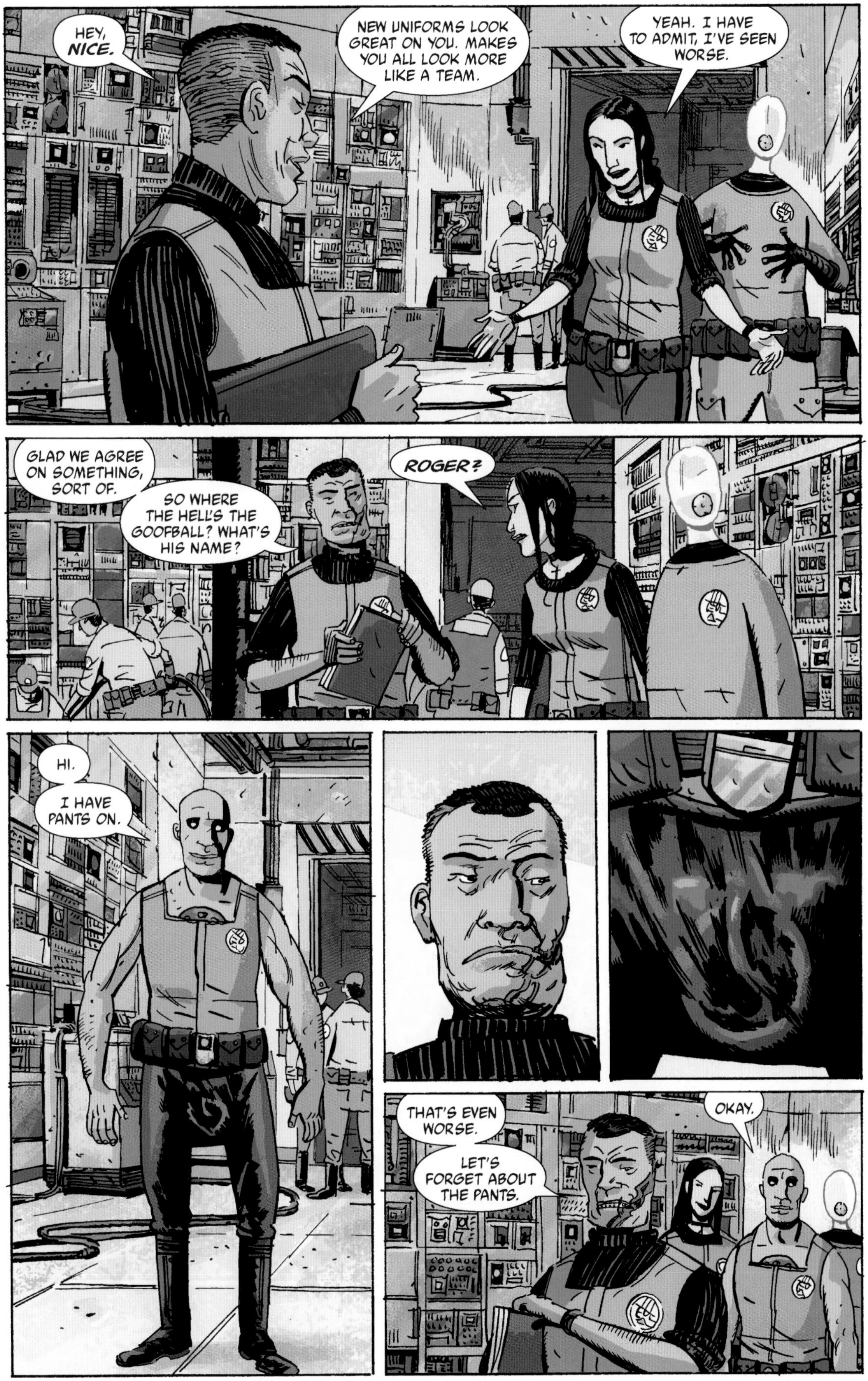
HEY, *NICE.*
NEW UNIFORMS LOOK GREAT ON YOU. MAKES YOU ALL LOOK MORE LIKE A TEAM.
YEAH. I HAVE TO ADMIT, I'VE SEEN WORSE.
GLAD WE AGREE ON SOMETHING, SORT OF.
SO WHERE THE HELL'S THE GOOFBALL? WHAT'S HIS NAME?
ROGER?
HI.
I HAVE PANTS ON.
THAT'S EVEN WORSE.
LET'S FORGET ABOUT THE PANTS.
OKAY.

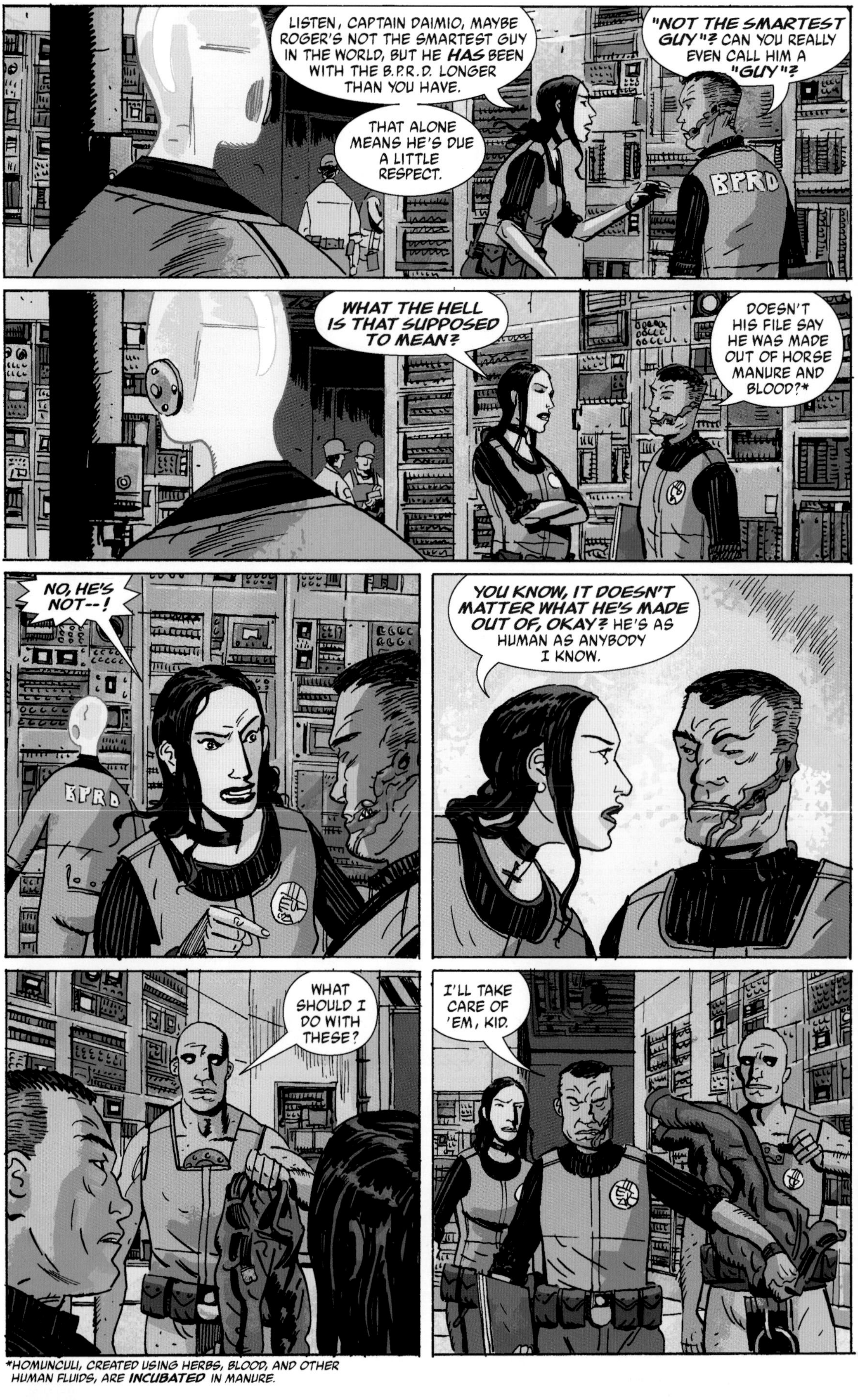
LISTEN, CAPTAIN DAIMIO, MAYBE ROGER'S NOT THE SMARTEST GUY IN THE WORLD, BUT HE HAS BEEN WITH THE B.P.R.D. LONGER THAN YOU HAVE.
THAT ALONE MEANS HE'S DUE A LITTLE RESPECT.
"NOT THE SMARTEST GUY"? CAN YOU REALLY EVEN CALL HIM A "GUY"?
BPRD
WHAT THE HELL IS THAT SUPPOSED TO MEAN?
DOESN'T HIS FILE SAY HE WAS MADE OUT OF HORSE MANURE AND BLOOD?*
NO, HE'S NOT--!
BPRD
YOU KNOW, IT DOESN'T MATTER WHAT HE'S MADE OUT OF, OKAY? HE'S AS HUMAN AS ANYBODY I KNOW.
WHAT SHOULD I DO WITH THESE?
I'LL TAKE CARE OF 'EM, KID.

*HOMUNCULI, CREATED USING HERBS, BLOOD, AND OTHER HUMAN FLUIDS, ARE **INCUBATED** IN MANURE.

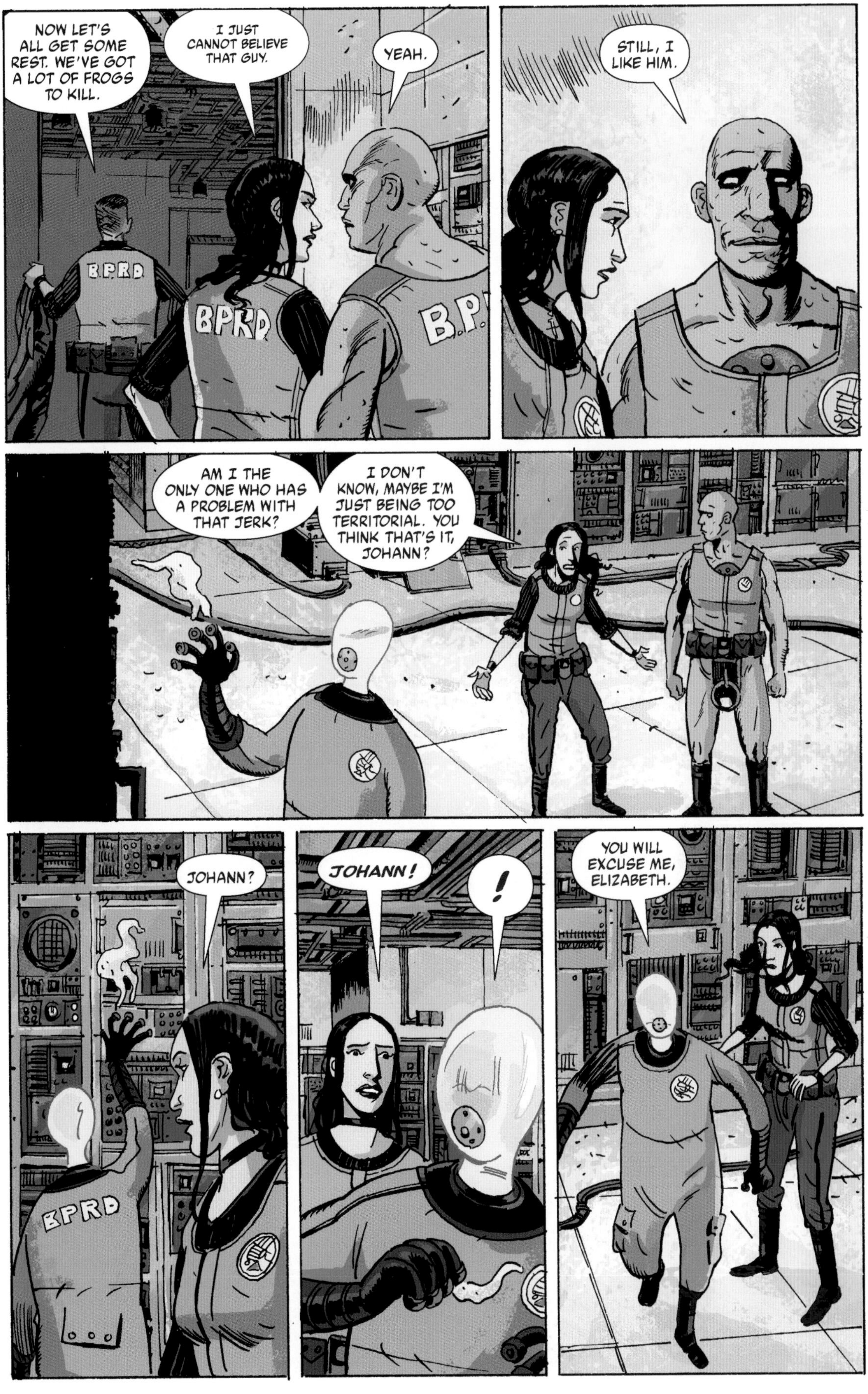
NOW LET'S ALL GET SOME REST. WE'VE GOT A LOT OF FROGS TO KILL.
I JUST CANNOT BELIEVE THAT GUY.
YEAH.
STILL, I LIKE HIM.
AM I THE ONLY ONE WHO HAS A PROBLEM WITH THAT JERK?
I DON'T KNOW, MAYBE I'M JUST BEING TOO TERRITORIAL. YOU THINK THAT'S IT, JOHANN?
JOHANN?
JOHANN!
!
YOU WILL EXCUSE ME, ELIZABETH.

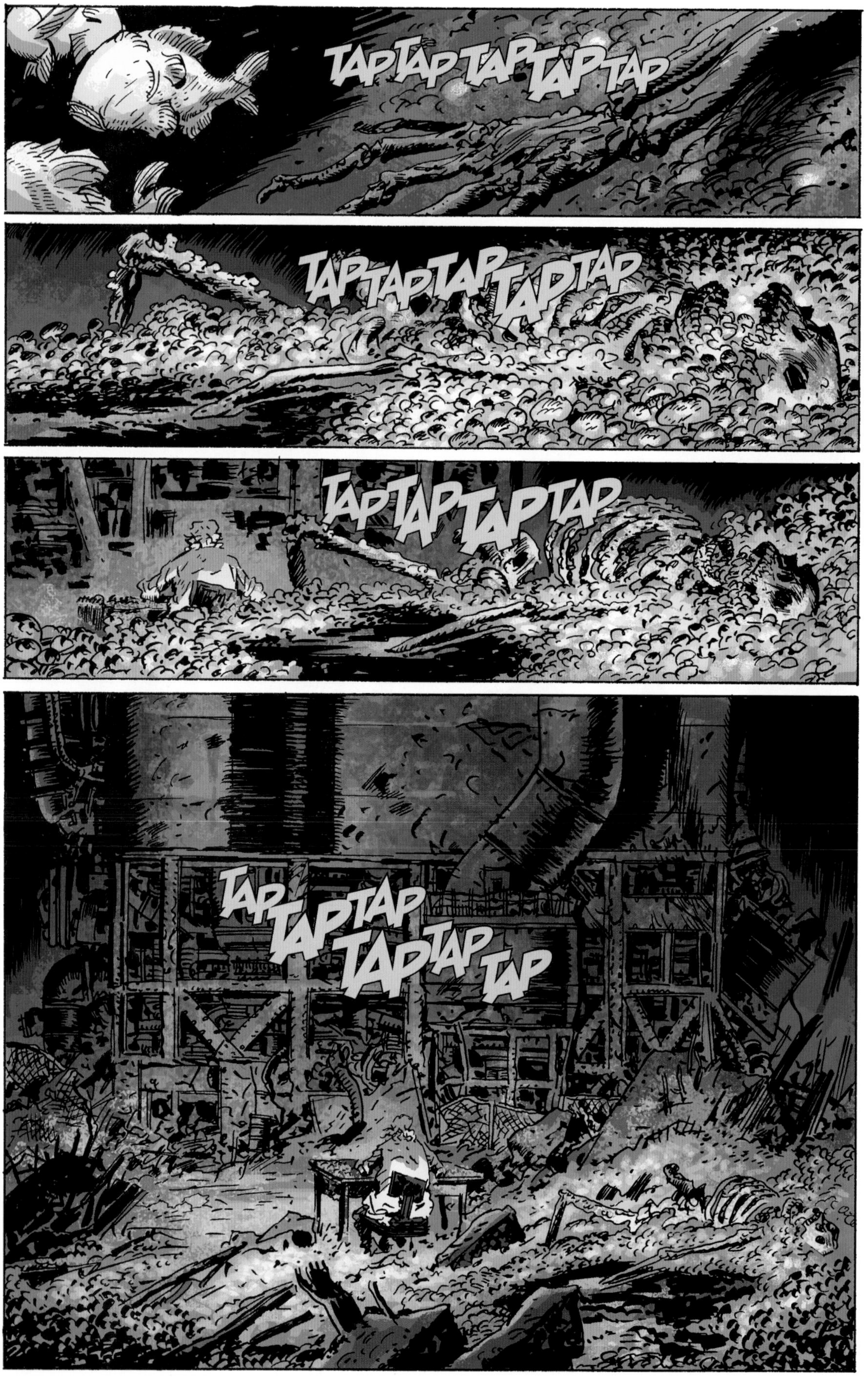
TAP TAP TAP TAP TAP
TAP TAP TAP TAP TAP
TAP TAP TAP TAP
TAP TAP TAP TAP TAP TAP

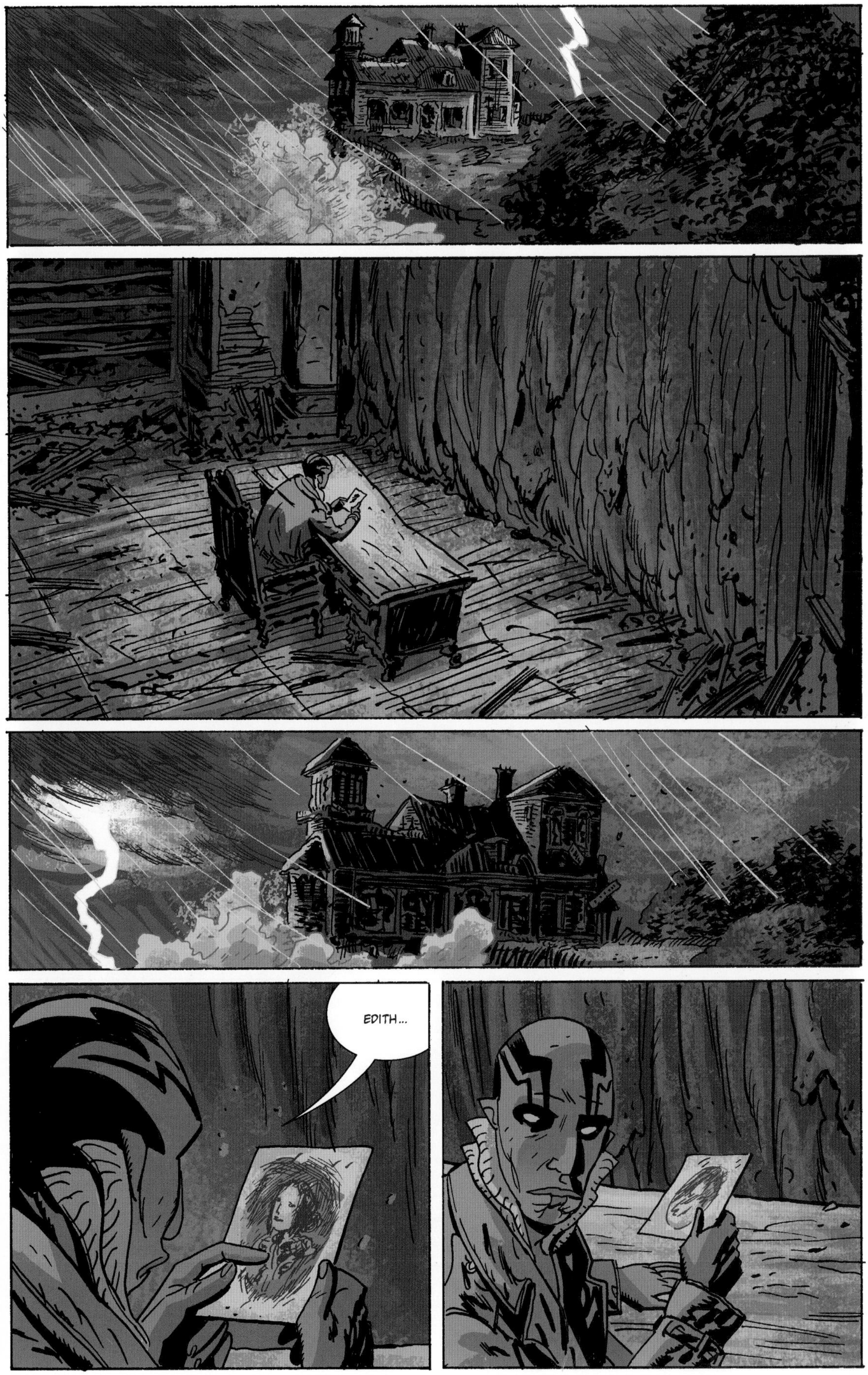
EDITH...

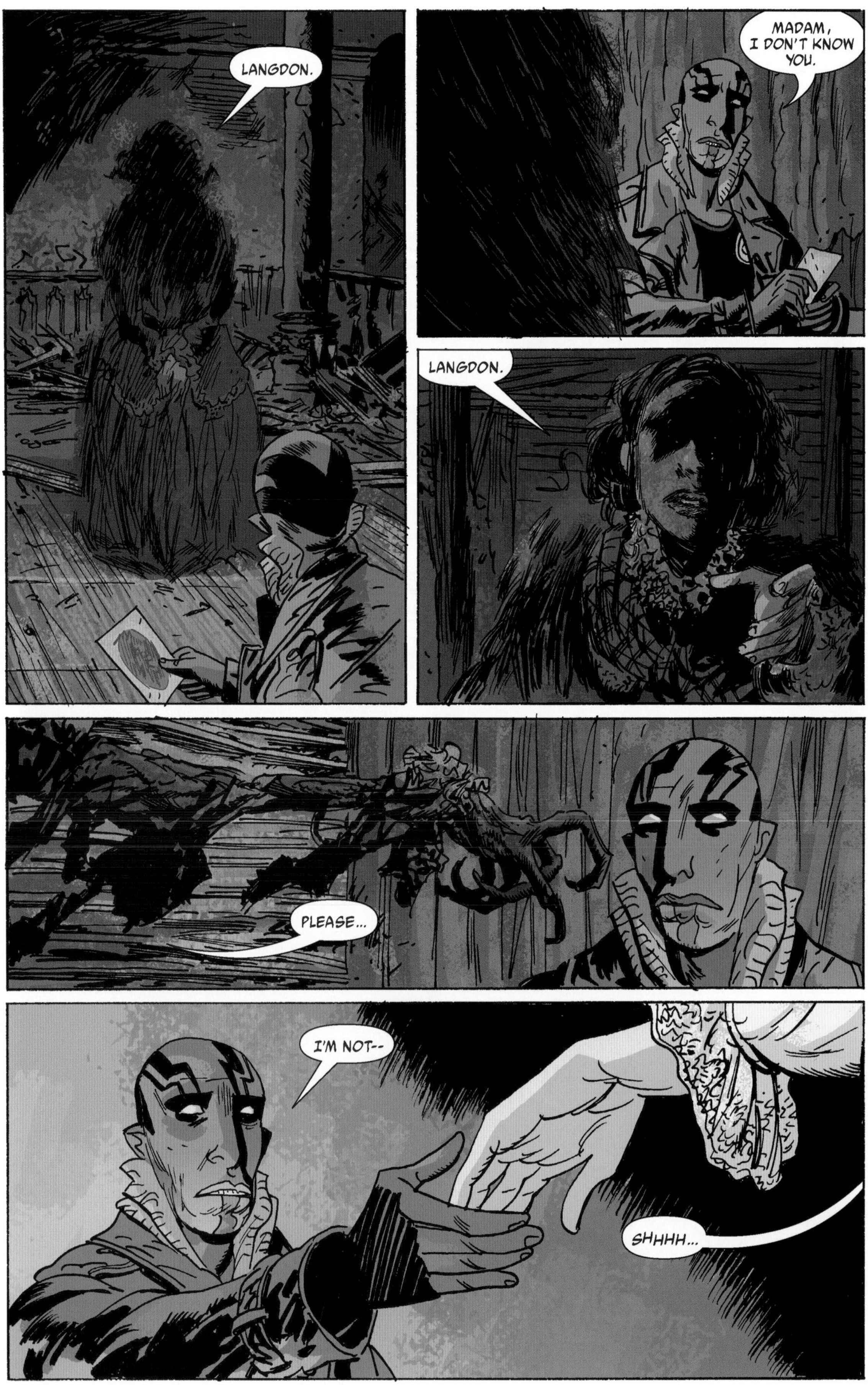
LANGDON.
MADAM, I DON'T KNOW YOU.
LANGDON.
PLEASE...
I'M NOT--
SHHHH...

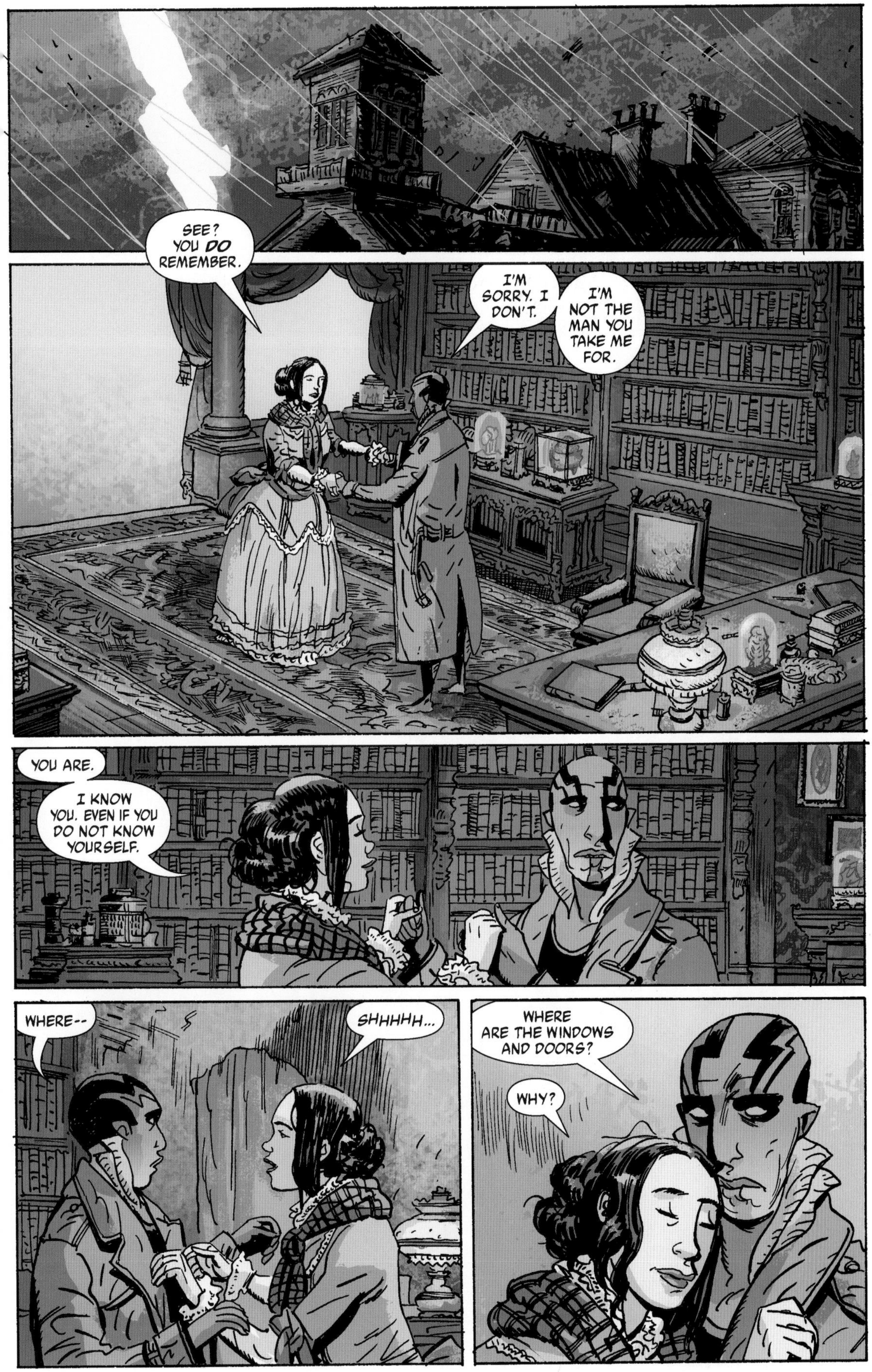
SEE? YOU *DO* REMEMBER.
I'M SORRY. I DON'T.
I'M NOT THE MAN YOU TAKE ME FOR.
YOU ARE.
I KNOW YOU. EVEN IF YOU DO NOT KNOW YOURSELF.
WHERE--
SHHHHH...
WHERE ARE THE WINDOWS AND DOORS?
WHY?

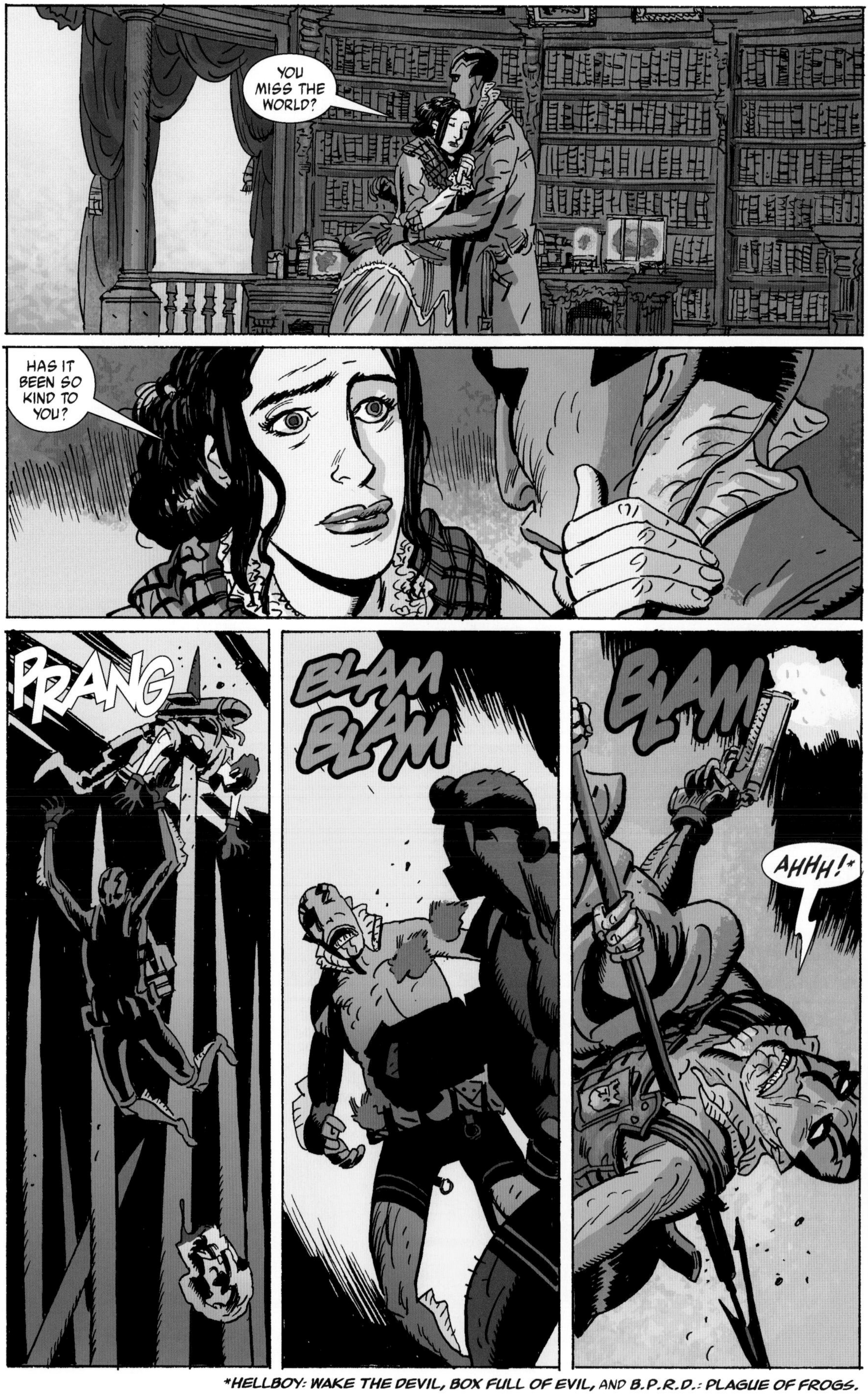
YOU MISS THE WORLD?
HAS IT BEEN SO KIND TO YOU?
PRANG
BLAM BLAM
BLAM
AHHH!*

*HELLBOY: WAKE THE DEVIL, BOX FULL OF EVIL, AND B.P.R.D.: PLAGUE OF FROGS.

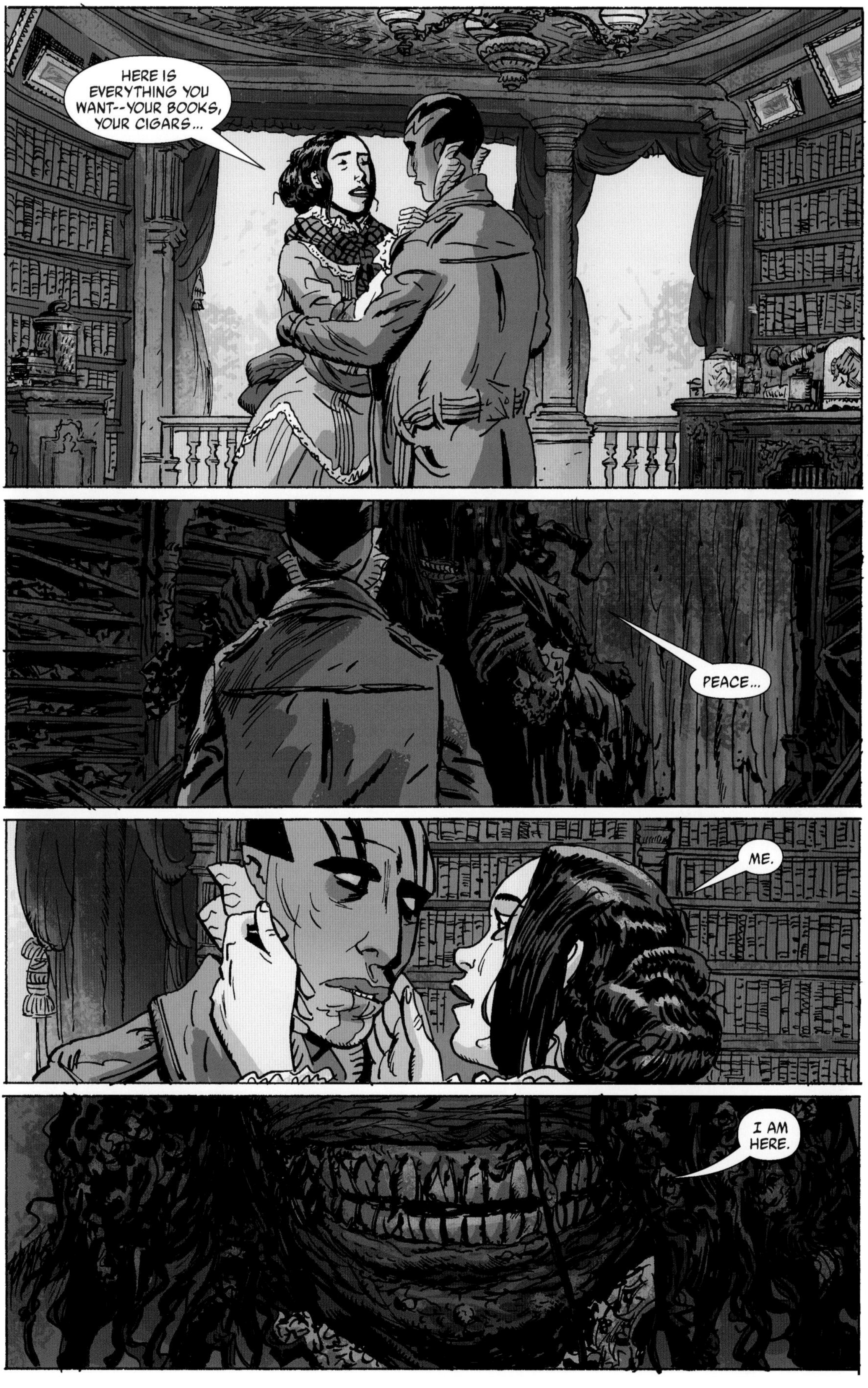
HERE IS EVERYTHING YOU WANT--YOUR BOOKS, YOUR CIGARS...
PEACE...
ME.
I AM HERE.

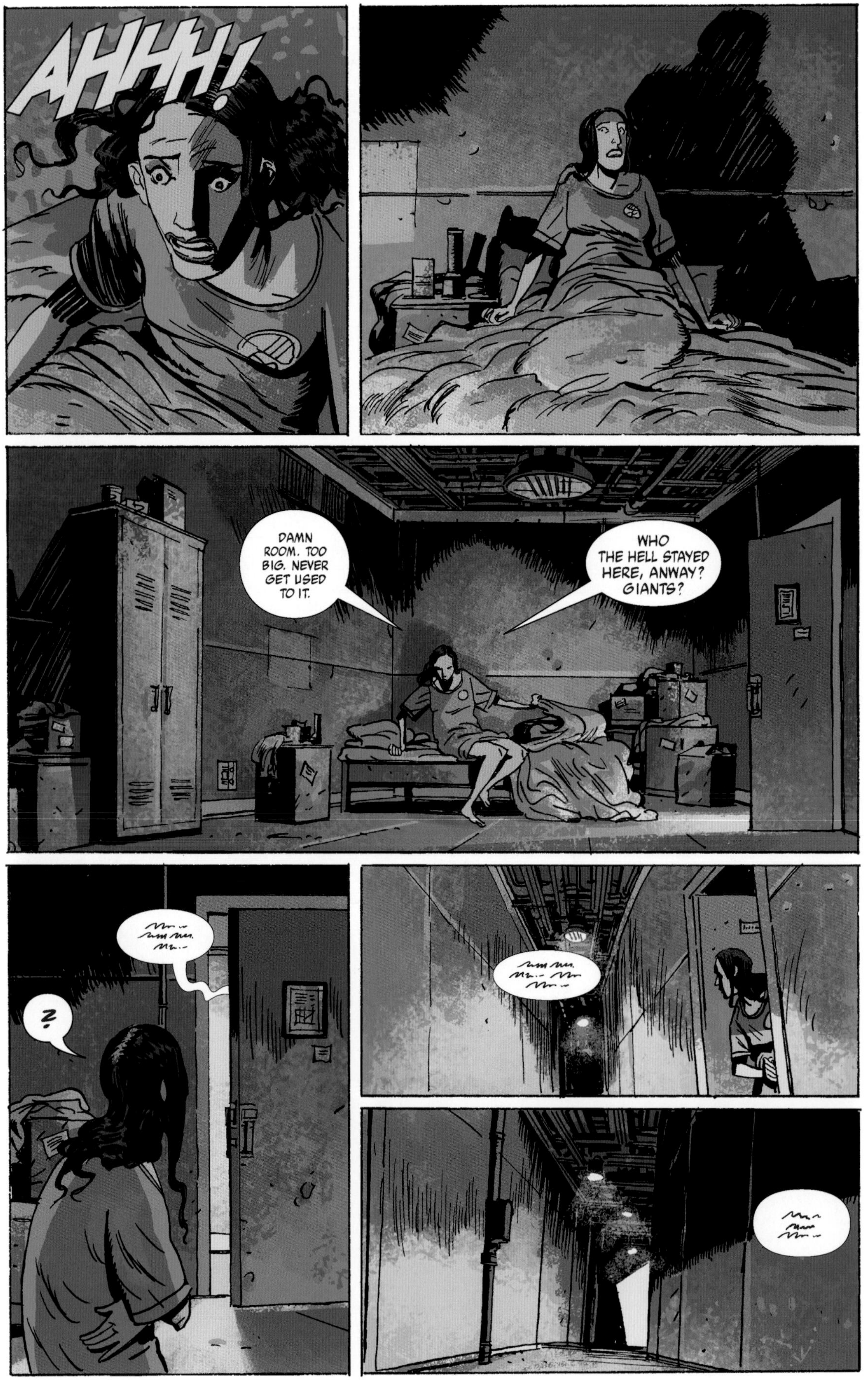
AHHH!
DAMN ROOM. TOO BIG. NEVER GET USED TO IT.
WHO THE HELL STAYED HERE, ANWAY? GIANTS?
?

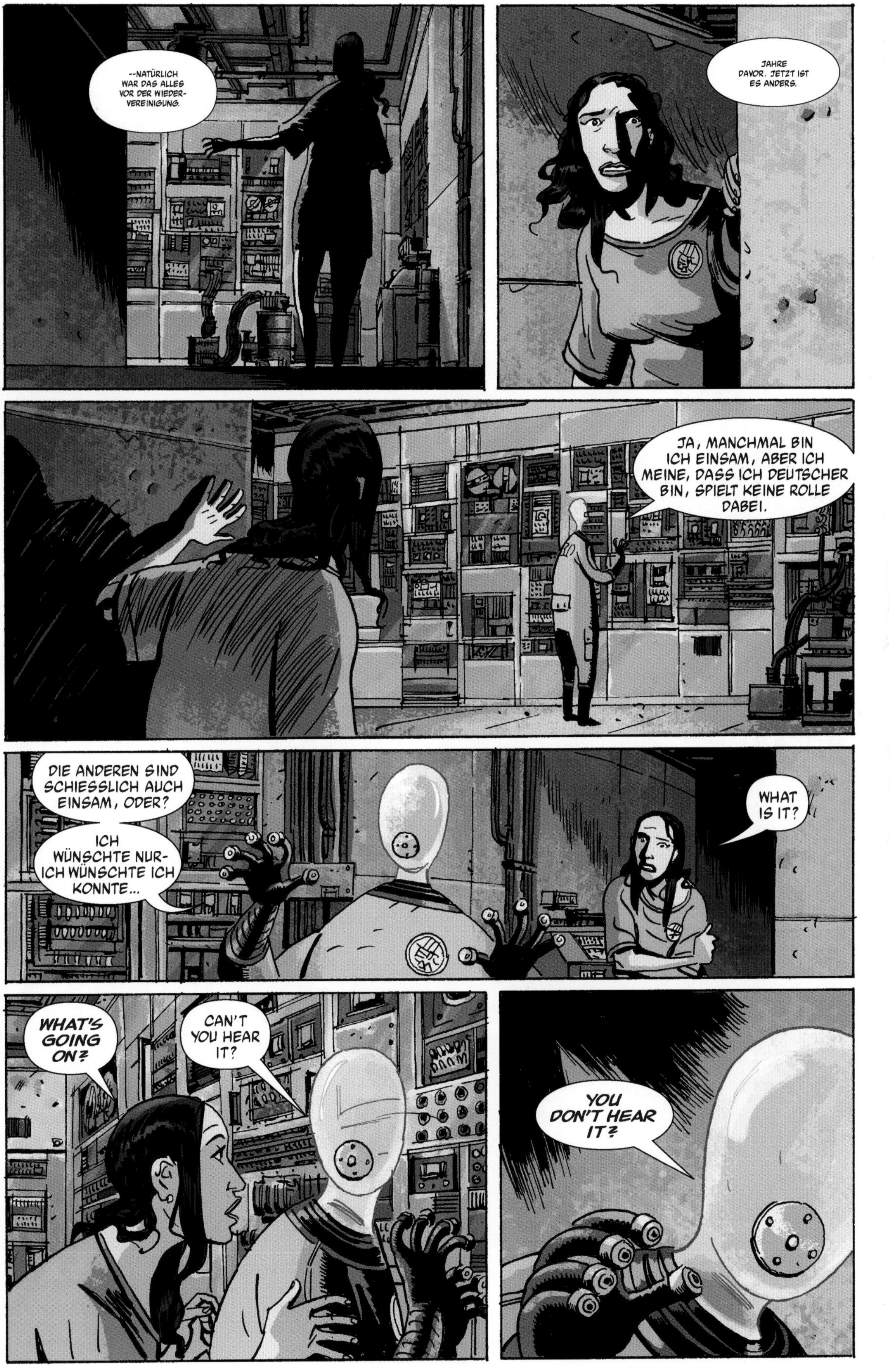
--NATÜRLICH WAR DAS ALLES VOR DER WIEDER-VEREINIGUNG.
JAHRE DAVOR. JETZT IST ES ANDERS.
JA, MANCHMAL BIN ICH EINSAM, ABER ICH MEINE, DASS ICH DEUTSCHER BIN, SPIELT KEINE ROLLE DABEI.
DIE ANDEREN SIND SCHIESSLICH AUCH EINSAM, ODER?
ICH WÜNSCHTE NUR-ICH WÜNSCHTE ICH KONNTE...
WHAT IS IT?
WHAT'S GOING ON?
CAN'T YOU HEAR IT?
YOU DON'T HEAR IT?

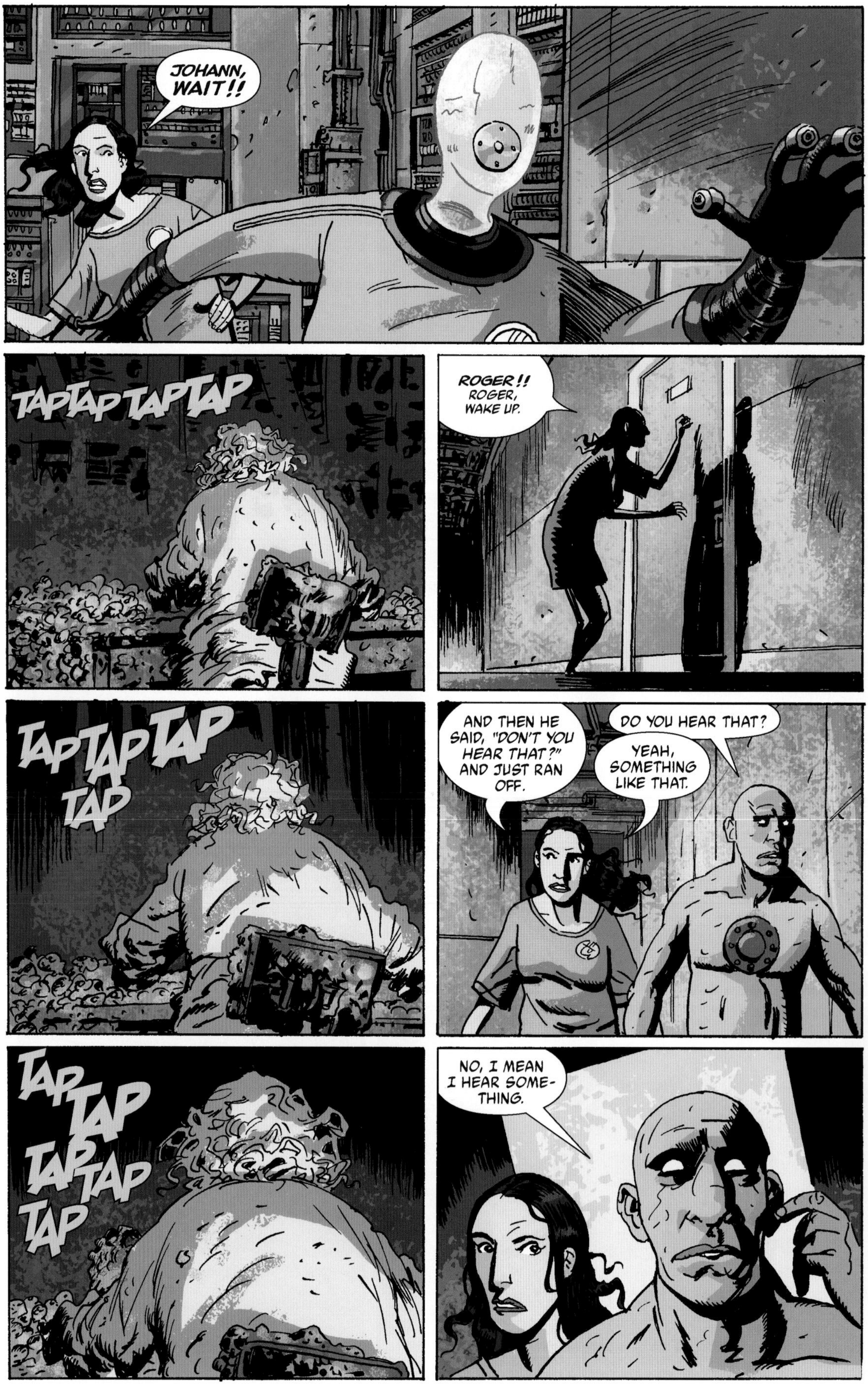
JOHANN, WAIT!!
TAPTAP TAPTAP
ROGER!! ROGER, WAKE UP.
TAPTAPTAP TAP
AND THEN HE SAID, "DON'T YOU HEAR THAT?" AND JUST RAN OFF.
DO YOU HEAR THAT?
YEAH, SOMETHING LIKE THAT.
TAP TAP TAP TAP TAP
NO, I MEAN I HEAR SOME-THING.

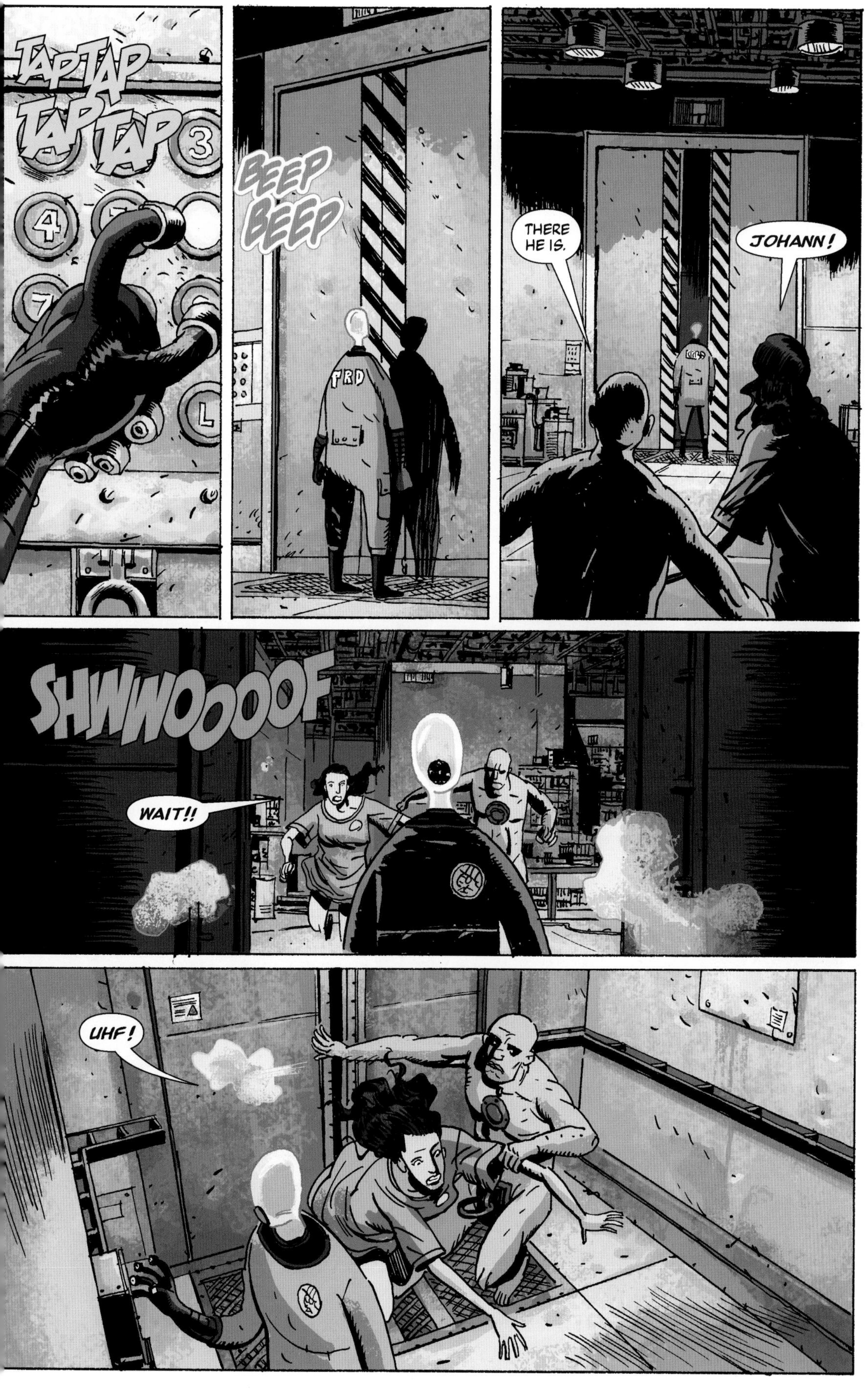
TAP TAP
TAP TAP
BEEP BEEP
THERE HE IS.
JOHANN!
SHWWOOOOF
WAIT!!
UHF!

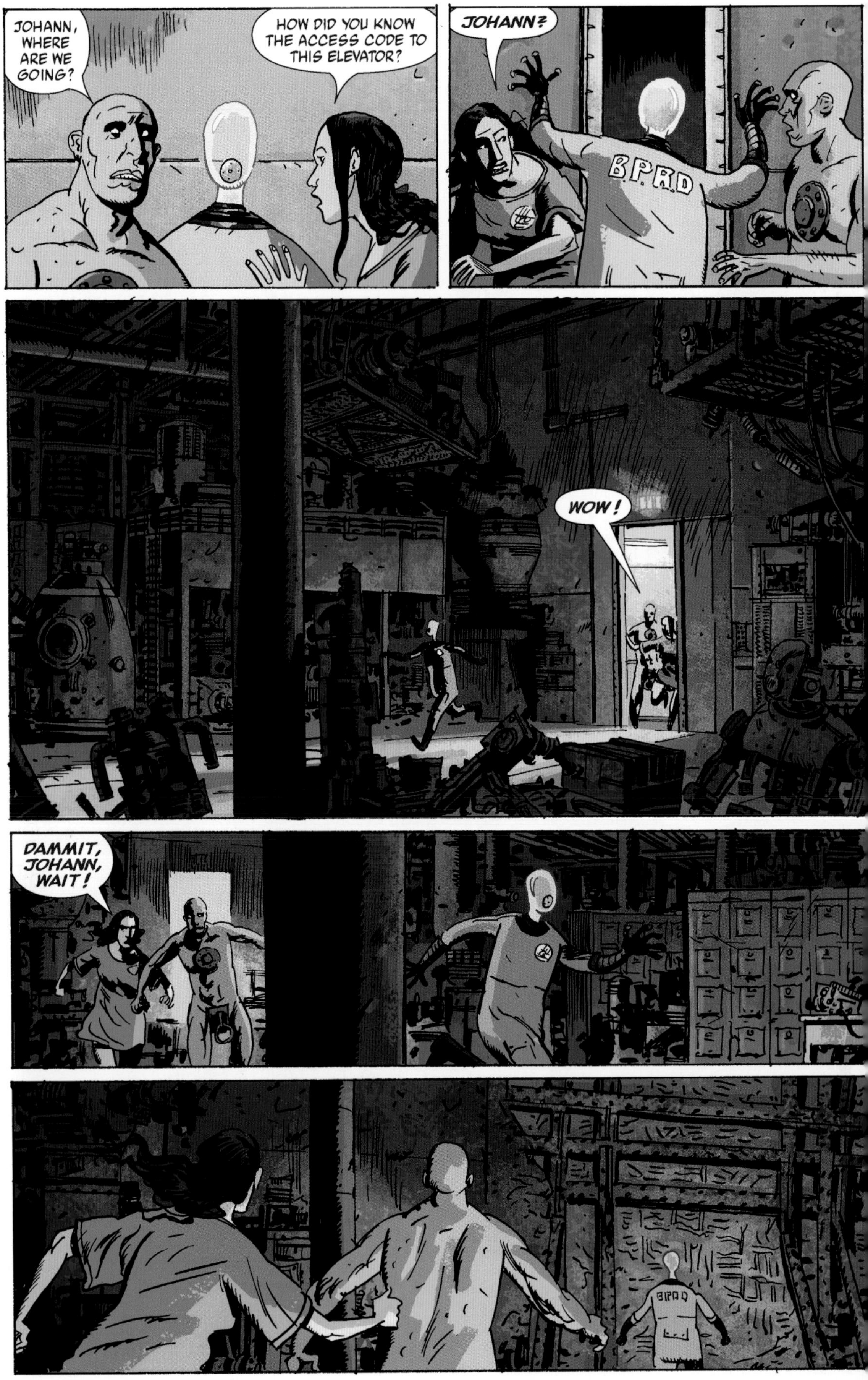
JOHANN, WHERE ARE WE GOING?
HOW DID YOU KNOW THE ACCESS CODE TO THIS ELEVATOR?
JOHANN?
B.P.R.D
WOW!
DAMMIT, JOHANN, WAIT!

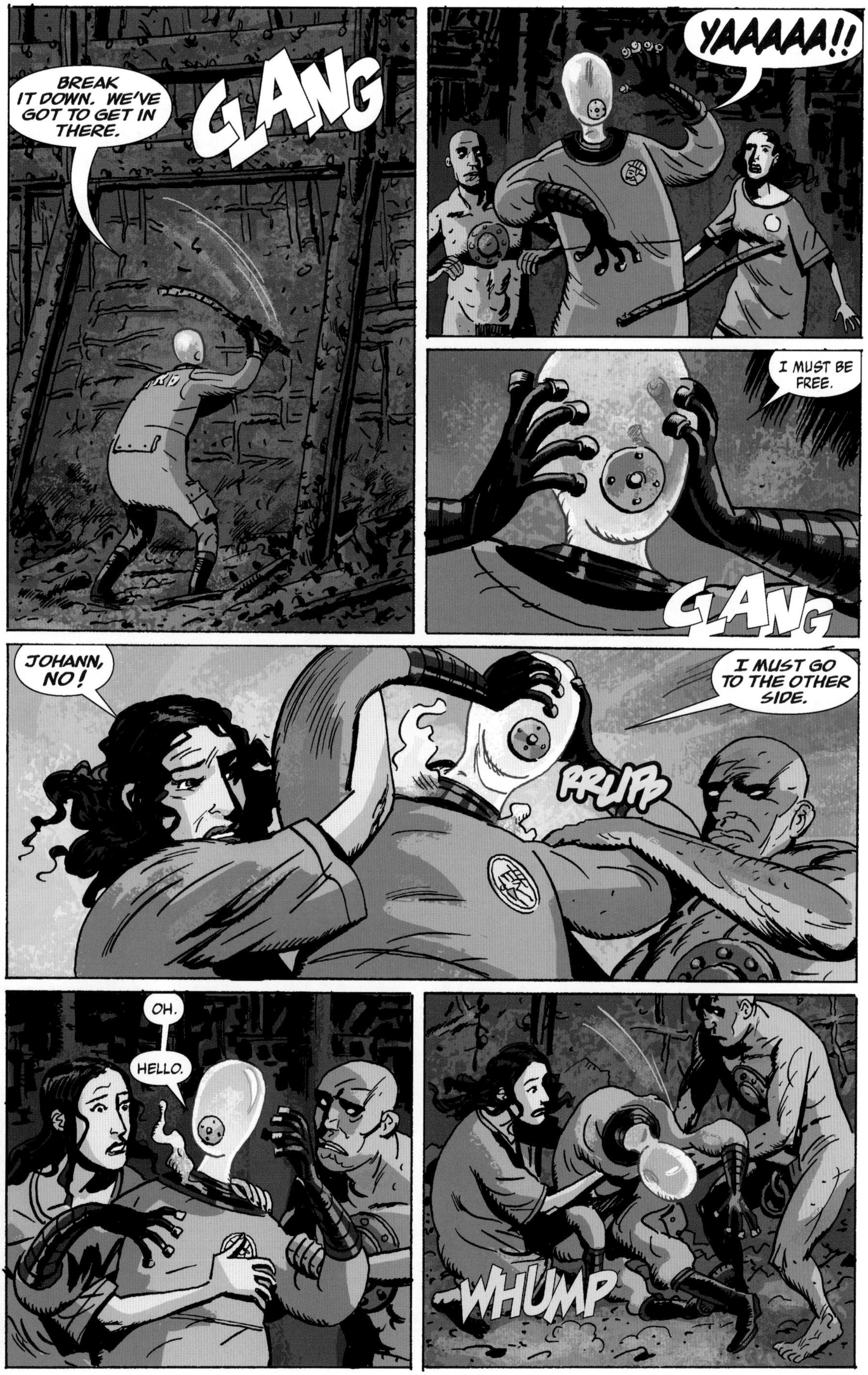
BREAK IT DOWN. WE'VE GOT TO GET IN THERE.
CLANG
YAAAAA!!
I MUST BE FREE.
CLANG
JOHANN, NO!
I MUST GO TO THE OTHER SIDE.
RRUPP
OH.
HELLO.
WHUMP

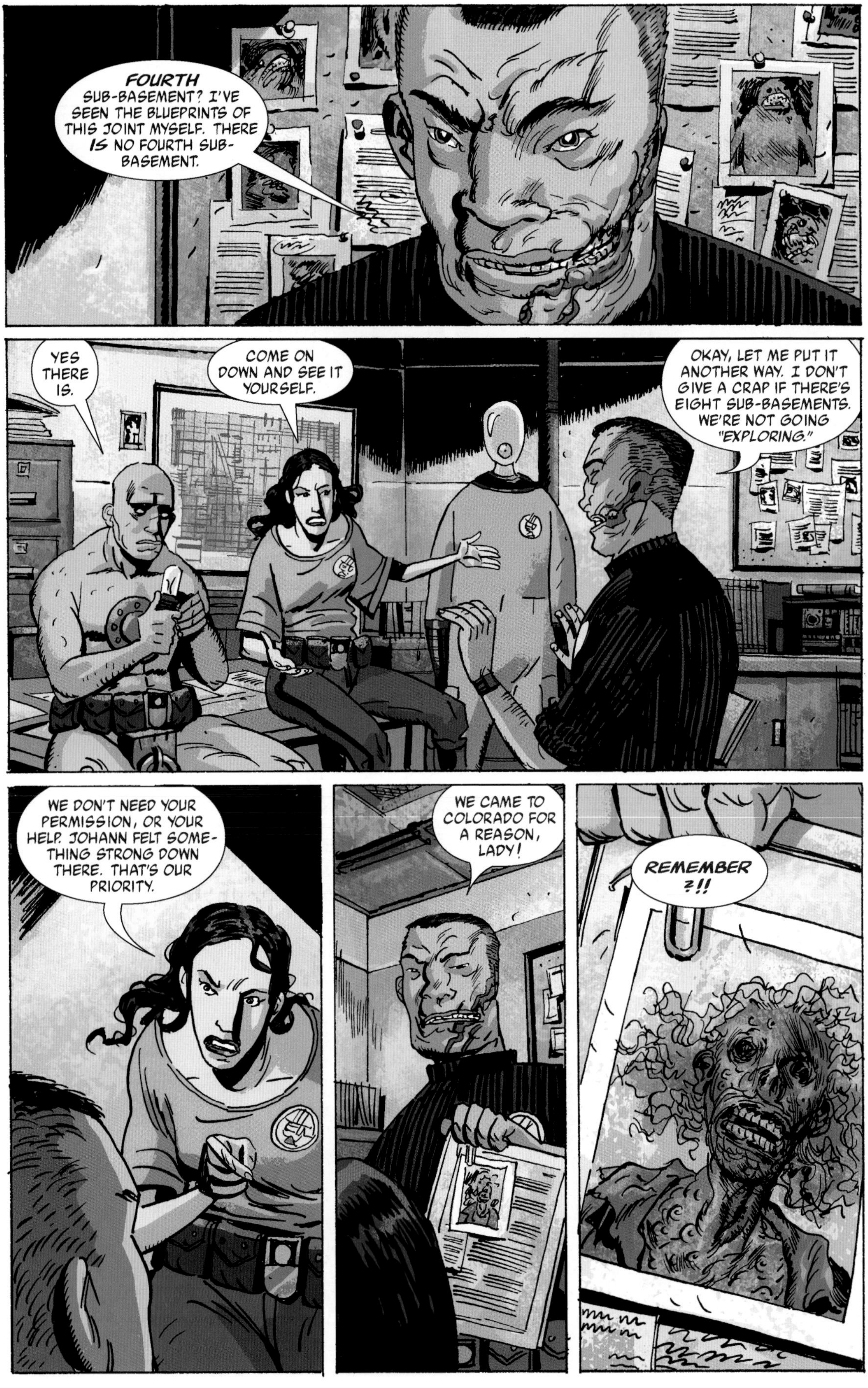
FOURTH SUB-BASEMENT? I'VE SEEN THE BLUEPRINTS OF THIS JOINT MYSELF. THERE IS NO FOURTH SUB-BASEMENT.
YES THERE IS.
COME ON DOWN AND SEE IT YOURSELF.
OKAY, LET ME PUT IT ANOTHER WAY. I DON'T GIVE A CRAP IF THERE'S EIGHT SUB-BASEMENTS. WE'RE NOT GOING "EXPLORING."
WE DON'T NEED YOUR PERMISSION, OR YOUR HELP. JOHANN FELT SOMETHING STRONG DOWN THERE. THAT'S OUR PRIORITY.
WE CAME TO COLORADO FOR A REASON, LADY!
REMEMBER?!!

THOSE THINGS ARE SPREADING ALL OVER.

"MORE OF 'EM EVERY DAY. I DON'T KNOW *HOW* THERE ARE MORE, BUT THERE ARE.

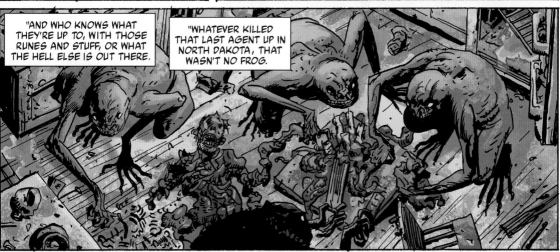

"AND WHO KNOWS WHAT THEY'RE UP TO, WITH THOSE RUNES AND STUFF, OR WHAT THE HELL ELSE IS OUT THERE.

"WHATEVER KILLED THAT LAST AGENT UP IN NORTH DAKOTA, THAT WASN'T NO FROG.

"I DON'T WANNA GET SIDE TRACKED, BECAUSE MY JOB--*YOUR* JOB--IS TO STOP THOSE THINGS.

"*NOW.*

"BEFORE IT GETS PLENTY WORSE."

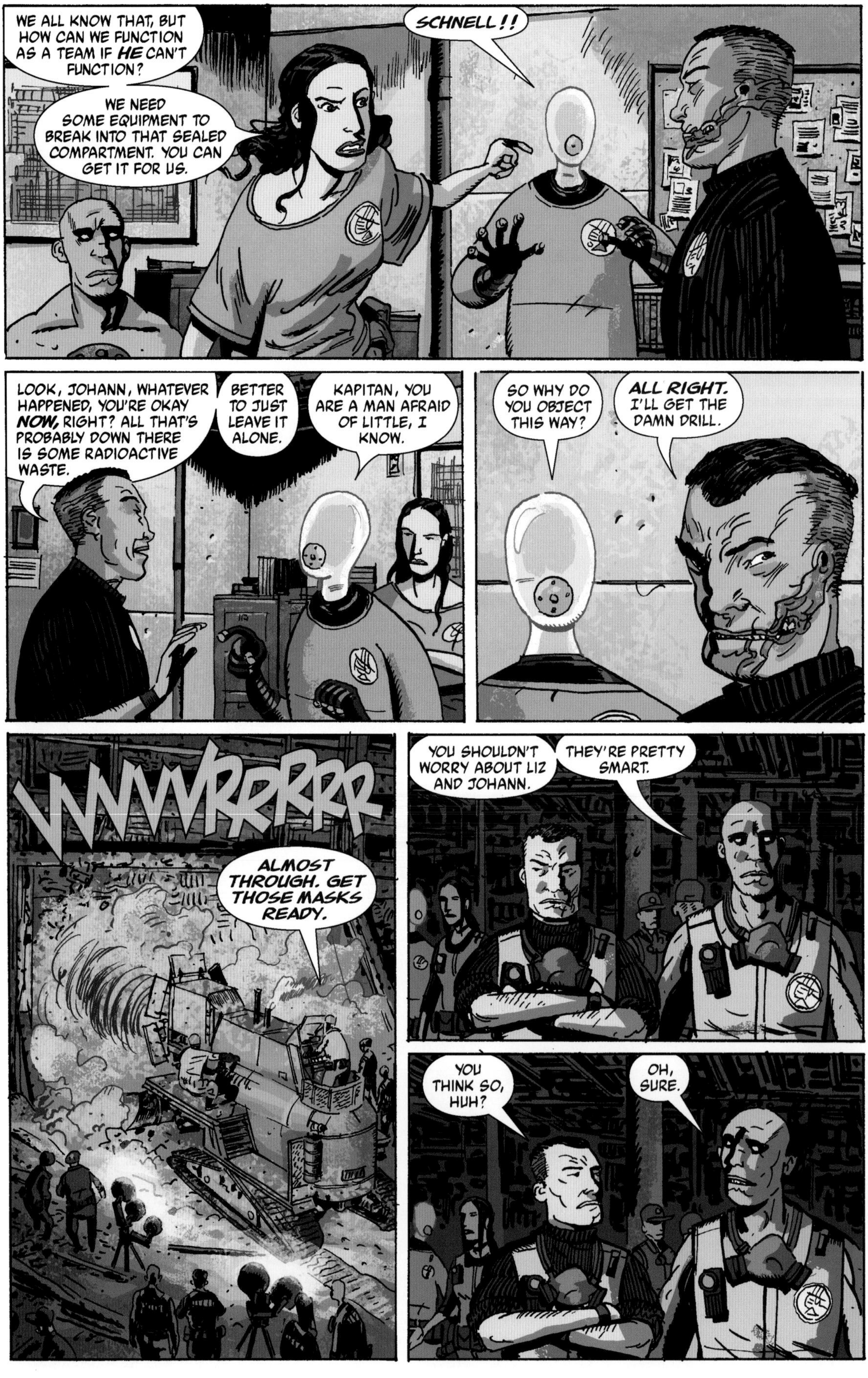
WE ALL KNOW THAT, BUT HOW CAN WE FUNCTION AS A TEAM IF HE CAN'T FUNCTION?
WE NEED SOME EQUIPMENT TO BREAK INTO THAT SEALED COMPARTMENT. YOU CAN GET IT FOR US.
SCHNELL!!
LOOK, JOHANN, WHATEVER HAPPENED, YOU'RE OKAY NOW, RIGHT? ALL THAT'S PROBABLY DOWN THERE IS SOME RADIOACTIVE WASTE.
BETTER TO JUST LEAVE IT ALONE.
KAPITAN, YOU ARE A MAN AFRAID OF LITTLE, I KNOW.
SO WHY DO YOU OBJECT THIS WAY?
ALL RIGHT. I'LL GET THE DAMN DRILL.
VVVVVRRRRR
ALMOST THROUGH. GET THOSE MASKS READY.
YOU SHOULDN'T WORRY ABOUT LIZ AND JOHANN.
THEY'RE PRETTY SMART.
YOU THINK SO, HUH?
OH, SURE.

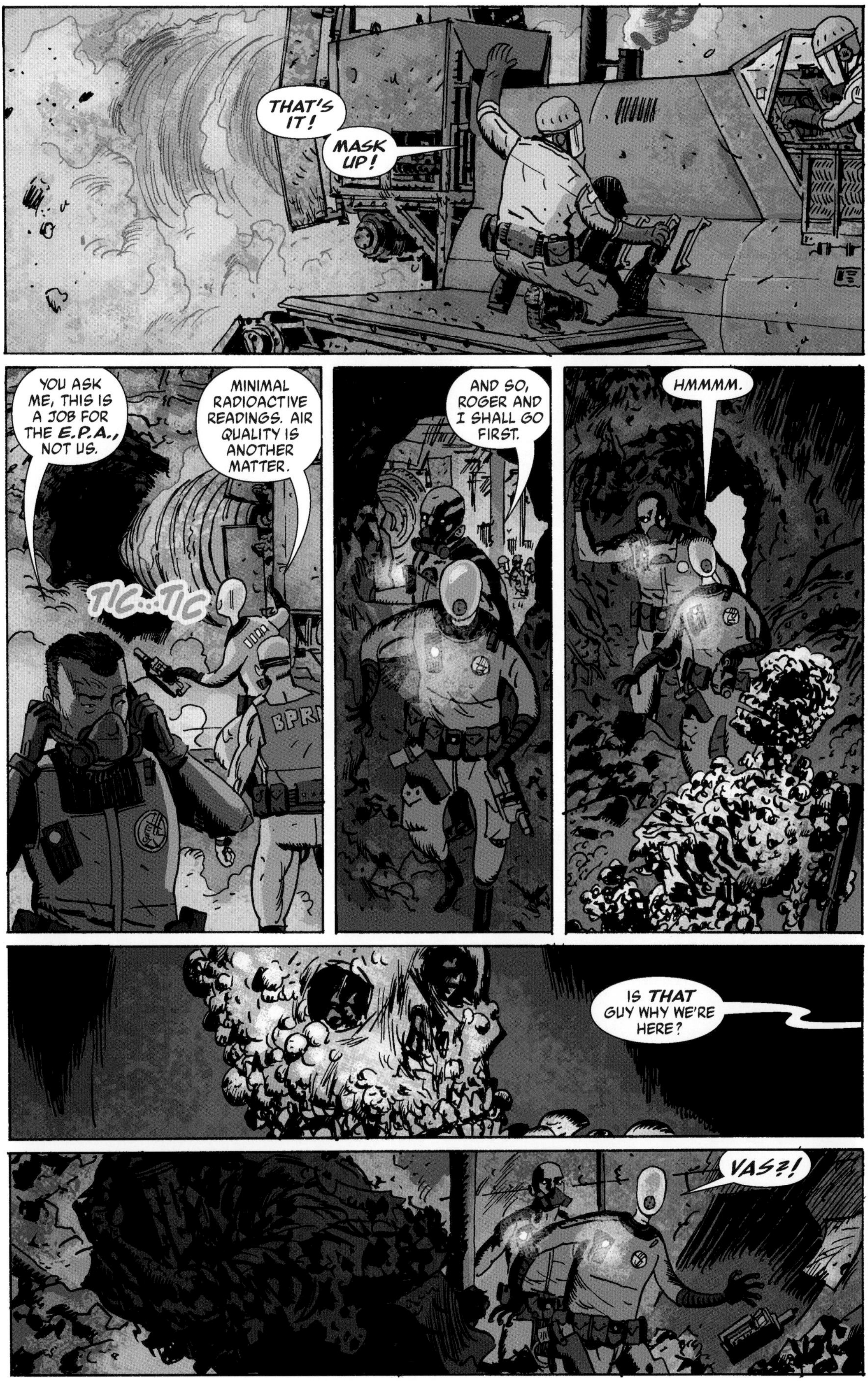
THAT'S IT!
MASK UP!
YOU ASK ME, THIS IS A JOB FOR THE E.P.A., NOT US.
MINIMAL RADIOACTIVE READINGS. AIR QUALITY IS ANOTHER MATTER.
TIC..TIC
BPRD
AND SO, ROGER AND I SHALL GO FIRST.
HMMMM.
IS THAT GUY WHY WE'RE HERE?
VAS?!

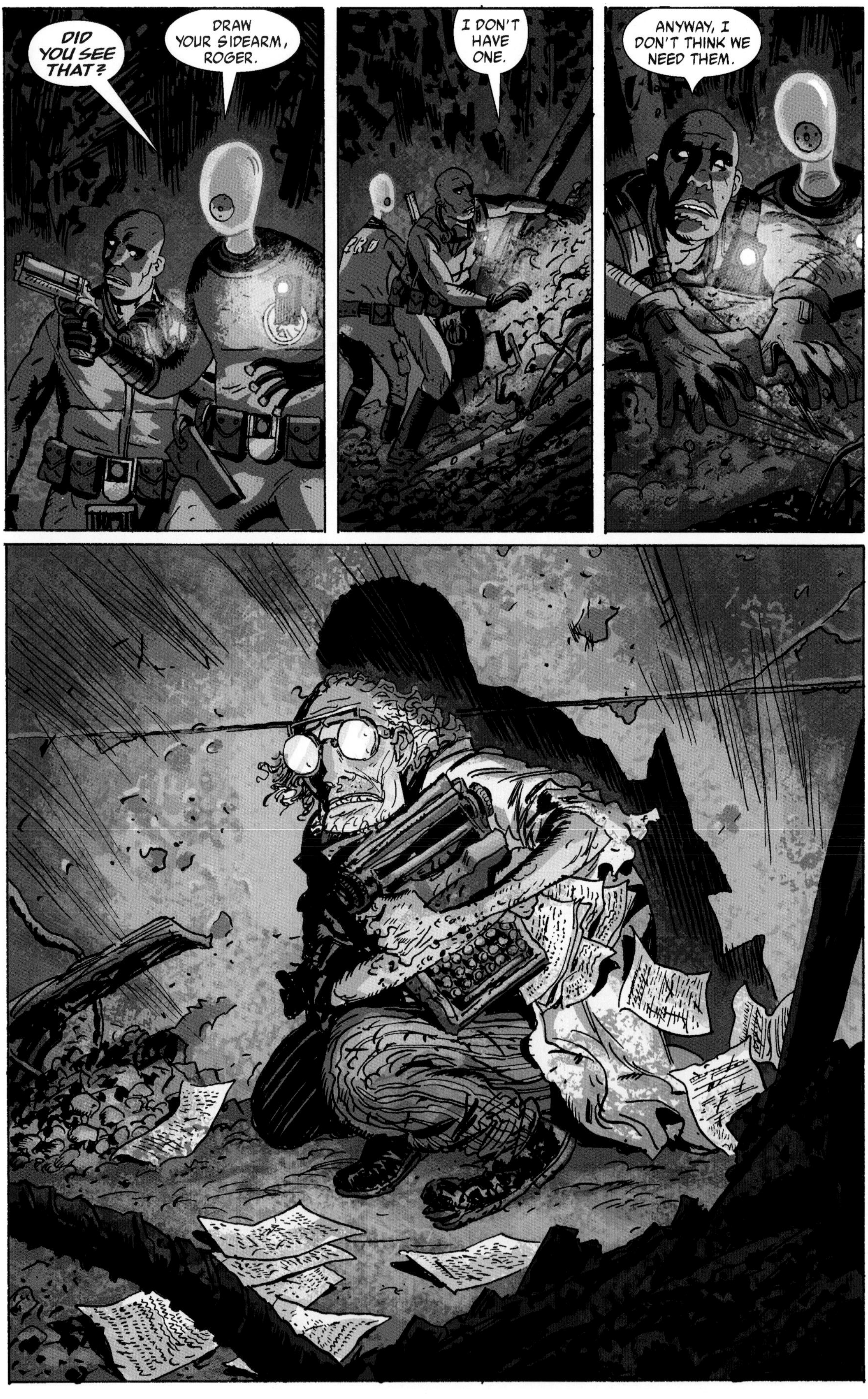
DID YOU SEE THAT?
DRAW YOUR SIDEARM, ROGER.
I DON'T HAVE ONE.
ANYWAY, I DON'T THINK WE NEED THEM.

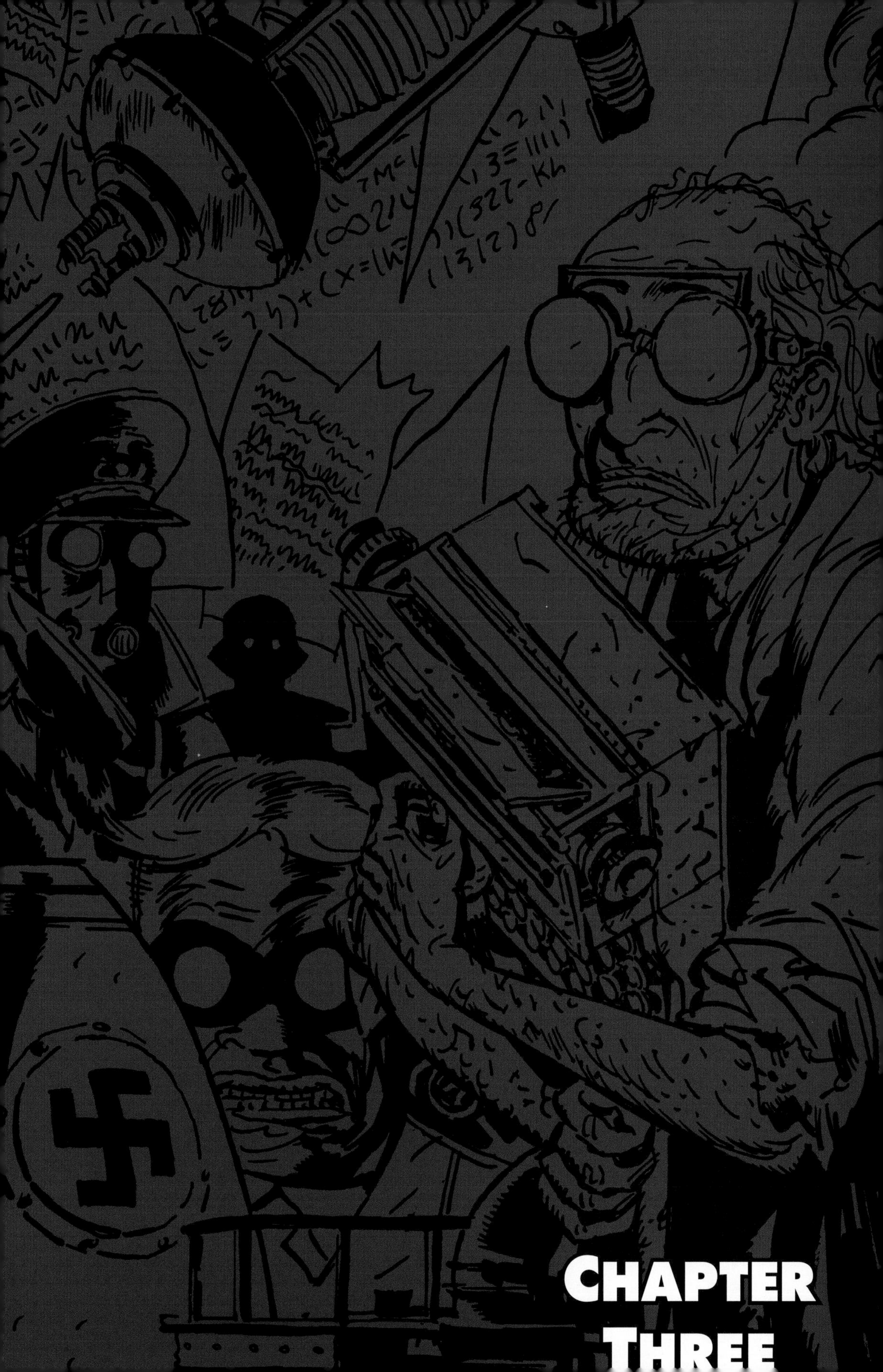

CHAPTER THREE

SO WHERE IS JOHANN NOW?

DOWN BELOW, IN THE SUB-BASEMENT, DOING A SITE ASSESSMENT.

WHY?

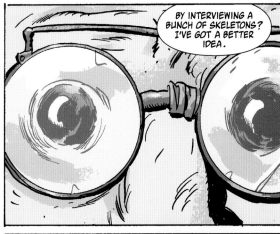

I MEAN, WE GOT THE GUY OUT, DIDN'T WE? WE'VE GOT SOME FROGS TO KILL, LADY.

YOU SAW THOSE BODIES DOWN THERE. SOMETHING HAPPENED. JOHANN MIGHT BE ABLE TO GET A READING.

BY INTERVIEWING A BUNCH OF SKELETONS? I'VE GOT A BETTER IDEA.

HEY, PAL. HOW YOU DOING?

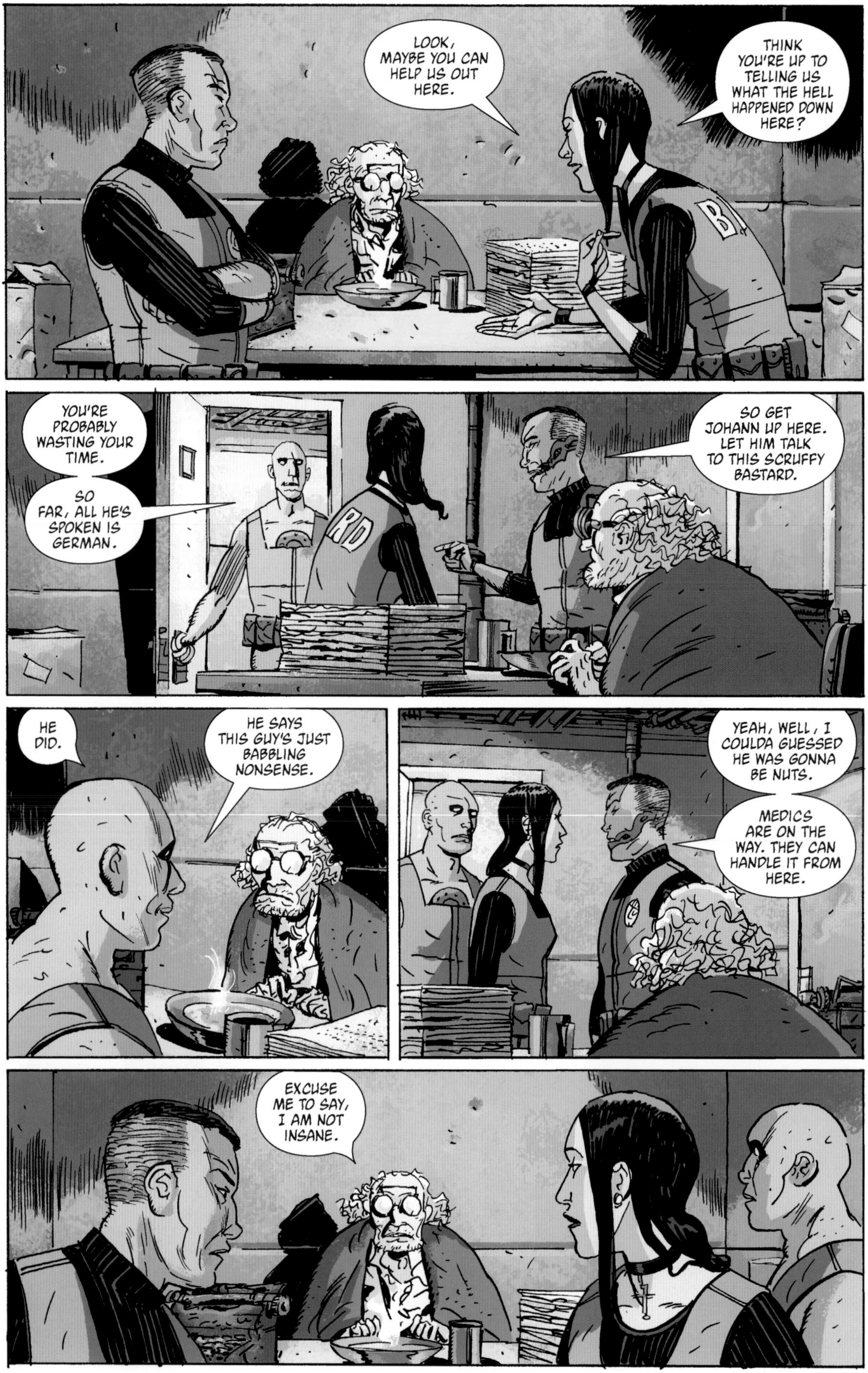
LOOK, MAYBE YOU CAN HELP US OUT HERE.
THINK YOU'RE UP TO TELLING US WHAT THE HELL HAPPENED DOWN HERE?
YOU'RE PROBABLY WASTING YOUR TIME.
SO FAR, ALL HE'S SPOKEN IS GERMAN.
SO GET JOHANN UP HERE. LET HIM TALK TO THIS SCRUFFY BASTARD.
HE DID.
HE SAYS THIS GUY'S JUST BABBLING NONSENSE.
YEAH, WELL, I COULDA GUESSED HE WAS GONNA BE NUTS.
MEDICS ARE ON THE WAY. THEY CAN HANDLE IT FROM HERE.
EXCUSE ME TO SAY, I AM NOT INSANE.

THE HUMAN REMAINS DO HINT--BUT EXPRESSLY SAY NOTHING.

--LARGE, AS YET UN-IDENTIFIED APPARATUS.

ONLY THIS IS NOT MY DEPARTMENT. THE TECHNICIANS, PERHAPS, MAY LEARN MORE.

BETTER TO BURY THEM QUICKLY, I THINK, AND FORGO ANY AUTOPSIES.

ONE NOTE--THE SUB-BASEMENT APPEARS ONLY HALF-FINISHED, CARVED OUT OF ROCK RATHER THAN CONSTRUCTED.

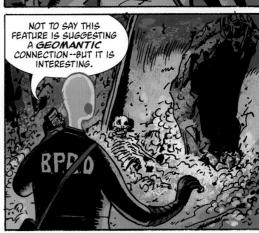

NOT TO SAY THIS FEATURE IS SUGGESTING A *GEOMANTIC* CONNECTION--BUT IT IS INTERESTING.

ALSO, THERE IS WRITING. THIS I HAD NOT NOTICED EARLIER.

EASY TO BELIEVE IT WAS SCRAWLED BY THE...AGITATED SUBJECT FOUND HERE.

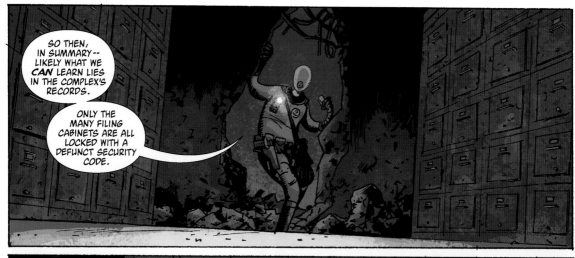

SO THEN, IN SUMMARY -- LIKELY WHAT WE **CAN** LEARN LIES IN THE COMPLEX'S RECORDS.

ONLY THE MANY FILING CABINETS ARE ALL LOCKED WITH A DEFUNCT SECURITY CODE.

SIMPLE ENOUGH TO PRY THEM OPEN, YES, IF NOT THAT CAPTAIN DAIMIO HAS OTHER--

CLANG

VORSICHT

YOU-- YOU SPEAK ENGLISH?

OF COURSE. HAVEN'T YOU READ MY NOTES?

IT IS ONLY THE LONG ISOLATION WHICH HAS MADE ME... CAUTIOUS.

AND WHEN I SAW *HIM* WITH THE BUBBLE-MAN COMING TO GET ME, I THOUGHT THE MONSTERS HAD TAKEN OVER.

THE MONSTERS?

THE CAPTAIN KNOWS WHAT I AM SAYING. HE KNOWS.

?

OKAY, SO YOU'RE NOT NUTS. THEN MAYBE YOU CAN TELL US WHAT WENT ON DOWN THERE IN YOUR LITTLE HIDEY HOLE.

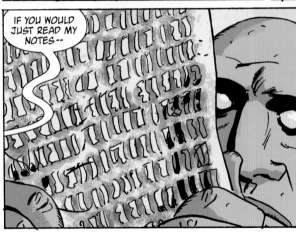

IF YOU WOULD JUST READ MY NOTES--

--BUT VERY WELL.

I AM DR. GUNTER EISS.

"I HAD JUST FINISHED MY PH.D. IN QUANTUM MECHANICS AT DRESDEN'S PLANCK UNIVERSITY WHEN I WAS CALLED BY THE GERMAN DEFENSE DEPARTMENT.

"THEY STARTED TO RECRUIT PHYSICISTS FROM THE UNIVERSITIES TO REPLACE THOSE KILLED WHEN THE SPACE PROGRAM FAILED IN 1939.

"A STROKE OF FORTUNE, I THOUGHT.

"THERE WERE FACTIONS WITHIN THE DEPARTMENT.

"COMPETITION FOR THE FUEHRER'S REICHS MARKS.

"THE PROJECT I WAS ASSIGNED TO WAS TO MY LIKING.

"OPERATION HIMMEL-MACHT WAS OUR AIM TO TAP THE DIVINE INFINITE FOR ASSISTANCE IN THE DEFENSE OF GERMANY.

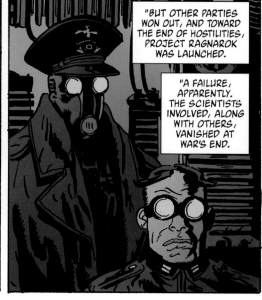

"BUT OTHER PARTIES WON OUT, AND TOWARD THE END OF HOSTILITIES, PROJECT RAGNAROK WAS LAUNCHED.

"A FAILURE, APPARENTLY. THE SCIENTISTS INVOLVED, ALONG WITH OTHERS, VANISHED AT WAR'S END.

"BUT TRUE SCIENCE KNOWS NO BORDERS. IT HAS NO POLITICAL POSITION.

"IN 1946, THE NEXT GREAT CHALLENGES WERE TO BE FOUND HERE.

"THAT'S WHEN THIS FACILITY WAS BUILT--BUILT REALLY, FOR US.

"THE EXPATRIATES, THE FUEHRER'S FINEST, NOW UNCLE SAM'S BOYS, YES?

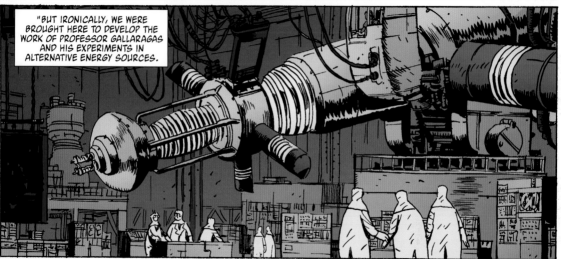

"BUT IRONICALLY, WE WERE BROUGHT HERE TO DEVELOP THE WORK OF PROFESSOR GALLARAGAS AND HIS EXPERIMENTS IN ALTERNATIVE ENERGY SOURCES.

"HE WAS A BRILLIANT MAN, NO QUESTION.

"BUT THE FEELING AMONG US CAME TO BE THAT WE WERE OUT OF OUR DEPTH IN ASSUMING HIS MANTLE.

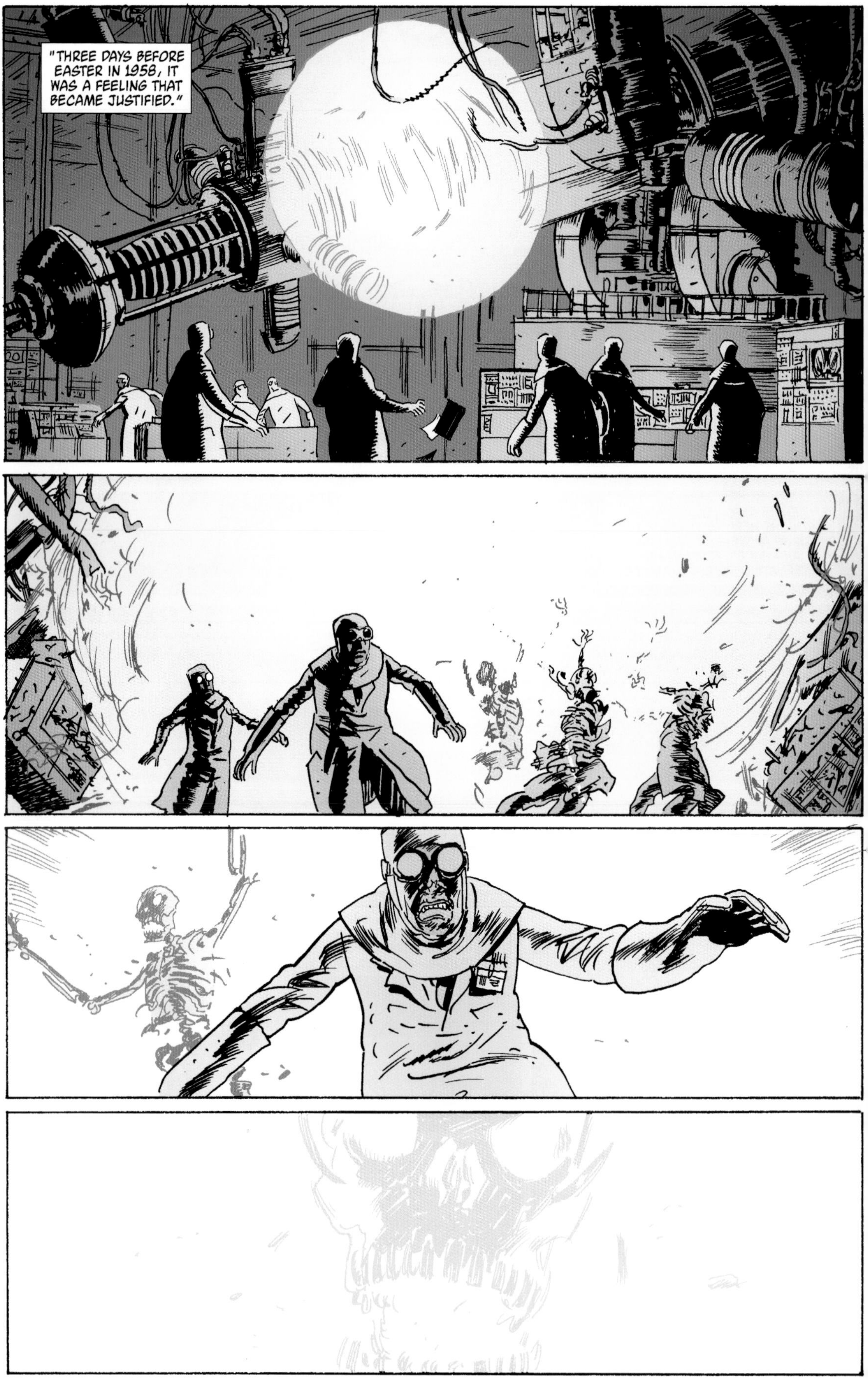
"THREE DAYS BEFORE EASTER IN 1958, IT WAS A FEELING THAT BECAME JUSTIFIED."

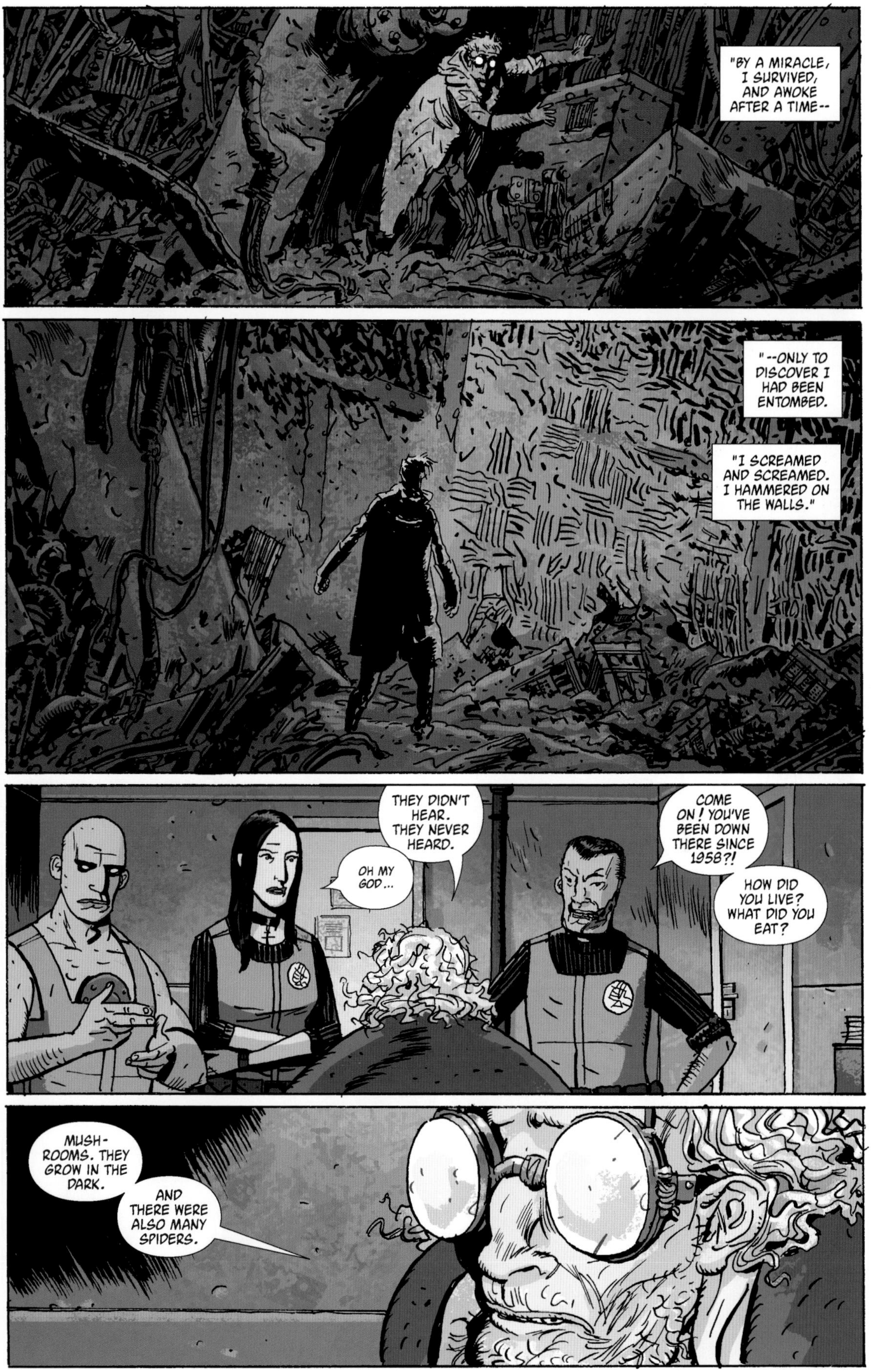
"BY A MIRACLE, I SURVIVED, AND AWOKE AFTER A TIME--
"--ONLY TO DISCOVER I HAD BEEN ENTOMBED.
"I SCREAMED AND SCREAMED. I HAMMERED ON THE WALLS."
THEY DIDN'T HEAR. THEY NEVER HEARD.
OH MY GOD...
COME ON! YOU'VE BEEN DOWN THERE SINCE 1958?!
HOW DID YOU LIVE? WHAT DID YOU EAT?
MUSH-ROOMS. THEY GROW IN THE DARK.
AND THERE WERE ALSO MANY SPIDERS.

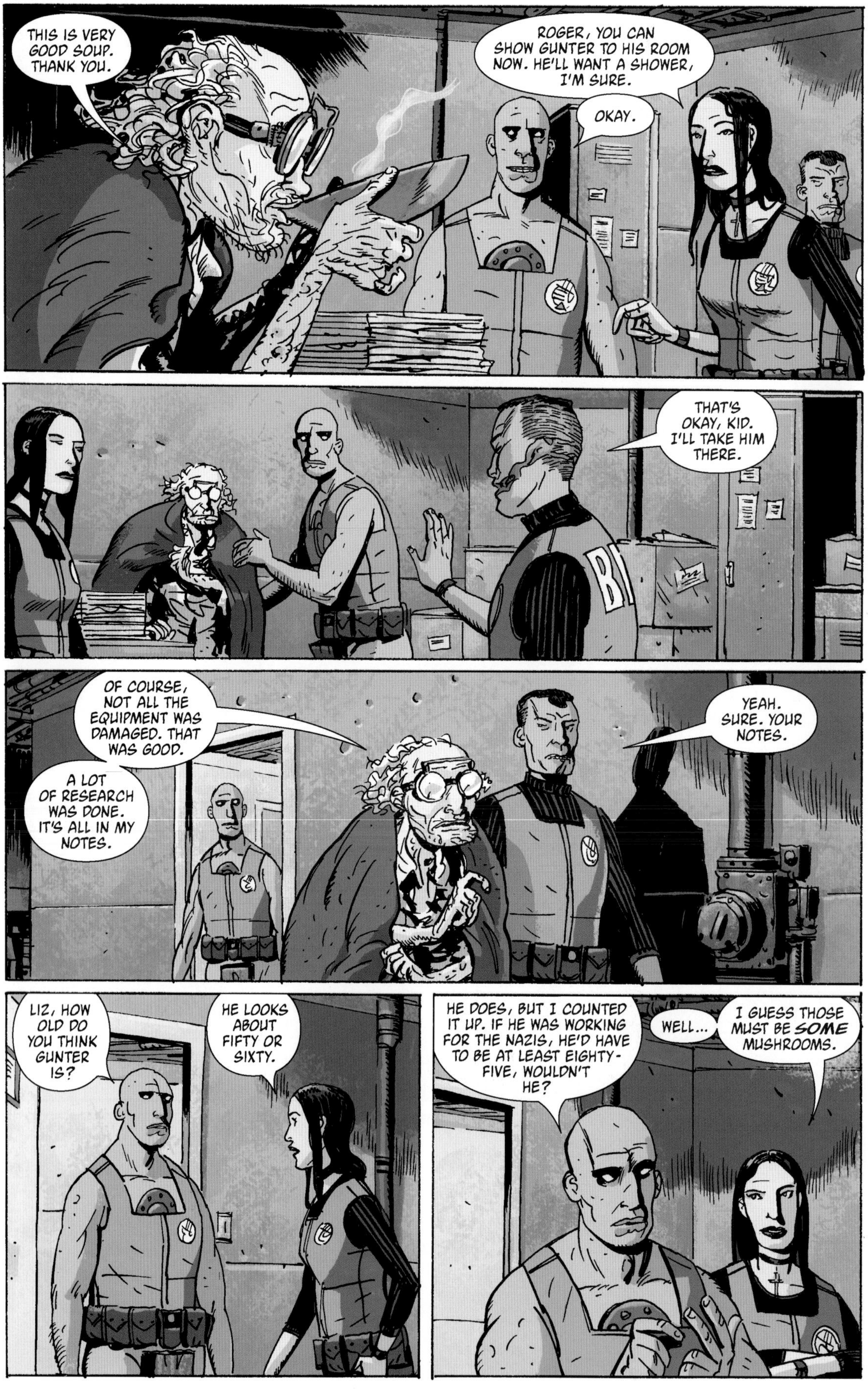
THIS IS VERY GOOD SOUP. THANK YOU.
ROGER, YOU CAN SHOW GUNTER TO HIS ROOM NOW. HE'LL WANT A SHOWER, I'M SURE.
OKAY.
THAT'S OKAY, KID. I'LL TAKE HIM THERE.
OF COURSE, NOT ALL THE EQUIPMENT WAS DAMAGED. THAT WAS GOOD.
A LOT OF RESEARCH WAS DONE. IT'S ALL IN MY NOTES.
YEAH. SURE. YOUR NOTES.
LIZ, HOW OLD DO YOU THINK GUNTER IS?
HE LOOKS ABOUT FIFTY OR SIXTY.
HE DOES, BUT I COUNTED IT UP. IF HE WAS WORKING FOR THE NAZIS, HE'D HAVE TO BE AT LEAST EIGHTY-FIVE, WOULDN'T HE?
WELL...
I GUESS THOSE MUST BE *SOME* MUSHROOMS.

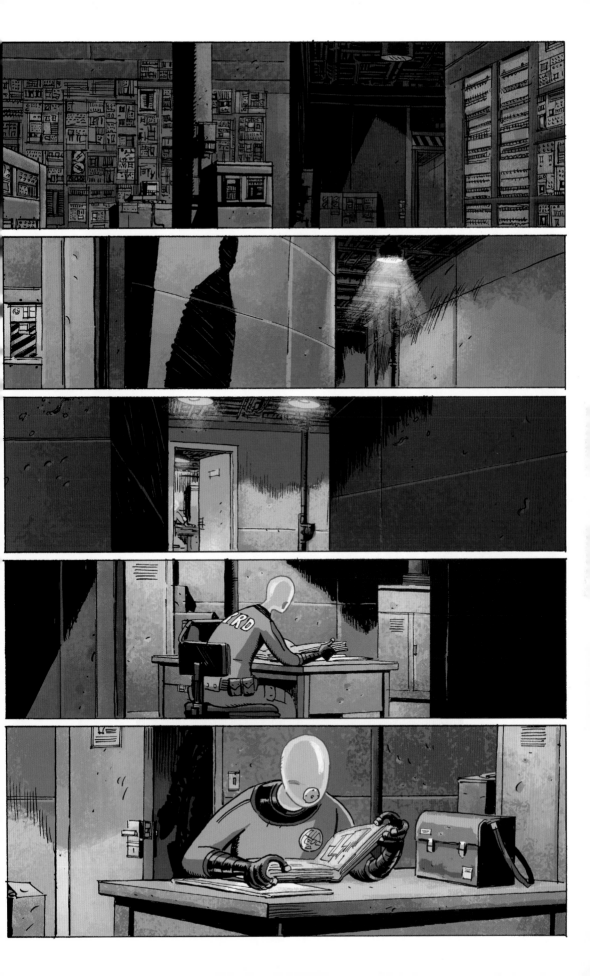

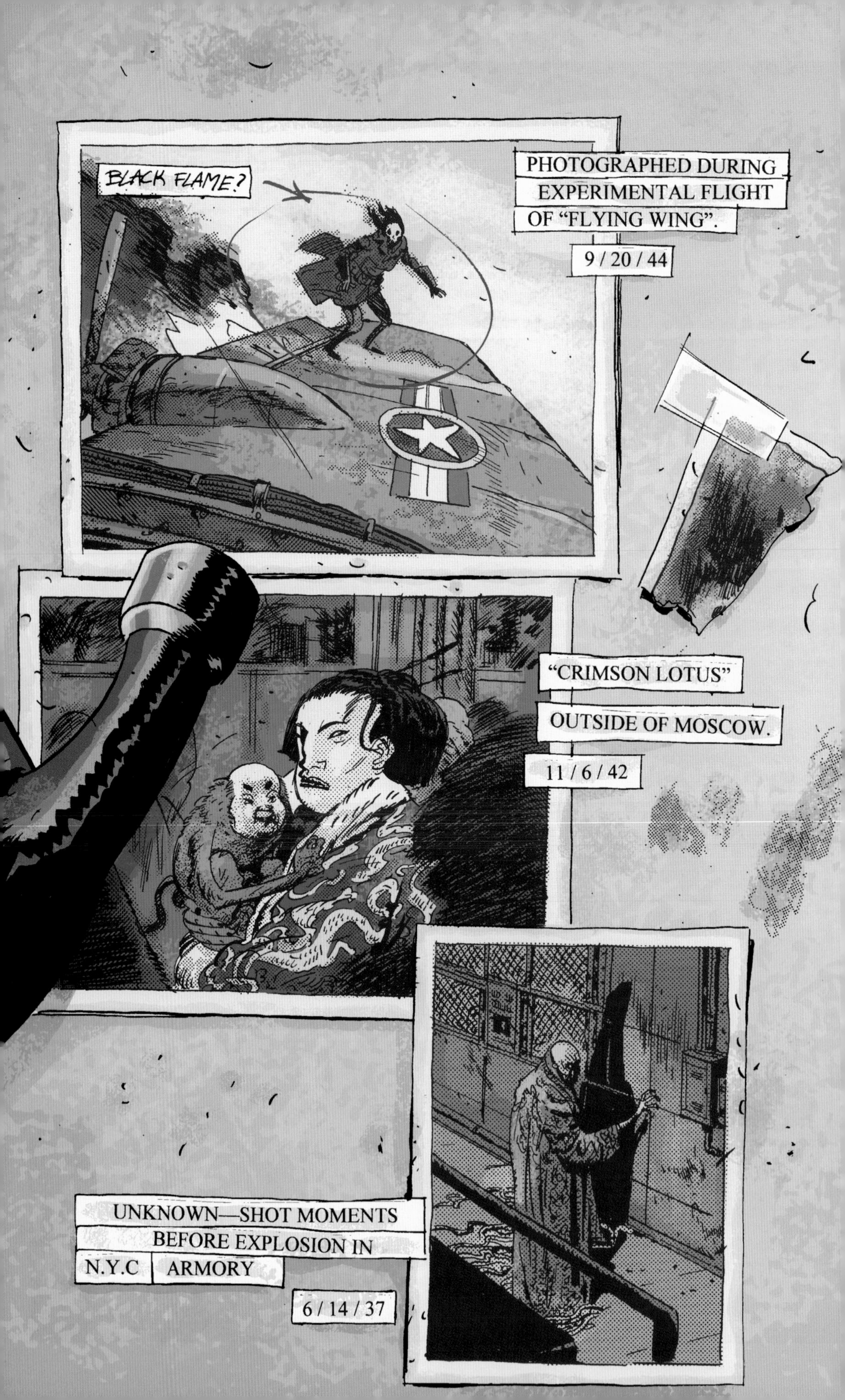
BLACK FLAME?
PHOTOGRAPHED DURING
EXPERIMENTAL FLIGHT
OF "FLYING WING".
9 / 20 / 44
"CRIMSON LOTUS"
OUTSIDE OF MOSCOW.
11 / 6 / 42
UNKNOWN—SHOT MOMENTS
BEFORE EXPLOSION IN
N.Y.C ARMORY
6 / 14 / 37

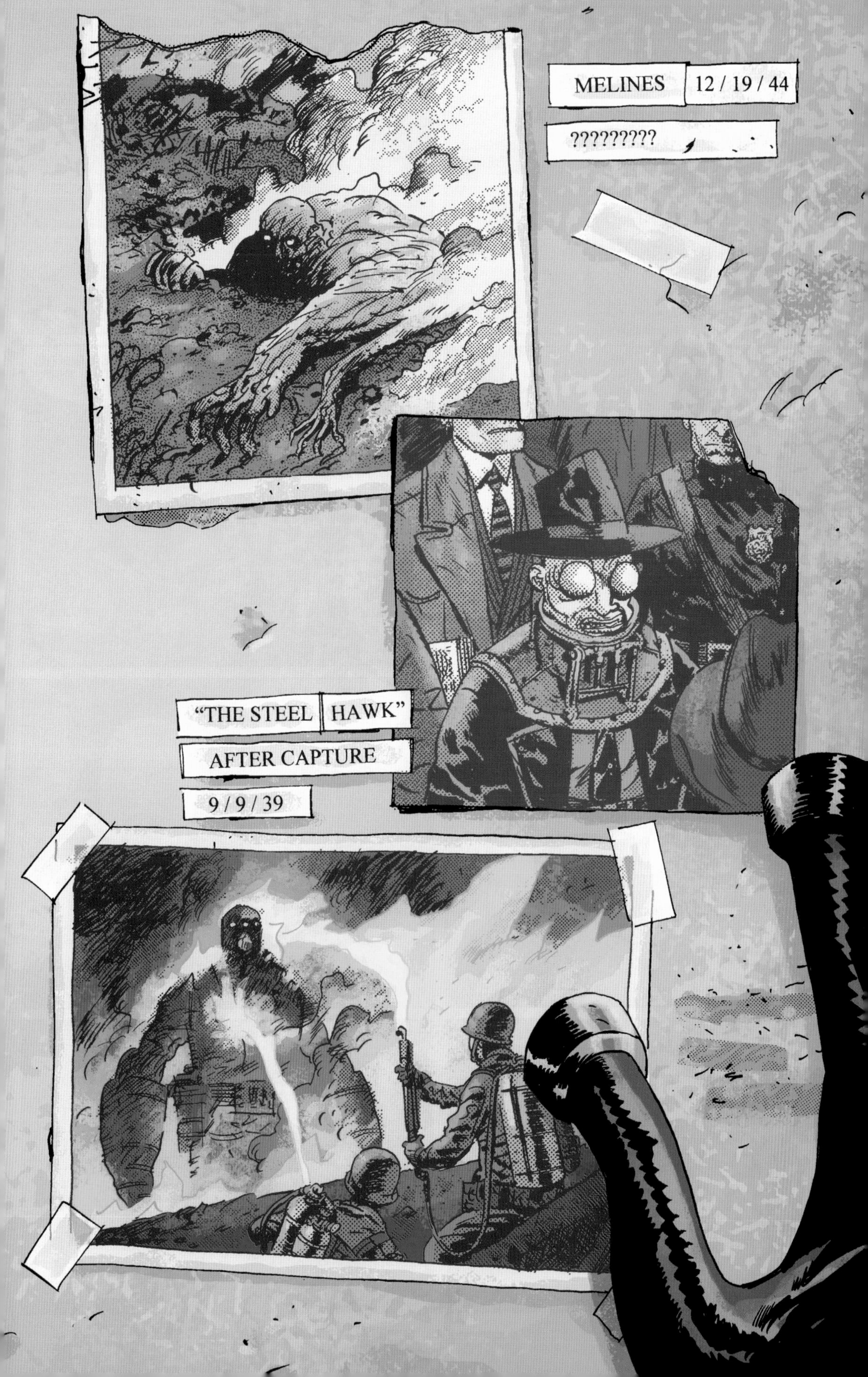
MELINES
12 / 19 / 44
?????????
"THE STEEL HAWK"
AFTER CAPTURE
9 / 9 / 39

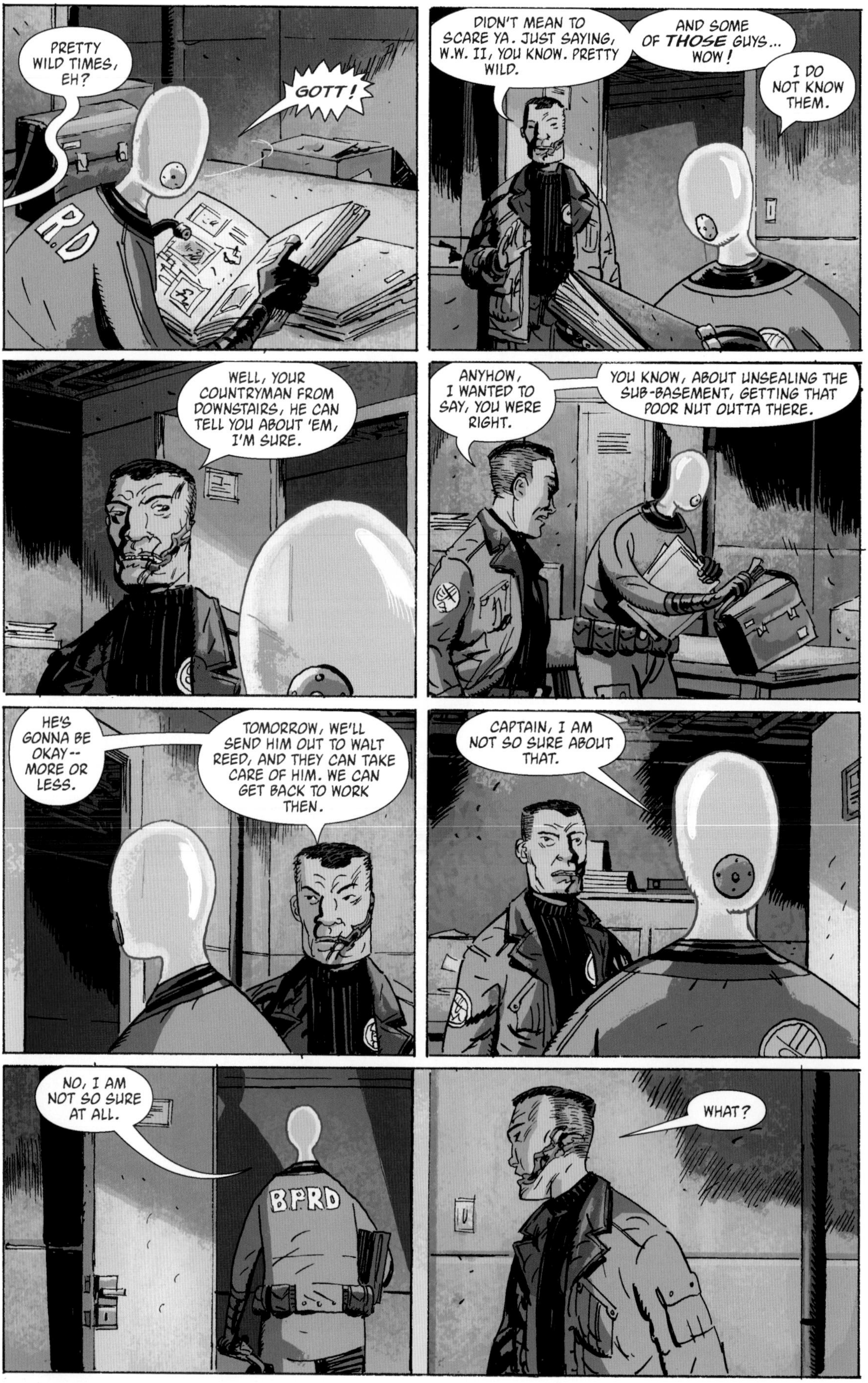
PRETTY WILD TIMES, EH?
GOTT!
DIDN'T MEAN TO SCARE YA. JUST SAYING, W.W. II, YOU KNOW. PRETTY WILD.
AND SOME OF THOSE GUYS... WOW!
I DO NOT KNOW THEM.
WELL, YOUR COUNTRYMAN FROM DOWNSTAIRS, HE CAN TELL YOU ABOUT 'EM, I'M SURE.
ANYHOW, I WANTED TO SAY, YOU WERE RIGHT.
YOU KNOW, ABOUT UNSEALING THE SUB-BASEMENT, GETTING THAT POOR NUT OUTTA THERE.
HE'S GONNA BE OKAY-- MORE OR LESS.
TOMORROW, WE'LL SEND HIM OUT TO WALT REED, AND THEY CAN TAKE CARE OF HIM. WE CAN GET BACK TO WORK THEN.
CAPTAIN, I AM NOT SO SURE ABOUT THAT.
NO, I AM NOT SO SURE AT ALL.
B.P.R.D
WHAT?

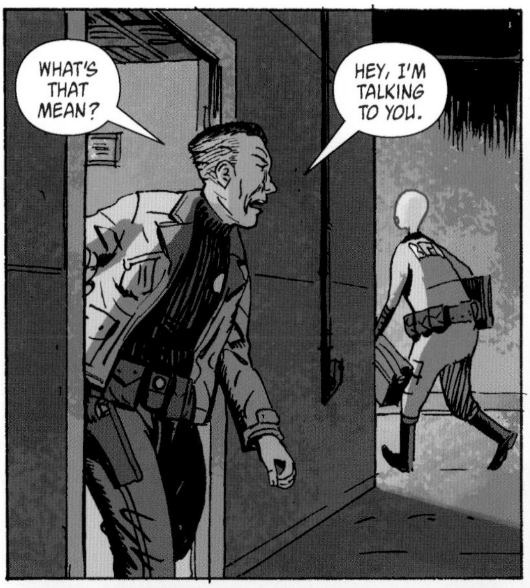
WHAT'S THAT MEAN?
HEY, I'M TALKING TO YOU.
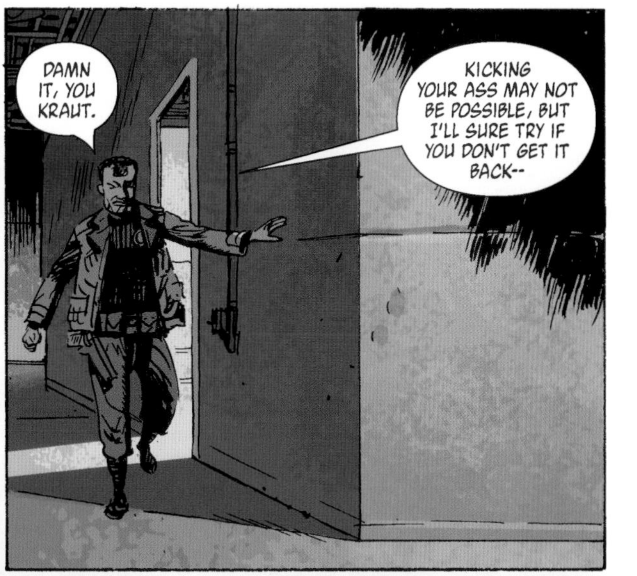
DAMN IT, YOU KRAUT.
KICKING YOUR ASS MAY NOT BE POSSIBLE, BUT I'LL SURE TRY IF YOU DON'T GET IT BACK--
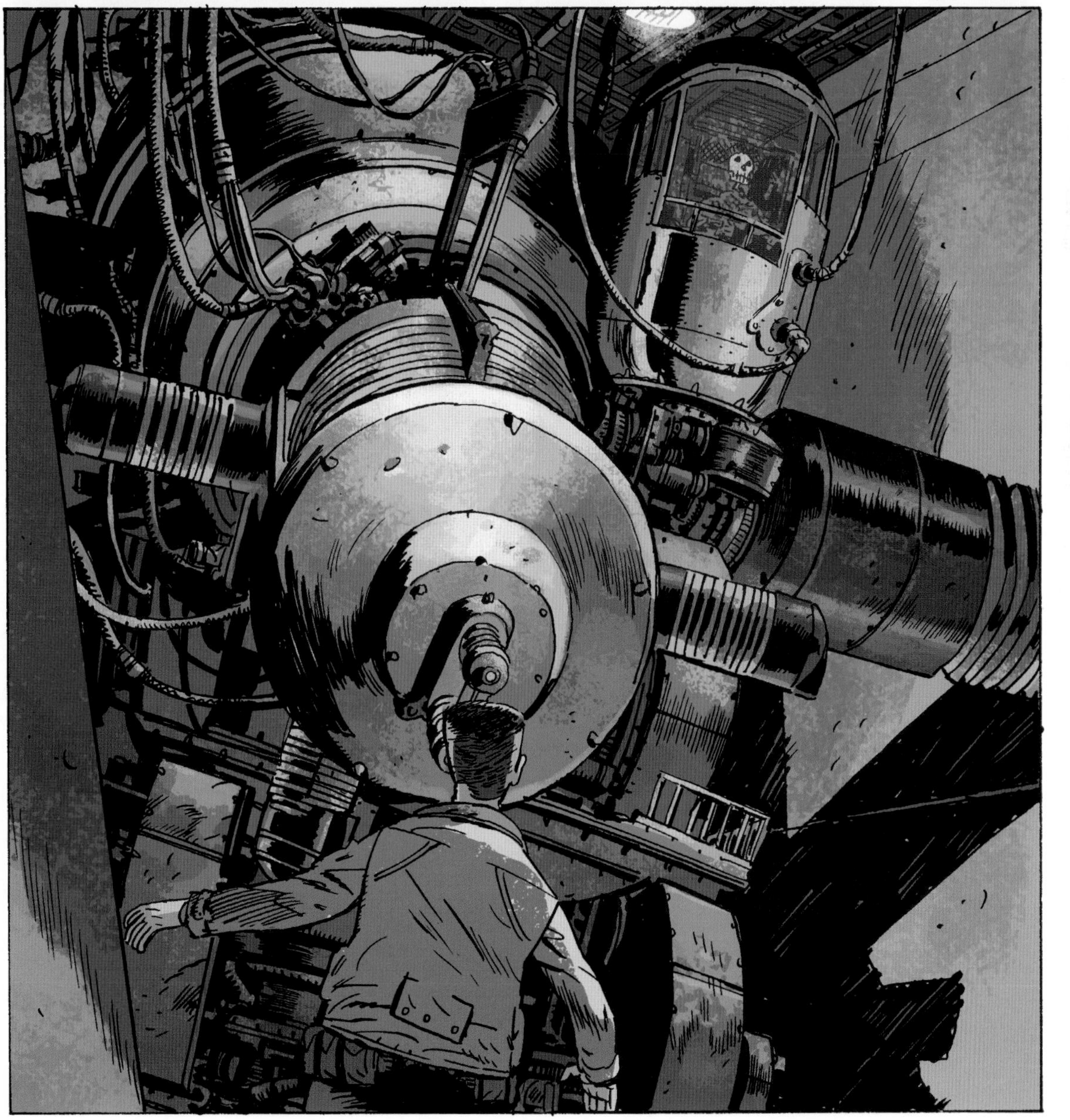

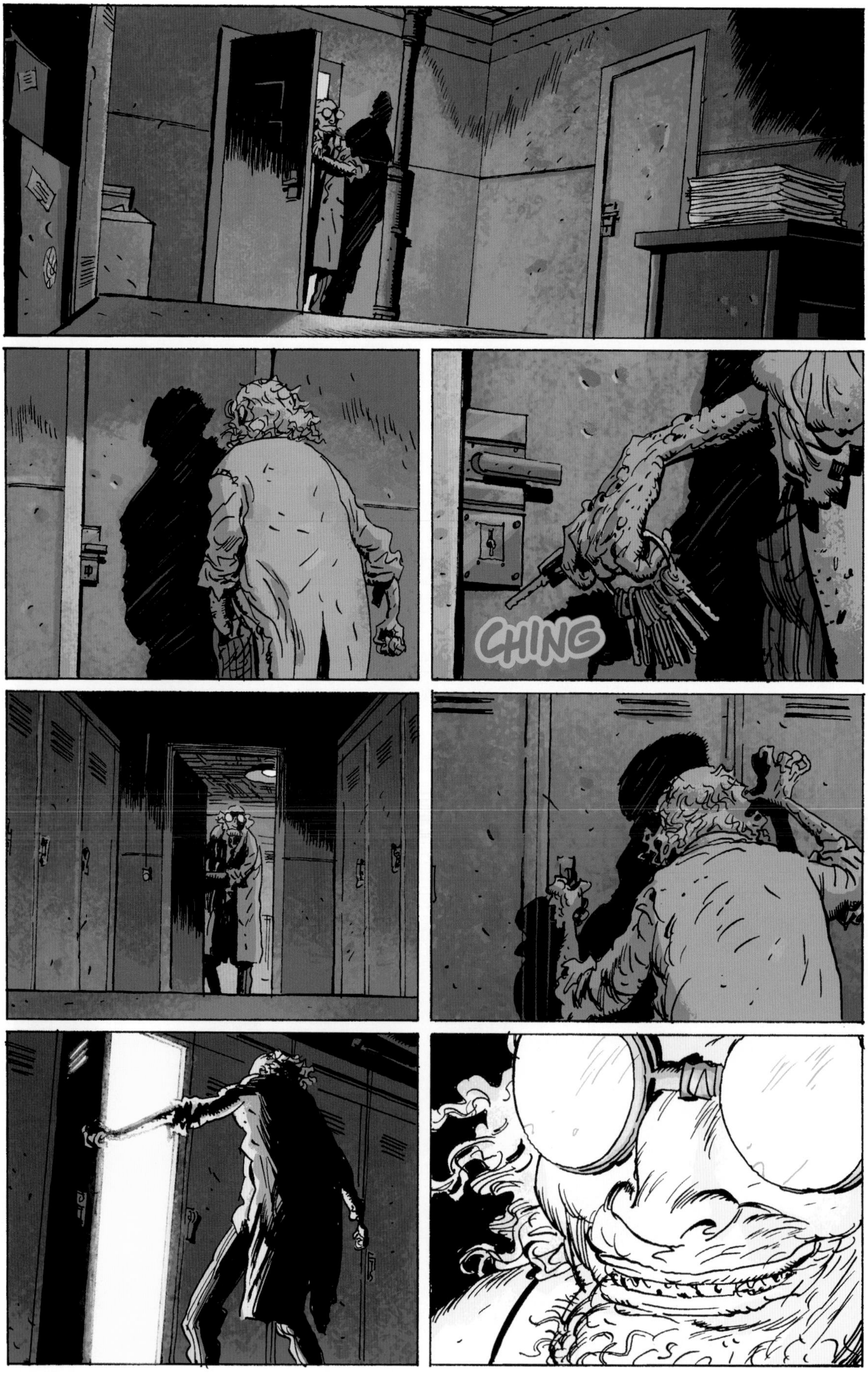
CHING

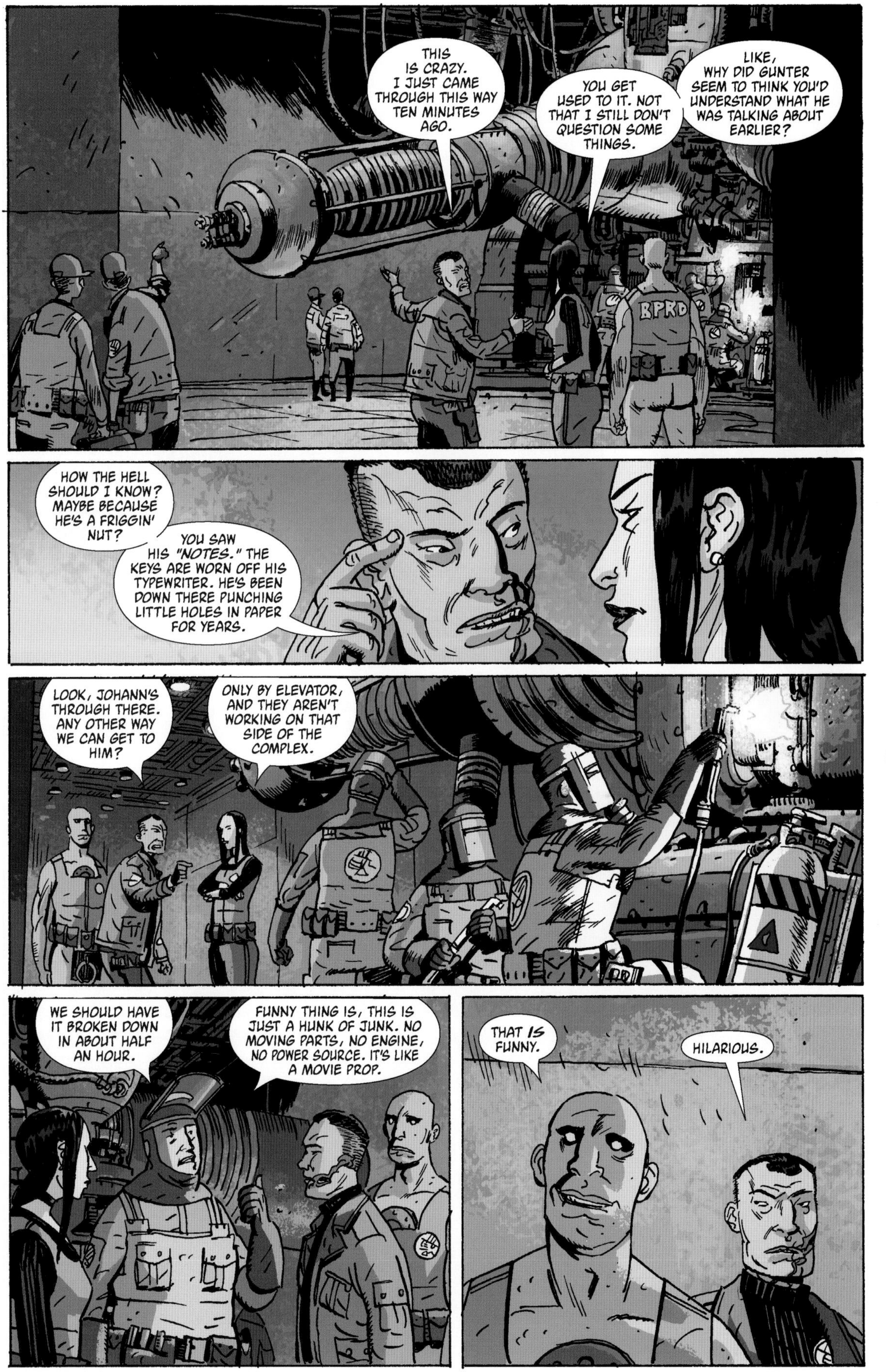
THIS IS CRAZY. I JUST CAME THROUGH THIS WAY TEN MINUTES AGO.
YOU GET USED TO IT. NOT THAT I STILL DON'T QUESTION SOME THINGS.
LIKE, WHY DID GUNTER SEEM TO THINK YOU'D UNDERSTAND WHAT HE WAS TALKING ABOUT EARLIER?
HOW THE HELL SHOULD I KNOW? MAYBE BECAUSE HE'S A FRIGGIN' NUT?
YOU SAW HIS "NOTES." THE KEYS ARE WORN OFF HIS TYPEWRITER. HE'S BEEN DOWN THERE PUNCHING LITTLE HOLES IN PAPER FOR YEARS.
LOOK, JOHANN'S THROUGH THERE. ANY OTHER WAY WE CAN GET TO HIM?
ONLY BY ELEVATOR, AND THEY AREN'T WORKING ON THAT SIDE OF THE COMPLEX.
WE SHOULD HAVE IT BROKEN DOWN IN ABOUT HALF AN HOUR.
FUNNY THING IS, THIS IS JUST A HUNK OF JUNK. NO MOVING PARTS, NO ENGINE, NO POWER SOURCE. IT'S LIKE A MOVIE PROP.
THAT IS FUNNY.
HILARIOUS.
BPRD

SSSZZZT
FLICK
PRD
PRD
HUMMMMMM

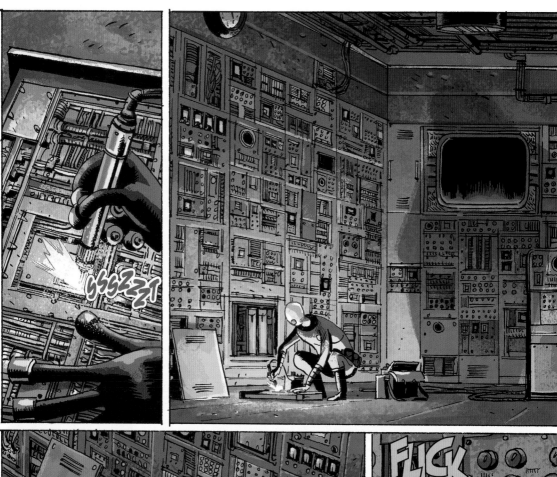

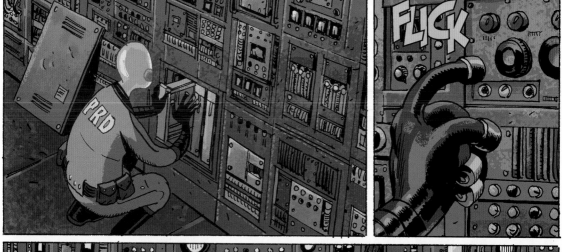

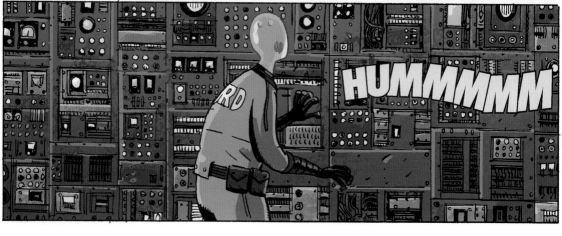

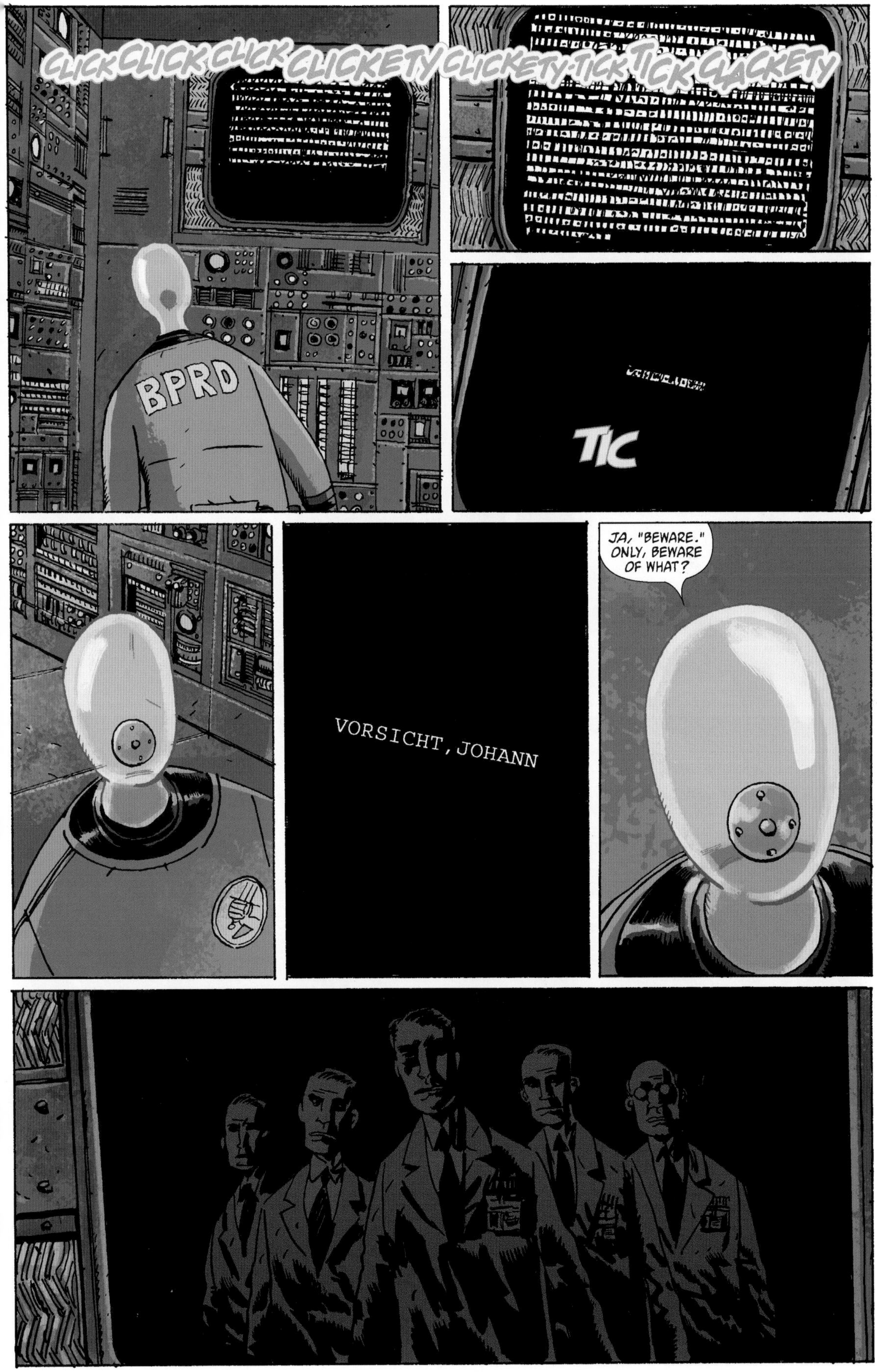
CLICK CLICK CLICK CLICKETY CLICKETY-TICK TICK CLACKETY
BPRD
TIC
VORSICHT, JOHANN
JA, "BEWARE." ONLY, BEWARE OF WHAT?

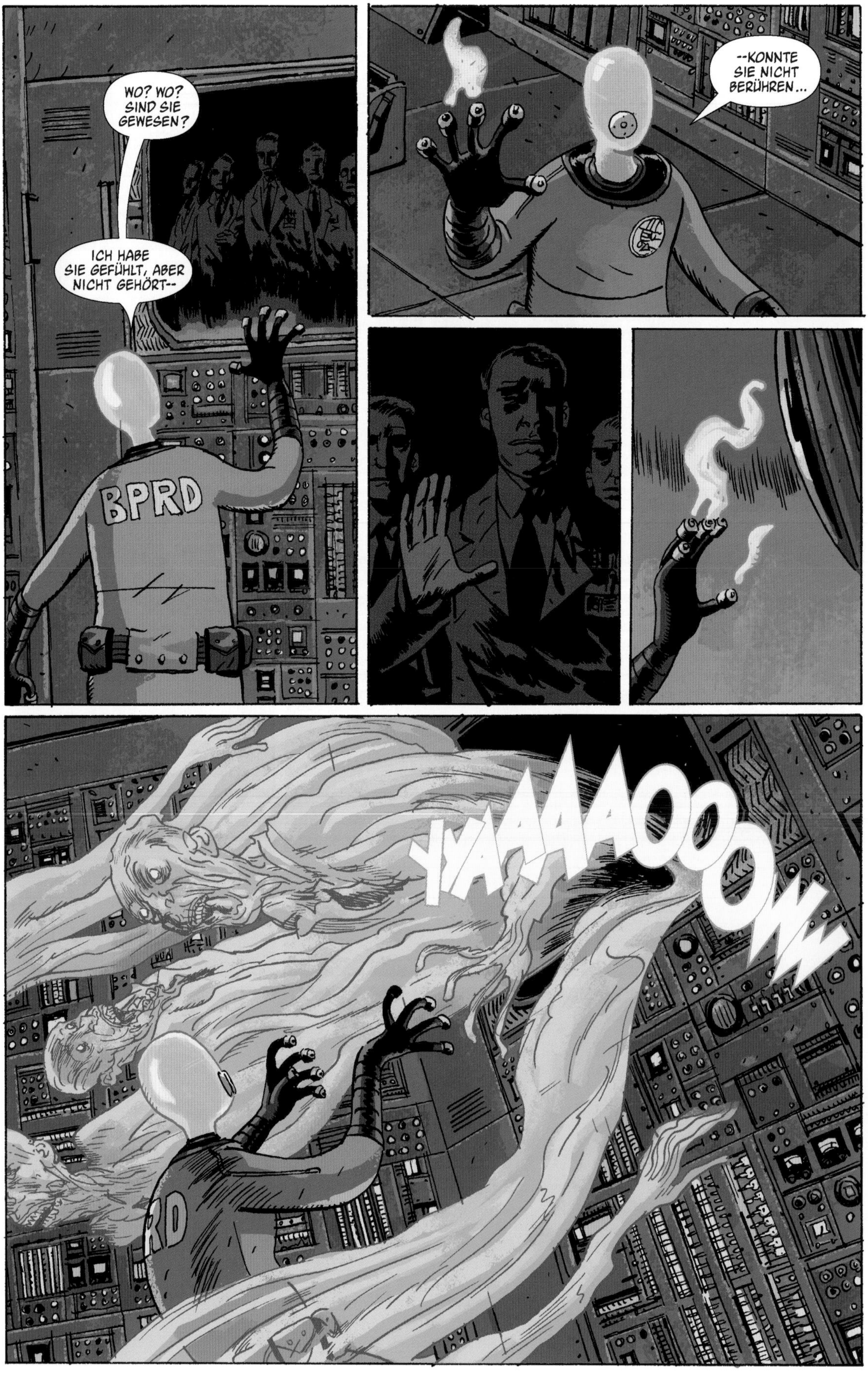
WO? WO? SIND SIE GEWESEN?
ICH HABE SIE GEFÜHLT, ABER NICHT GEHÖRT--
--KONNTE SIE NICHT BERÜHREN...
BPRD
YYAAAAOOOOW

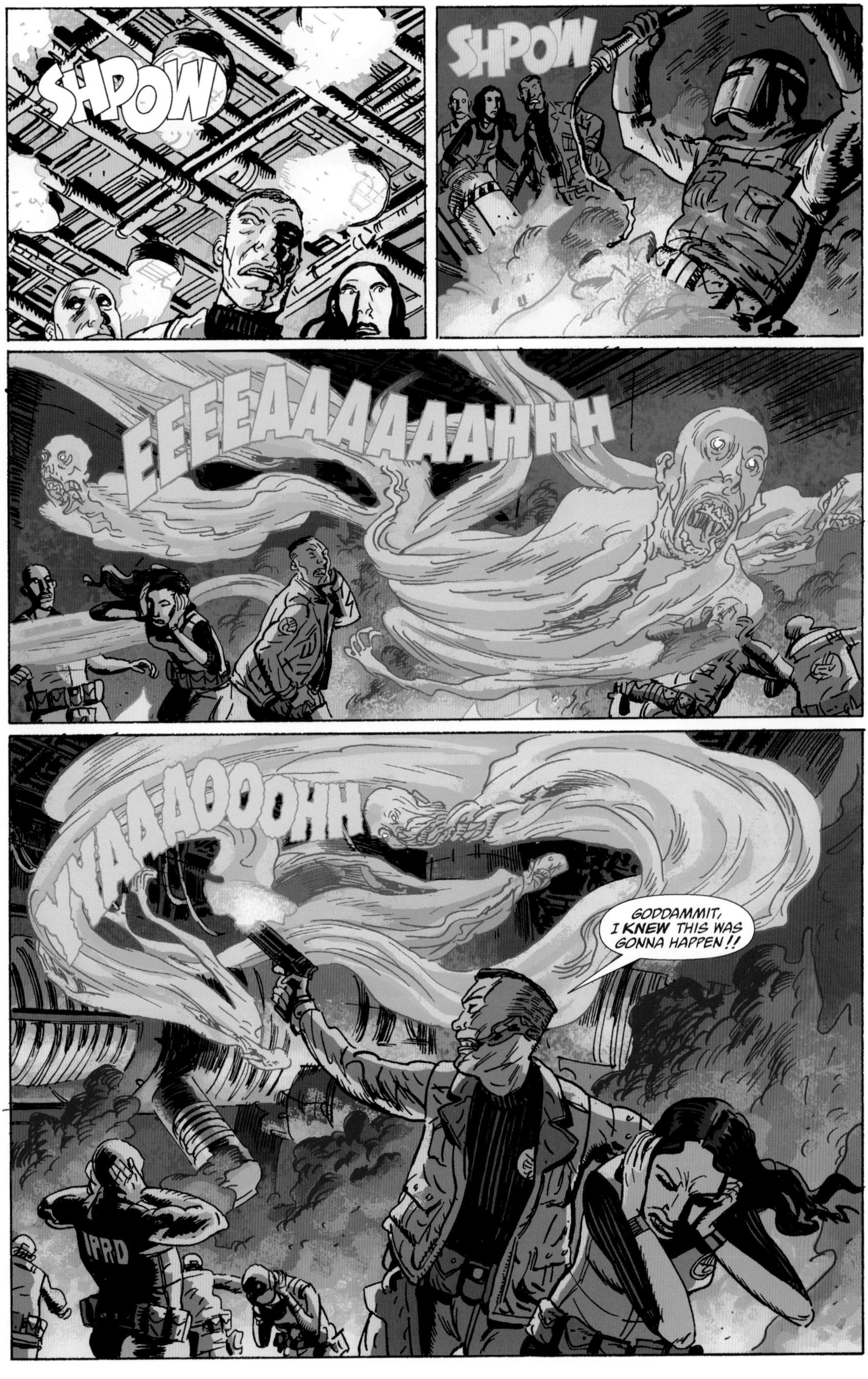
SHPOW
SHPOW
EEEEAAAAAAAHHH
WHAAAOOOOHH
GODDAMMIT, I KNEW THIS WAS GONNA HAPPEN!!
IPRD

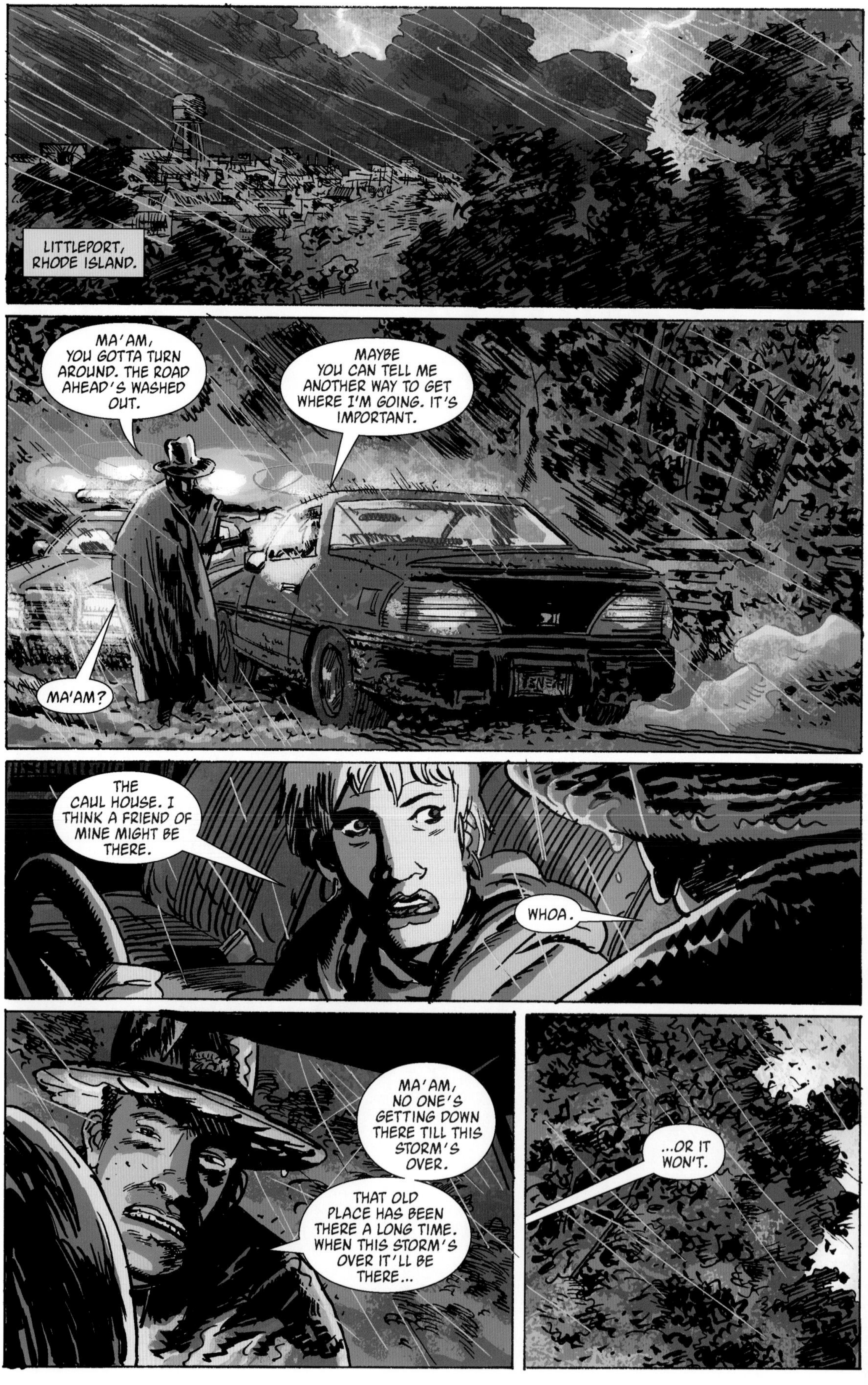
LITTLEPORT, RHODE ISLAND.
MA'AM, YOU GOTTA TURN AROUND. THE ROAD AHEAD'S WASHED OUT.
MAYBE YOU CAN TELL ME ANOTHER WAY TO GET WHERE I'M GOING. IT'S IMPORTANT.
MA'AM?
THE CAUL HOUSE. I THINK A FRIEND OF MINE MIGHT BE THERE.
WHOA.
MA'AM, NO ONE'S GETTING DOWN THERE TILL THIS STORM'S OVER.
THAT OLD PLACE HAS BEEN THERE A LONG TIME. WHEN THIS STORM'S OVER IT'LL BE THERE...
...OR IT WON'T.

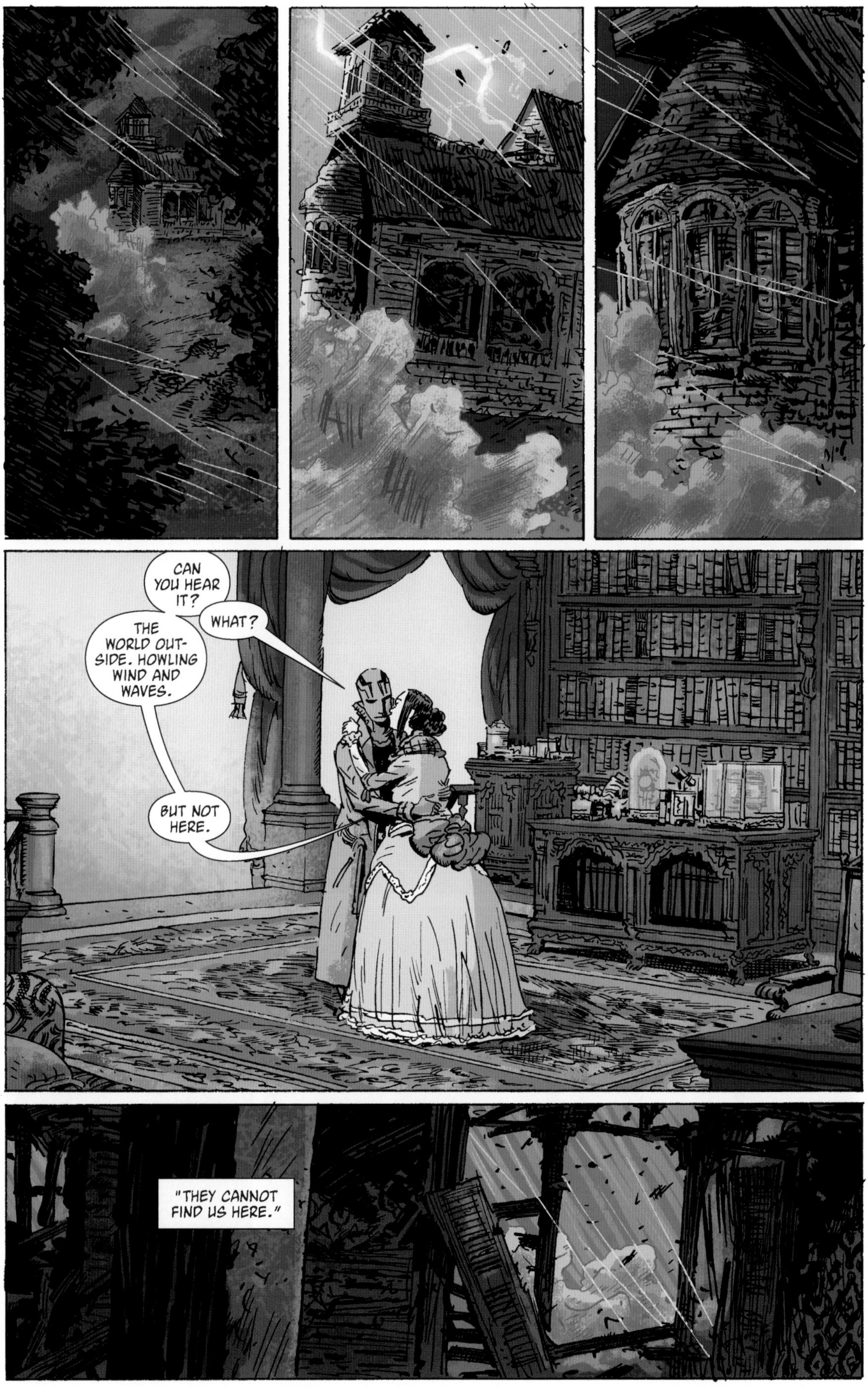
CAN YOU HEAR IT?
WHAT?
THE WORLD OUT-SIDE. HOWLING WIND AND WAVES.
BUT NOT HERE.
"THEY CANNOT FIND US HERE."

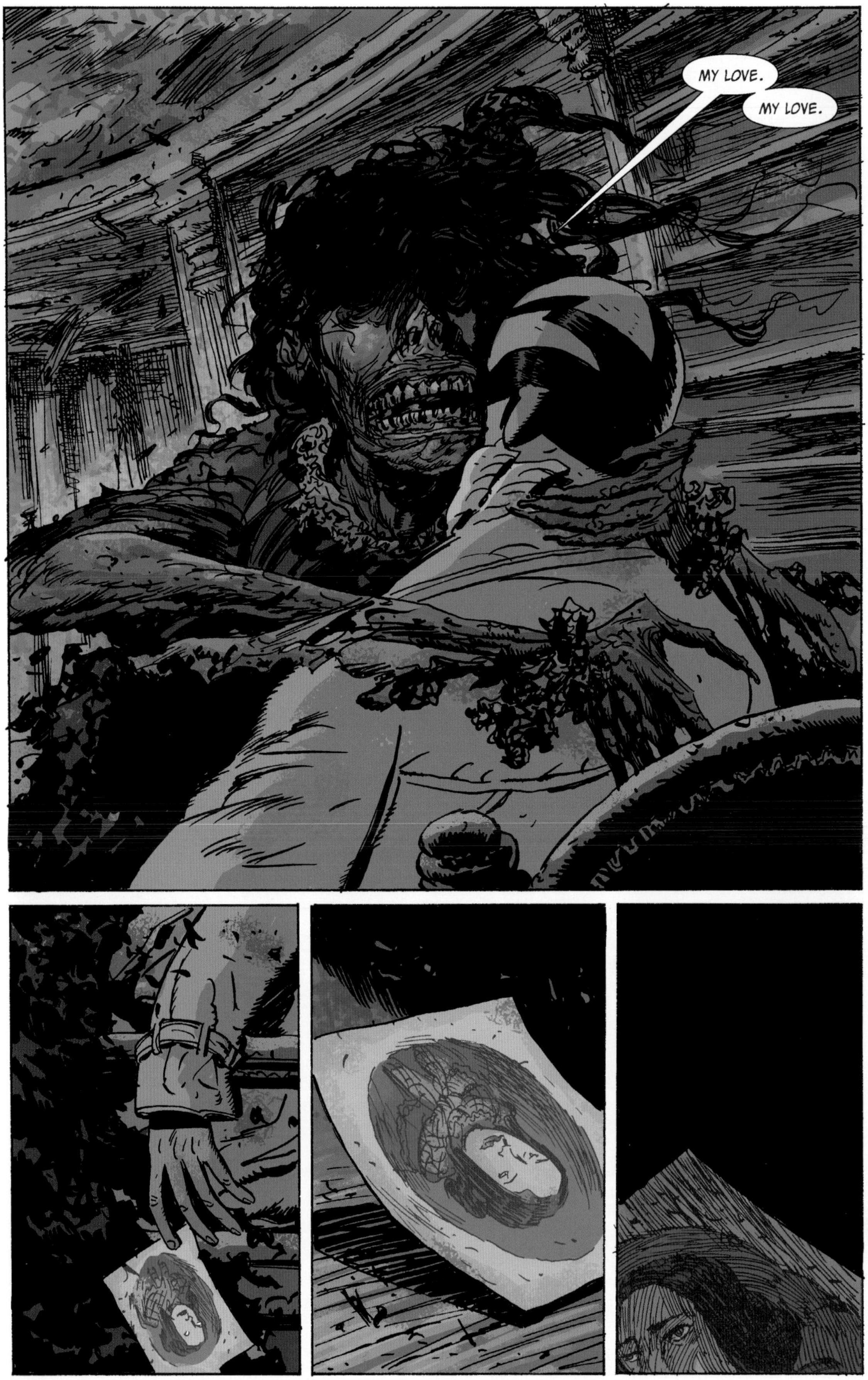
MY LOVE.
MY LOVE.

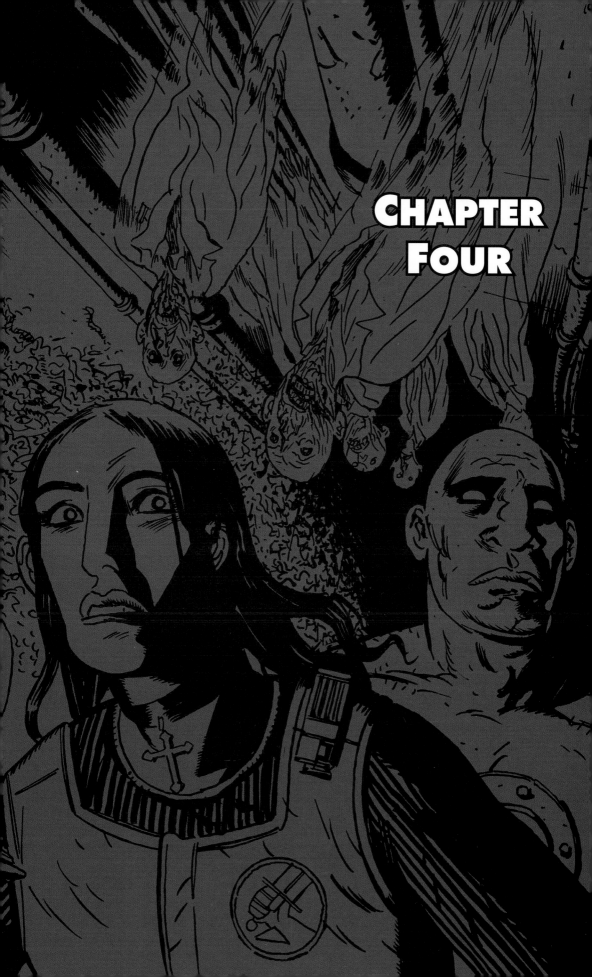

CHAPTER
FOUR

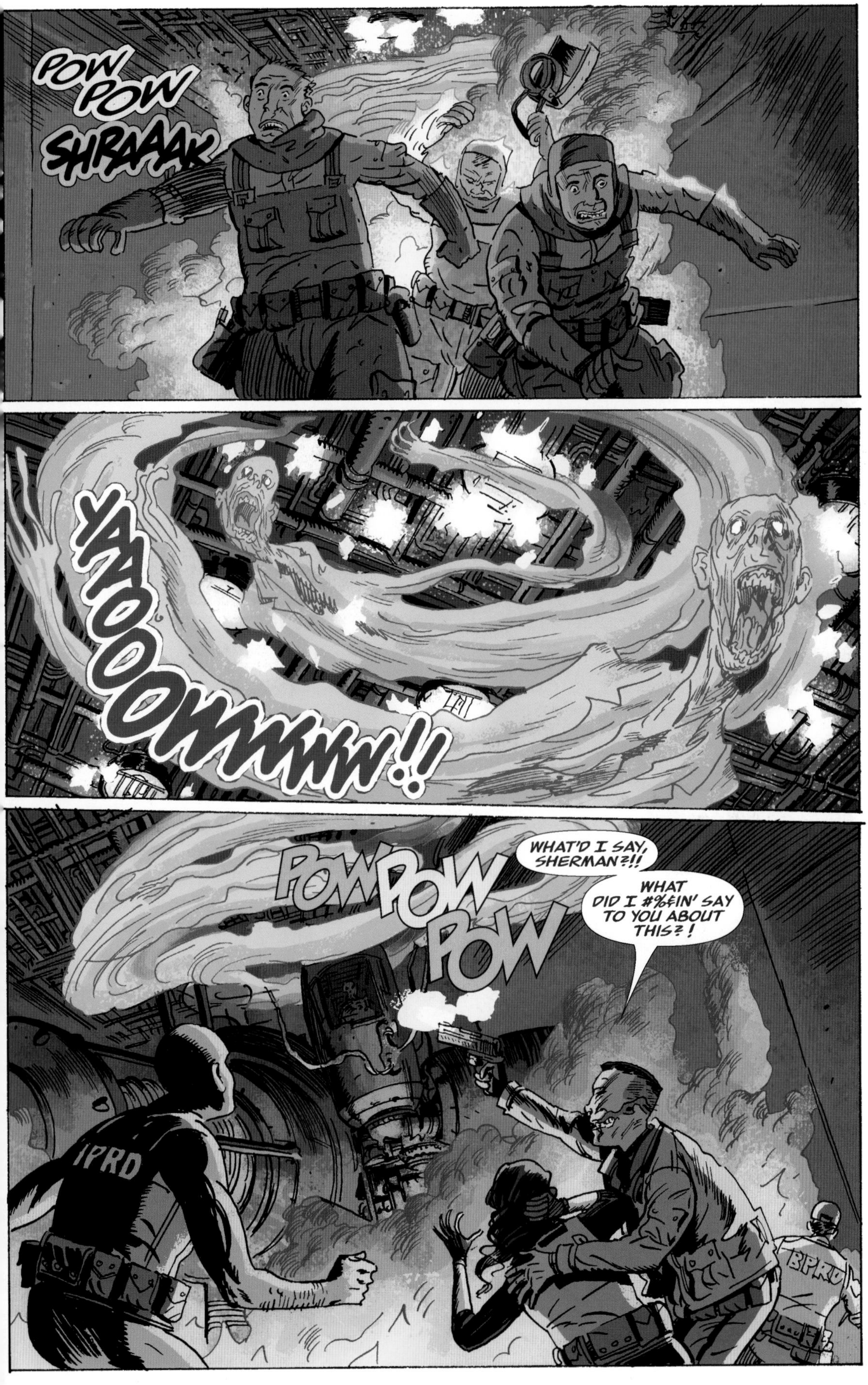
POW
POW
SHRAAAK
YAAOOOOWWWW!!
POW POW POW POW
WHAT'D I SAY, SHERMAN?!!
WHAT DID I #%¢IN' SAY TO YOU ABOUT THIS?!
BPRD
BPRD

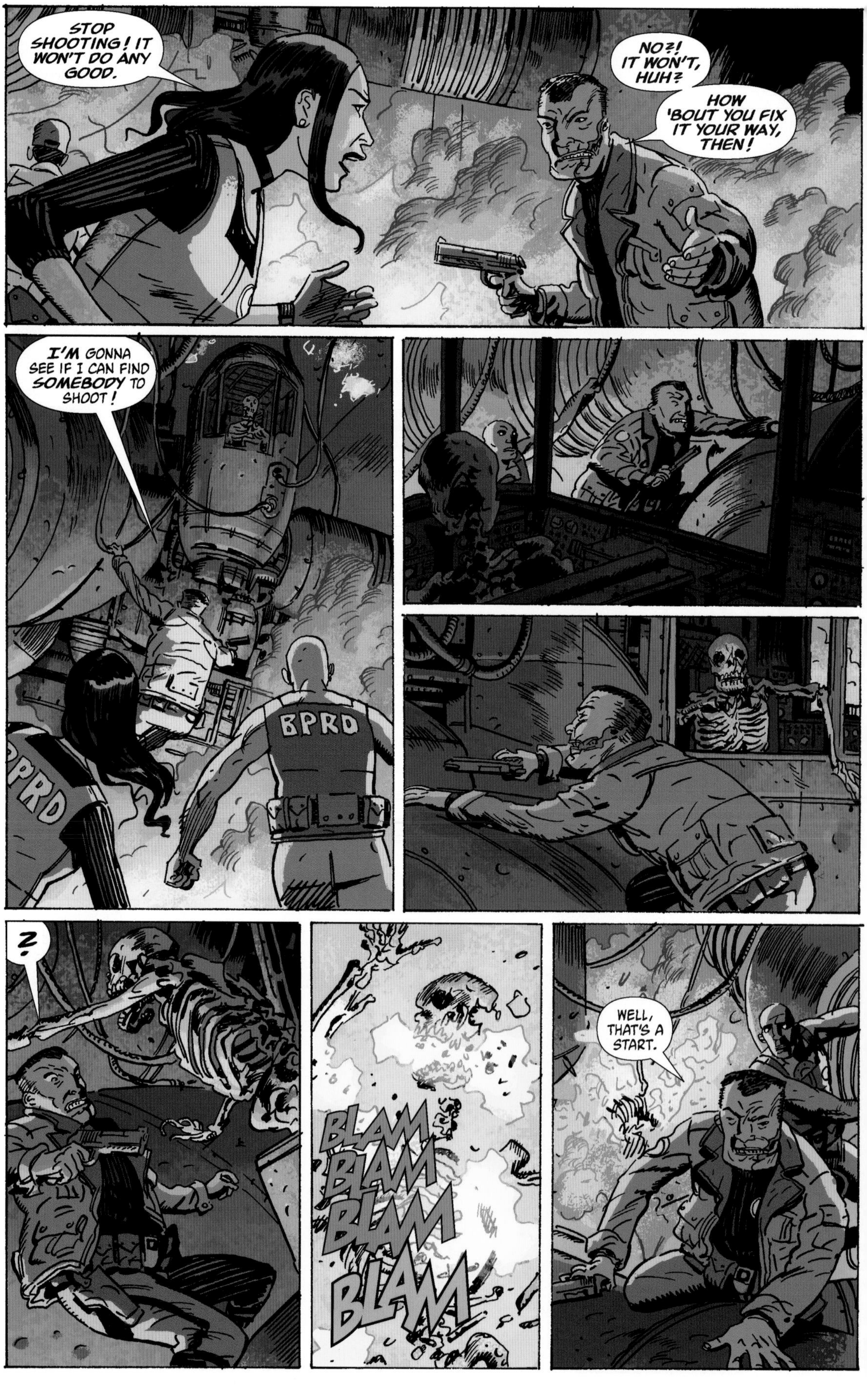
STOP SHOOTING! IT WON'T DO ANY GOOD.
NO?! IT WON'T, HUH?
HOW 'BOUT YOU FIX IT YOUR WAY, THEN!
I'M GONNA SEE IF I CAN FIND SOMEBODY TO SHOOT!
BPRD
BPRD
?
BLAM BLAM BLAM BLAM
WELL, THAT'S A START.

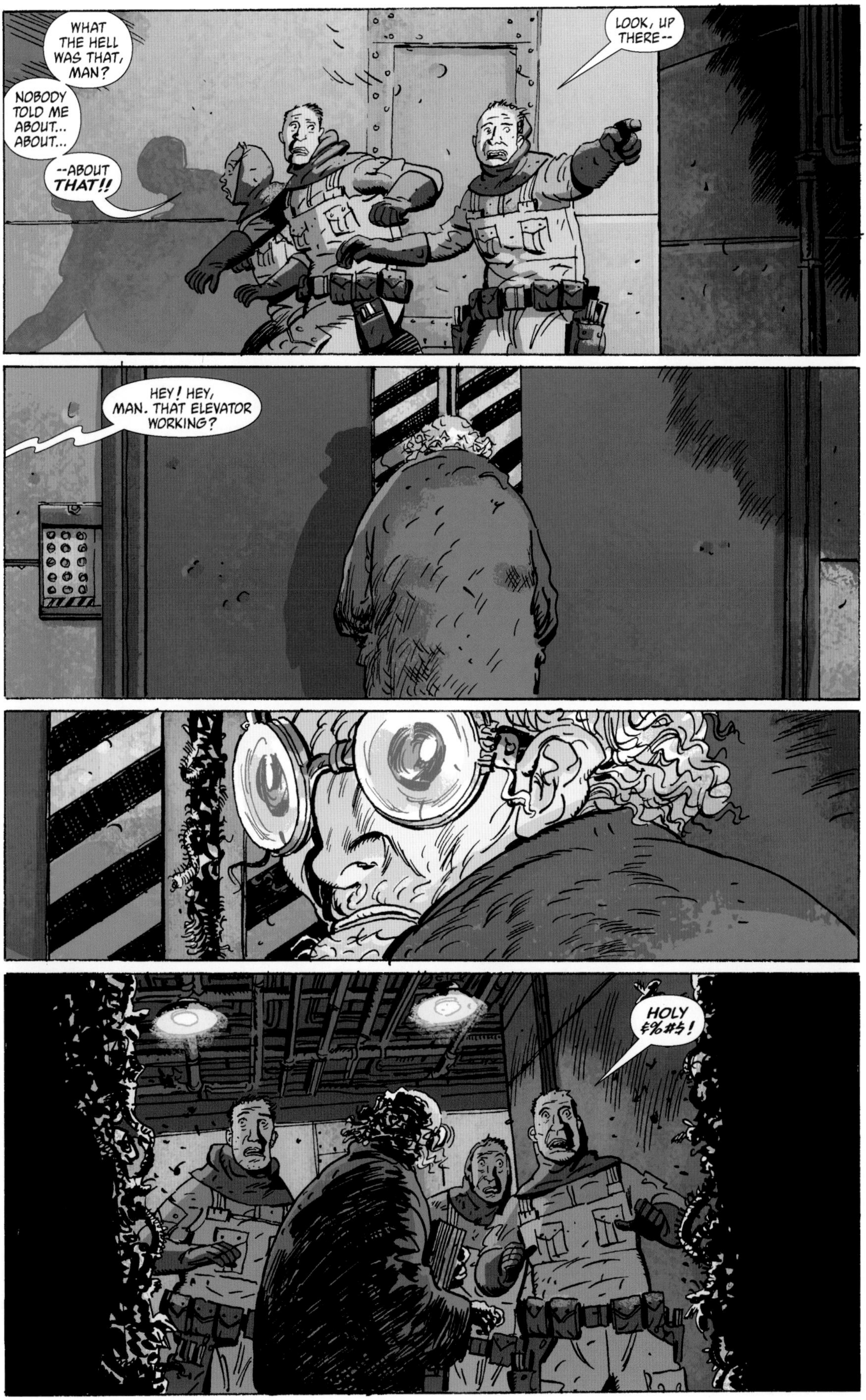
WHAT THE HELL WAS THAT, MAN?
NOBODY TOLD ME ABOUT... ABOUT...
--ABOUT THAT!!
LOOK, UP THERE--
HEY! HEY, MAN. THAT ELEVATOR WORKING?
HOLY ₤%#$!

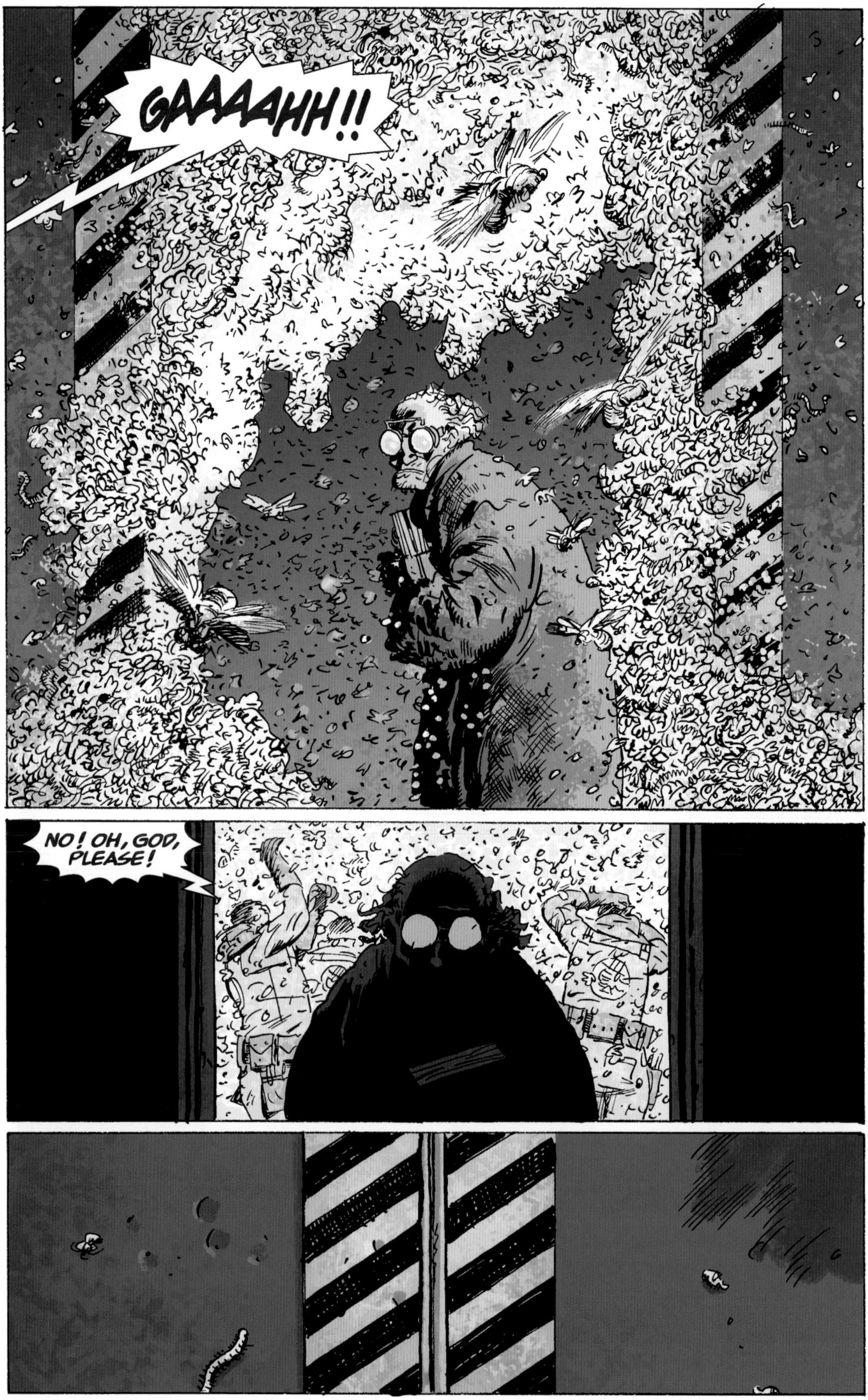
GAAAAHH!!
NO! OH, GOD, PLEASE!

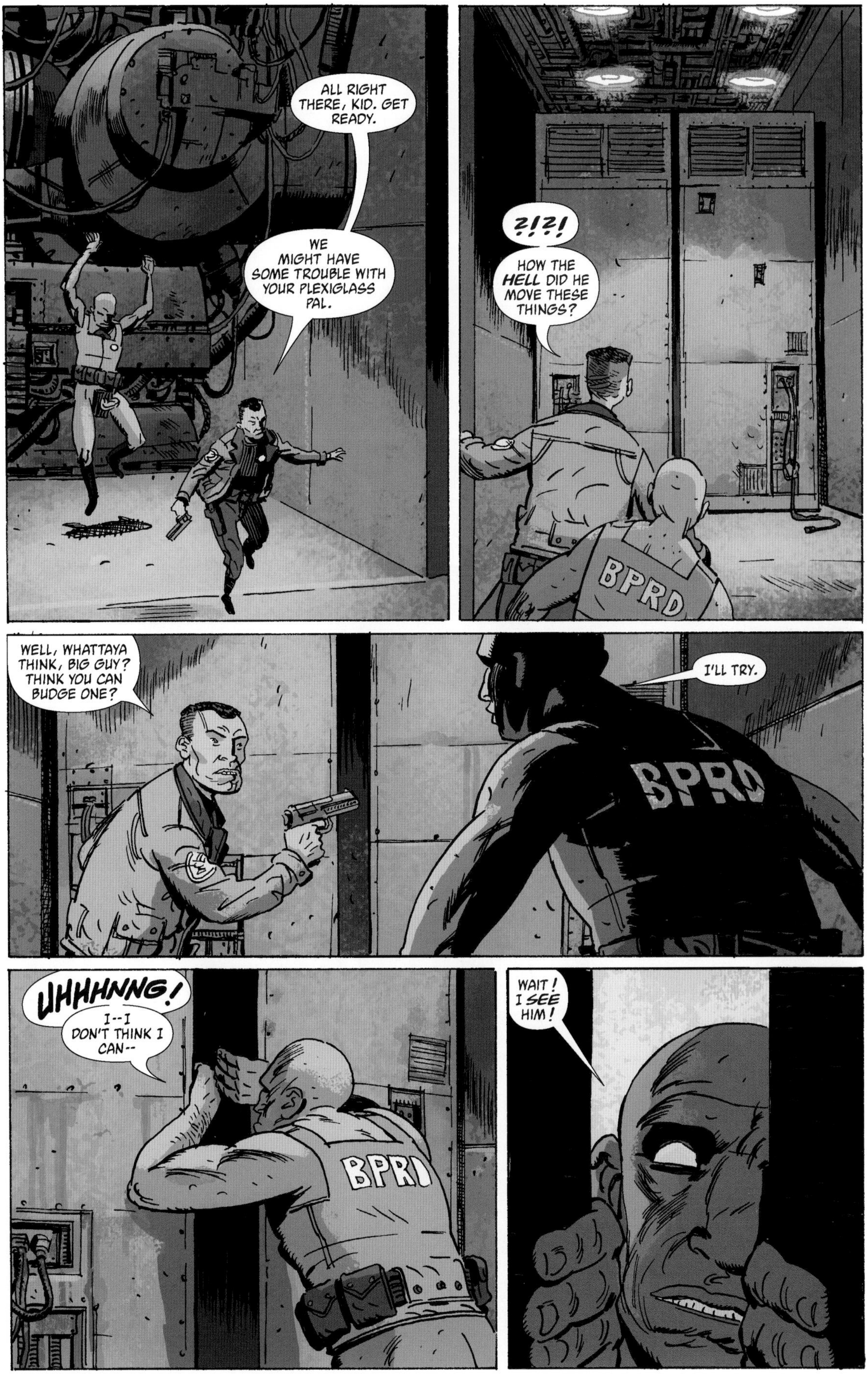
ALL RIGHT THERE, KID. GET READY.
WE MIGHT HAVE SOME TROUBLE WITH YOUR PLEXIGLASS PAL.
?!?!
HOW THE HELL DID HE MOVE THESE THINGS?
BPRD
WELL, WHATTAYA THINK, BIG GUY? THINK YOU CAN BUDGE ONE?
I'LL TRY.
BPRD
UHHHNNG!
I--I DON'T THINK I CAN--
BPRD
WAIT! I SEE HIM!

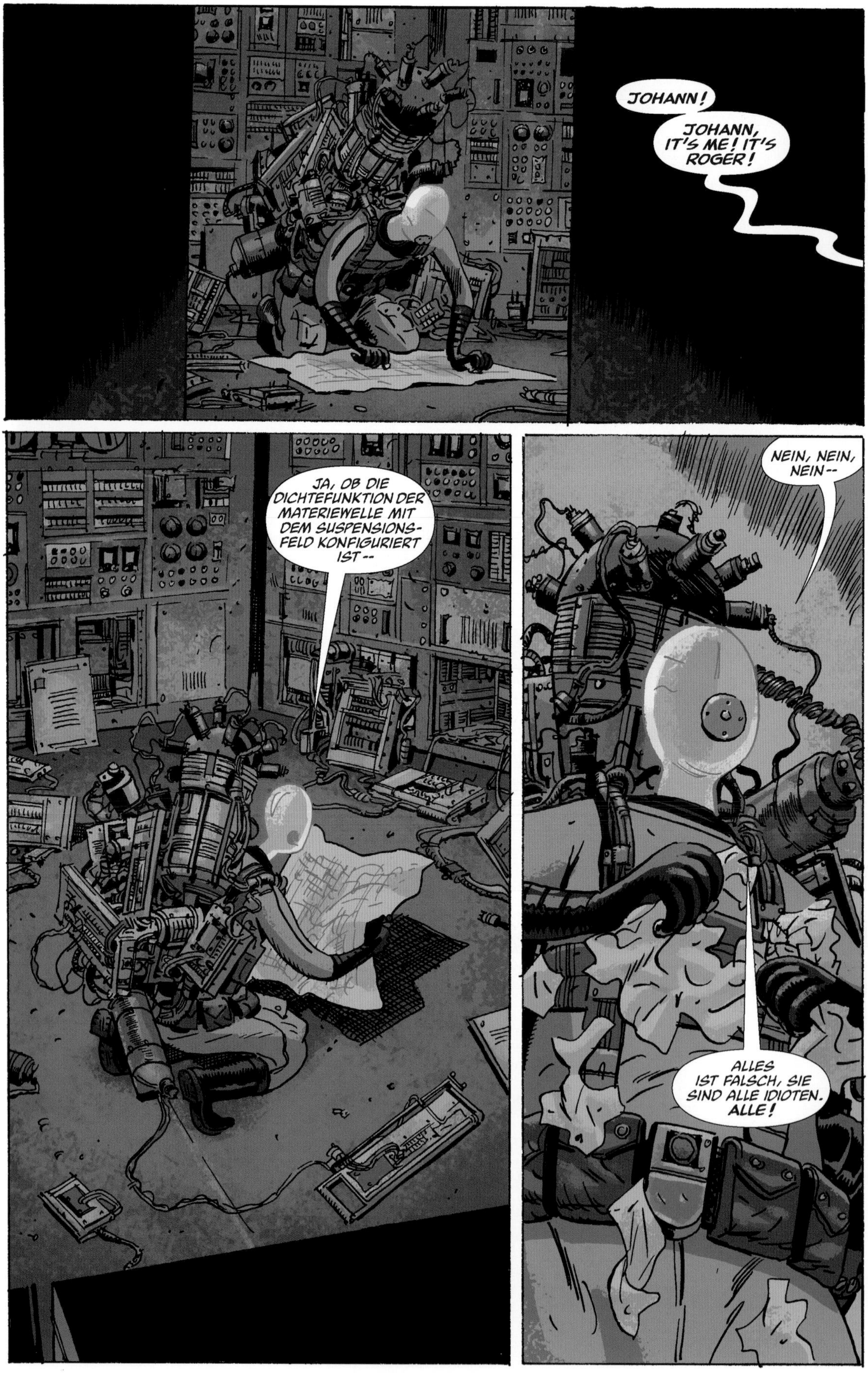
JOHANN!
JOHANN, IT'S ME! IT'S ROGER!
JA, OB DIE DICHTEFUNKTION DER MATERIEWELLE MIT DEM SUSPENSIONSFELD KONFIGURIERT IST --
NEIN, NEIN, NEIN --
ALLES IST FALSCH, SIE SIND ALLE IDIOTEN. ALLE!

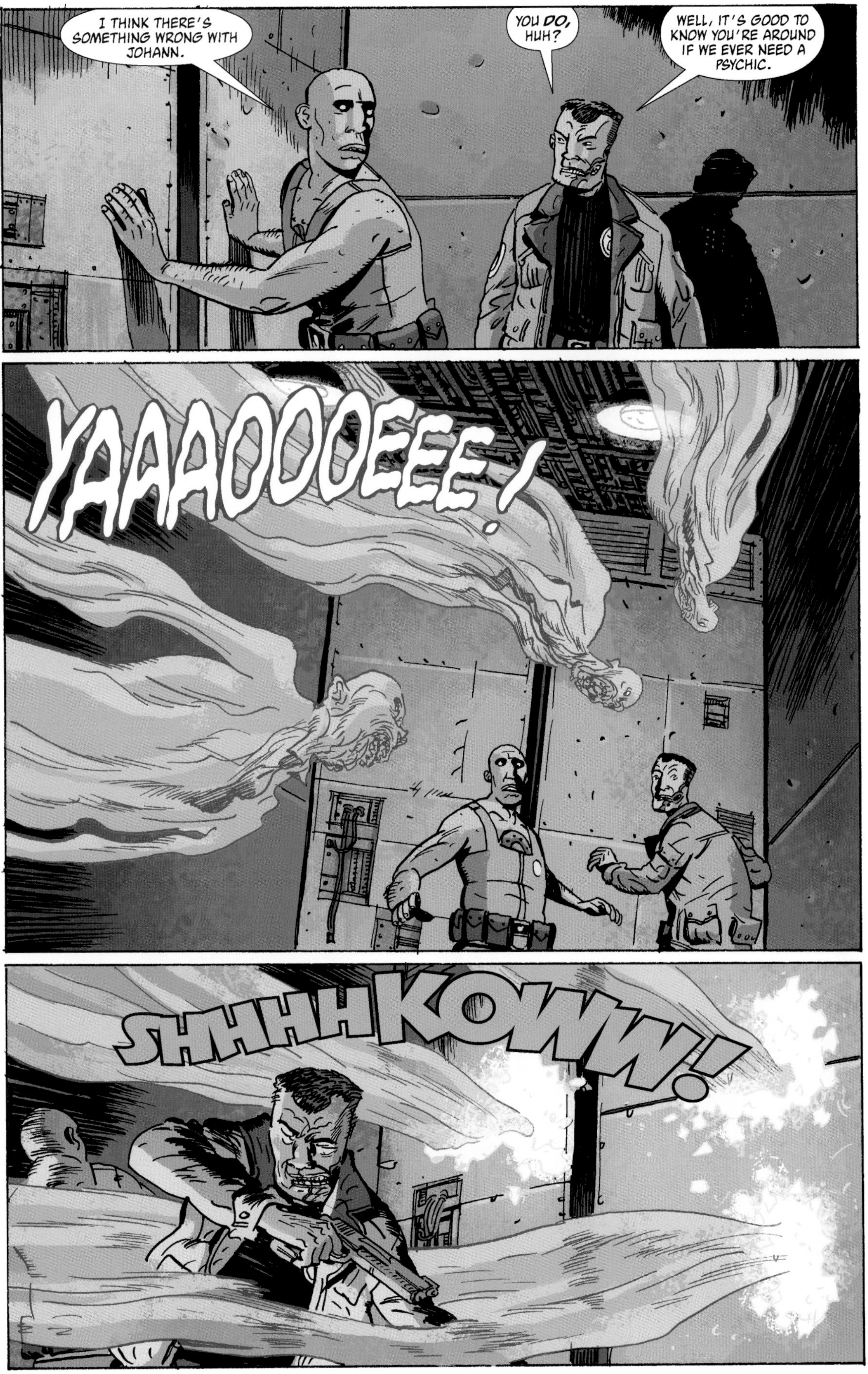
I THINK THERE'S SOMETHING WRONG WITH JOHANN.
YOU DO, HUH?
WELL, IT'S GOOD TO KNOW YOU'RE AROUND IF WE EVER NEED A PSYCHIC.
YAAAOOOEEE!
SHHHHKOWW!

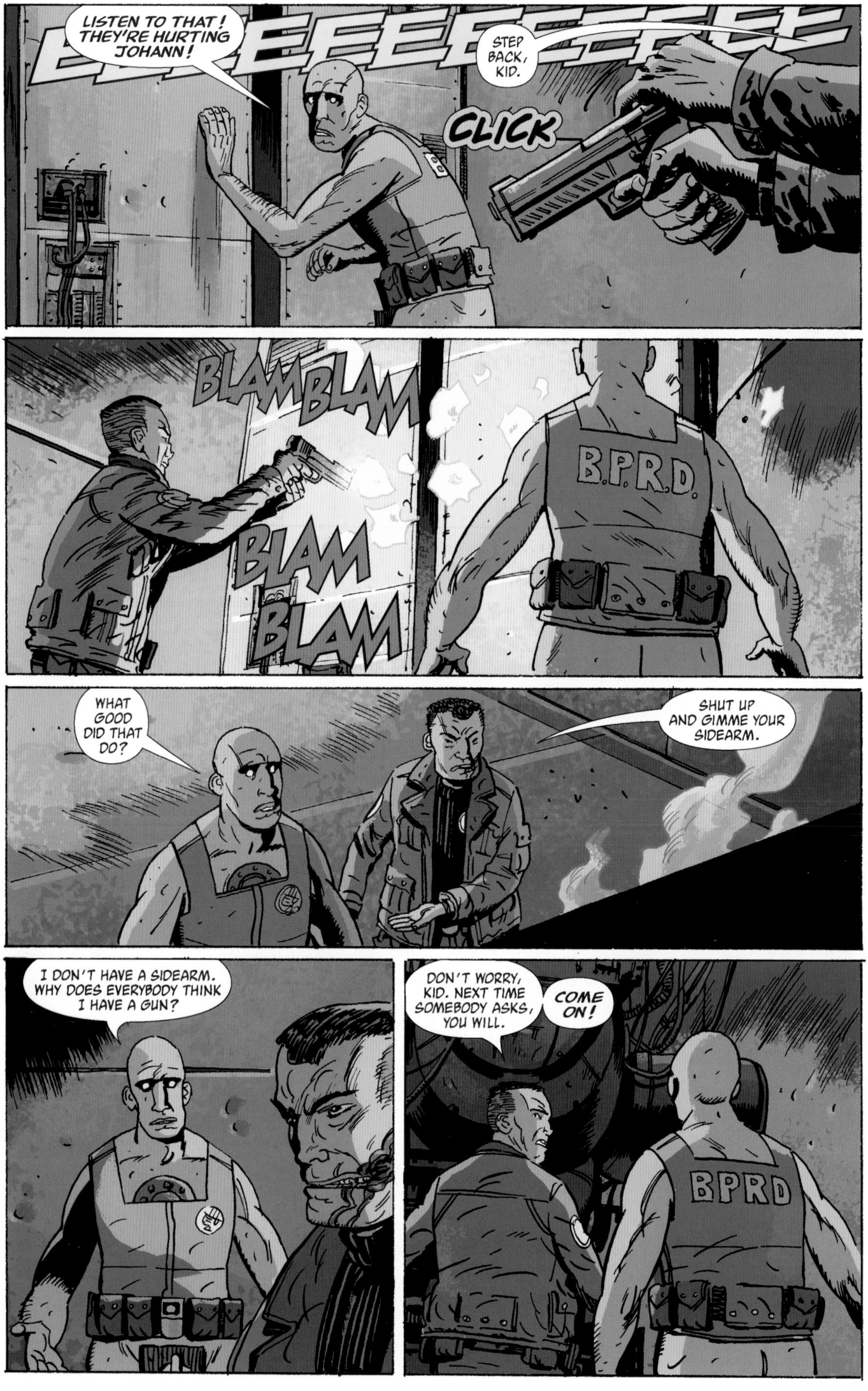

EEEEEEEEEEEEEE
LISTEN TO THAT! THEY'RE HURTING JOHANN!
STEP BACK, KID.
CLICK
BLAMBLAM
BLAM
BLAM
B.P.R.D.
WHAT GOOD DID THAT DO?
SHUT UP AND GIMME YOUR SIDEARM.
I DON'T HAVE A SIDEARM. WHY DOES EVERYBODY THINK I HAVE A GUN?
DON'T WORRY, KID. NEXT TIME SOMEBODY ASKS, YOU WILL.
COME ON!
BPRD

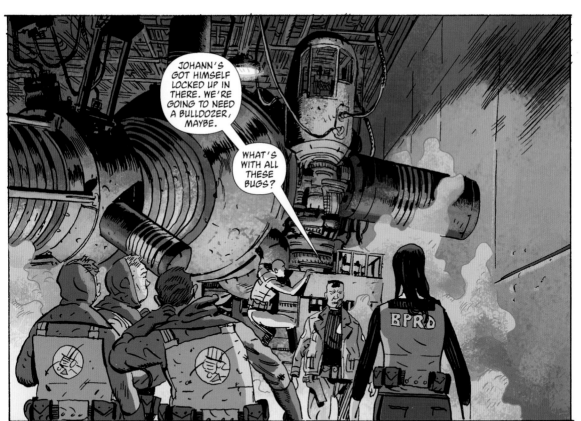

JOHANN'S GOT HIMSELF LOCKED UP IN THERE. WE'RE GOING TO NEED A BULLDOZER, MAYBE.

WHAT'S WITH ALL THESE BUGS?

YEAH, ABOUT THAT--

THE ELEVATOR. THEY CAME UP THROUGH THE ELEVATOR. THOUSANDS AND THOUSANDS OF THEM.

THAT OLD GUY? HE WAS STANDING THERE AT THE ELEVATOR, AND WHEN THE DOORS OPENED...

HE DIDN'T SAY A THING. THEY ALL CAME OUT, AND THEN HE JUST WALKED ONTO THE ELEVATOR--

--LIKE HE WAS JUST BEING POLITE, LIKE HE'D BEEN WAITING FOR THEM TO COME OFF.

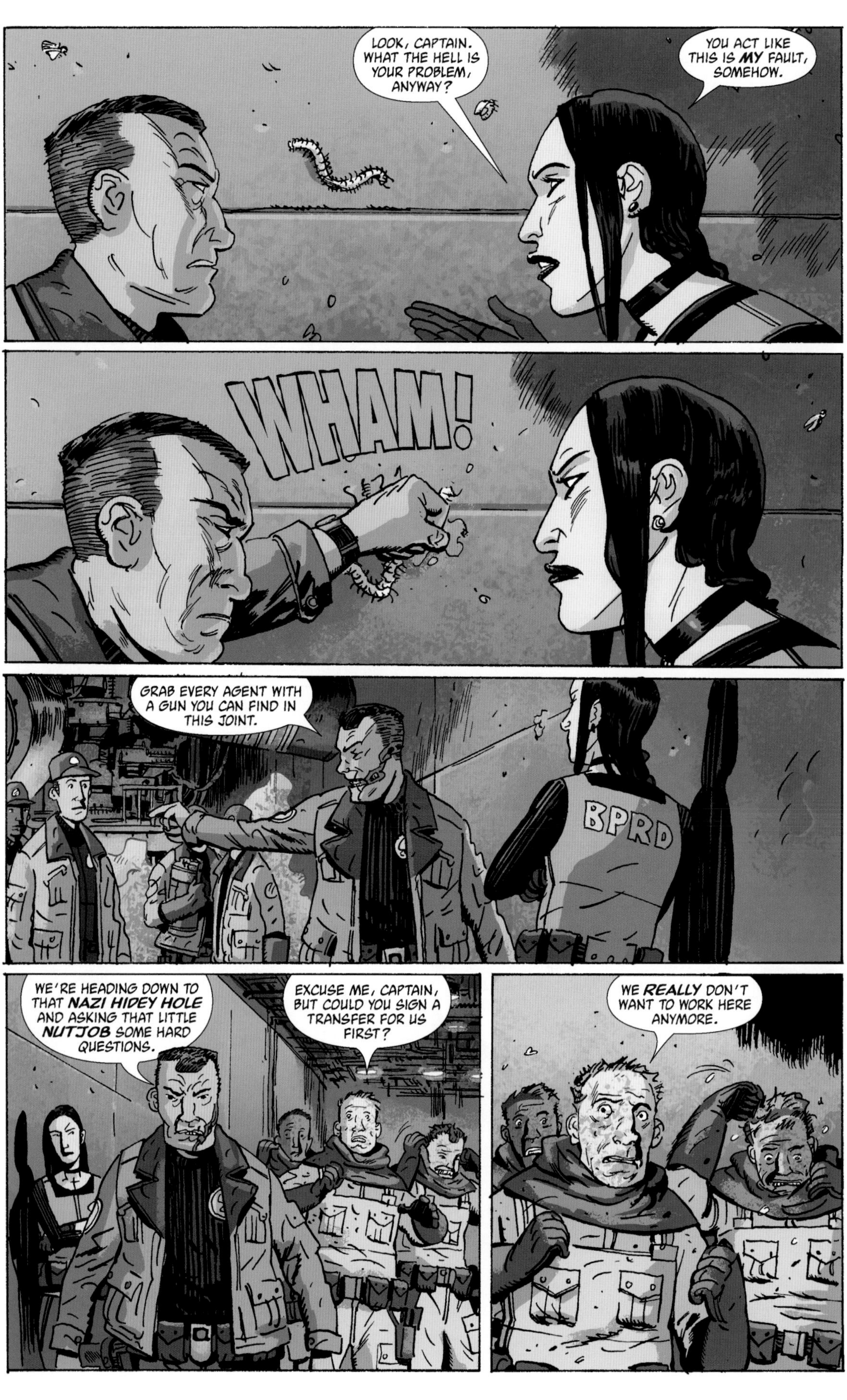

LOOK, CAPTAIN. WHAT THE HELL IS YOUR PROBLEM, ANYWAY?
YOU ACT LIKE THIS IS MY FAULT, SOMEHOW.
WHAM!
GRAB EVERY AGENT WITH A GUN YOU CAN FIND IN THIS JOINT.
BPRD
WE'RE HEADING DOWN TO THAT NAZI HIDEY HOLE AND ASKING THAT LITTLE NUTJOB SOME HARD QUESTIONS.
EXCUSE ME, CAPTAIN, BUT COULD YOU SIGN A TRANSFER FOR US FIRST?
WE REALLY DON'T WANT TO WORK HERE ANYMORE.

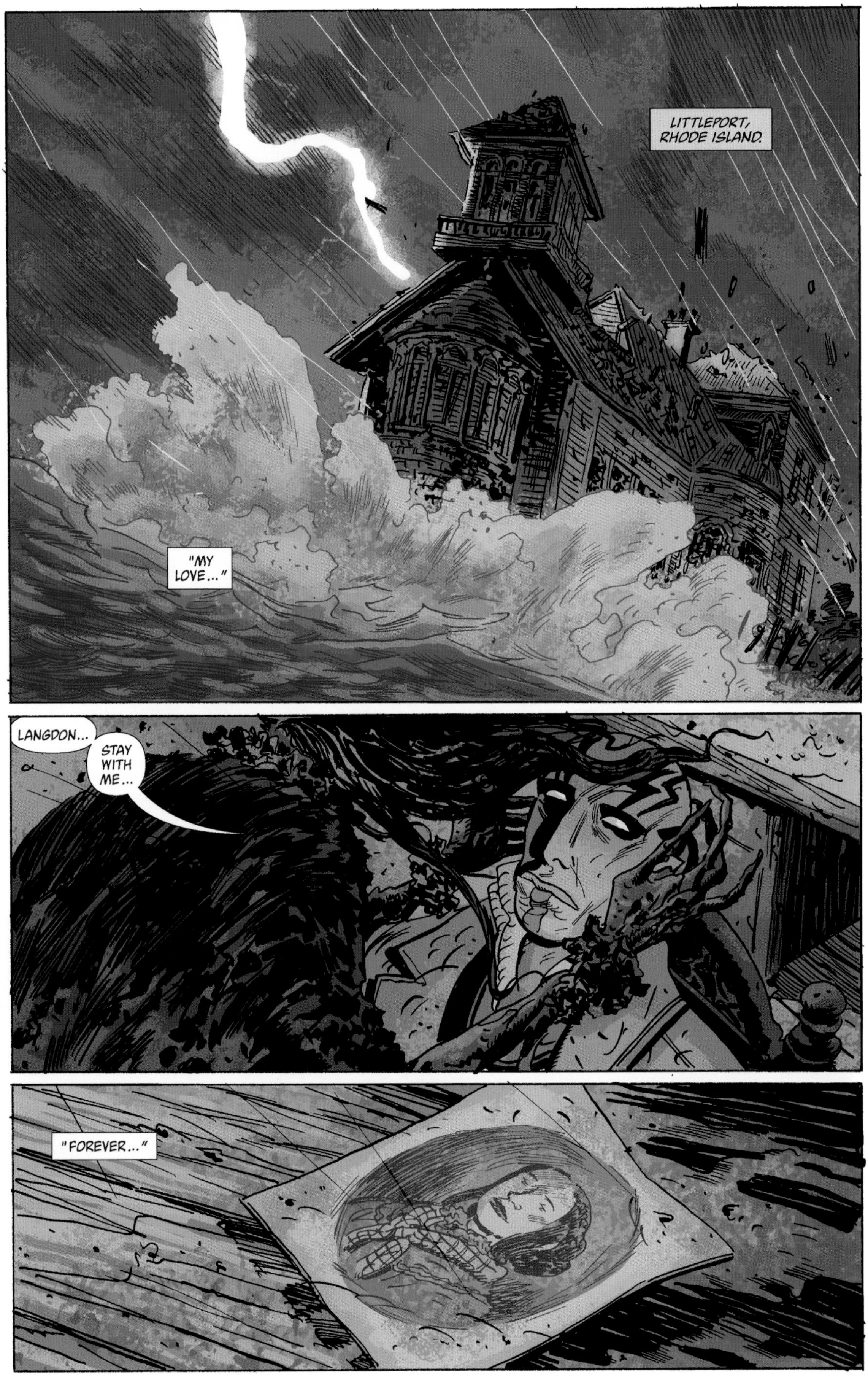
LITTLEPORT, RHODE ISLAND.
"MY LOVE..."
LANGDON...
STAY WITH ME...
"FOREVER..."

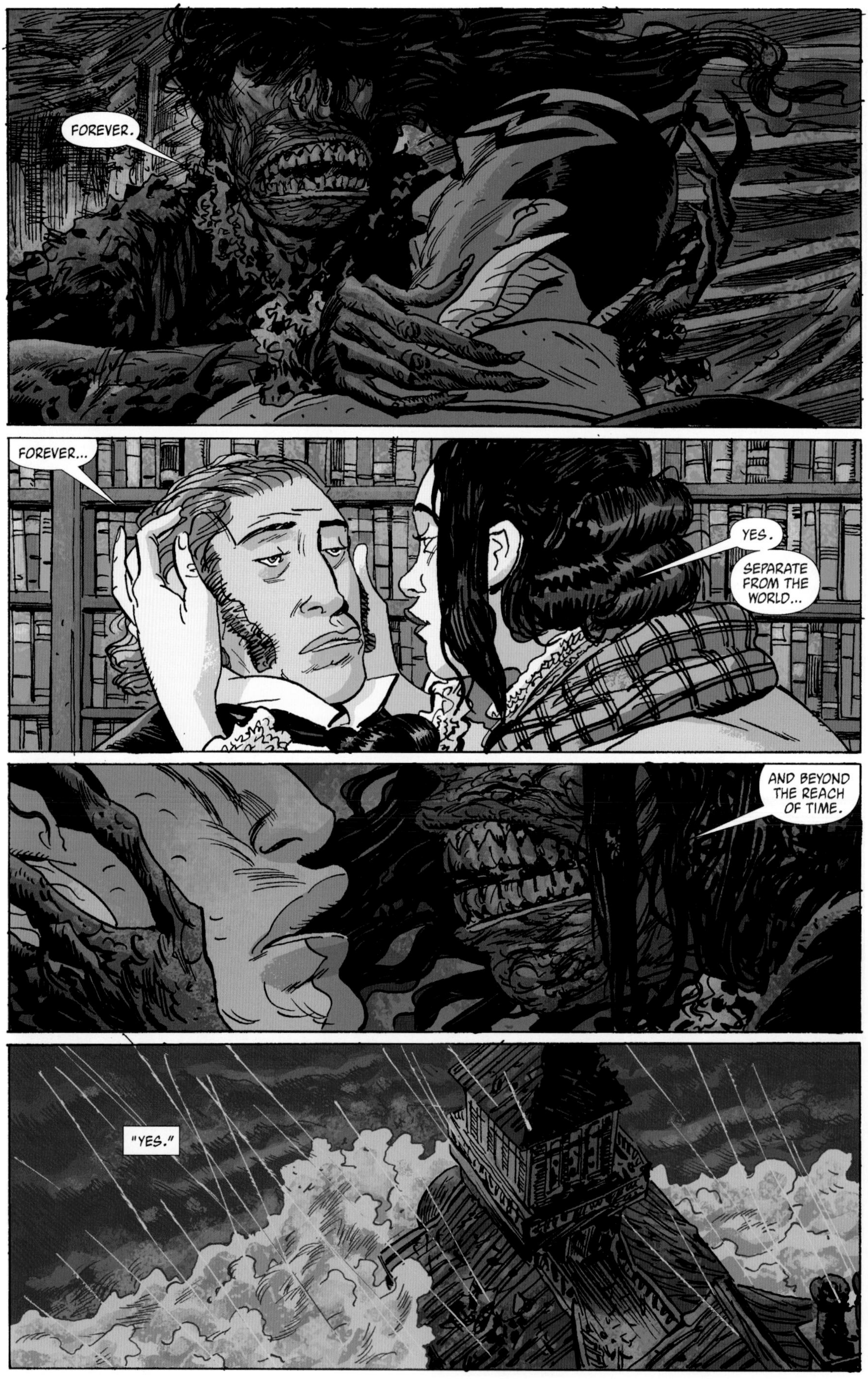
FOREVER.
FOREVER...
YES.
SEPARATE FROM THE WORLD...
AND BEYOND THE REACH OF TIME.
"YES."

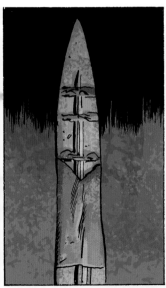

NICE.

REAL NICE OUTFIT.

STRANGE THINGS GOING ON HERE, GUNTER.

MY CRAZYBONE TELLS ME *YOU* GOT SOMETHING TO DO WITH ALL THAT.

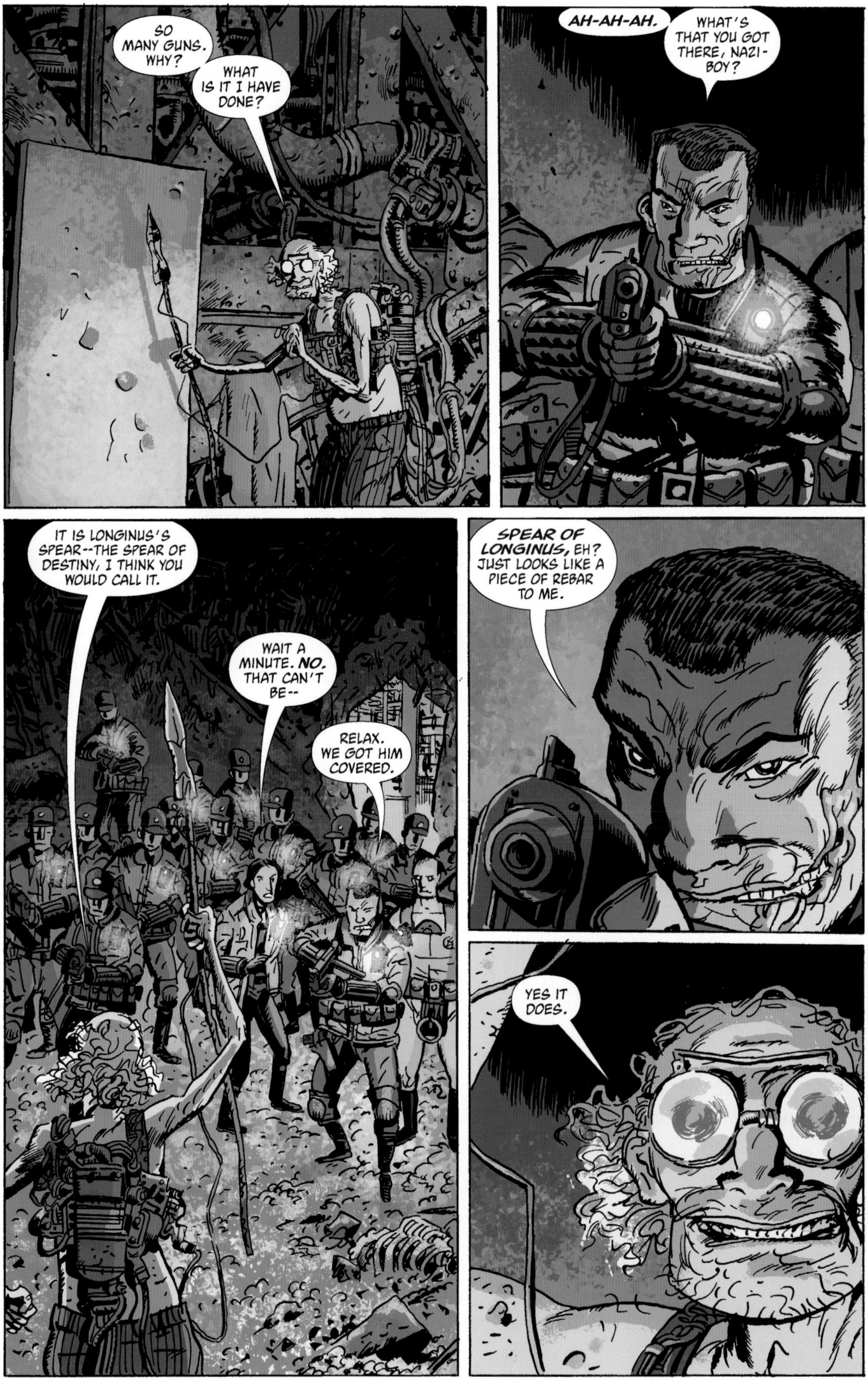
SO MANY GUNS. WHY?
WHAT IS IT I HAVE DONE?
AH-AH-AH.
WHAT'S THAT YOU GOT THERE, NAZI-BOY?
IT IS LONGINUS'S SPEAR--THE SPEAR OF DESTINY, I THINK YOU WOULD CALL IT.
WAIT A MINUTE. NO. THAT CAN'T BE--
RELAX. WE GOT HIM COVERED.
SPEAR OF LONGINUS, EH? JUST LOOKS LIKE A PIECE OF REBAR TO ME.
YES IT DOES.

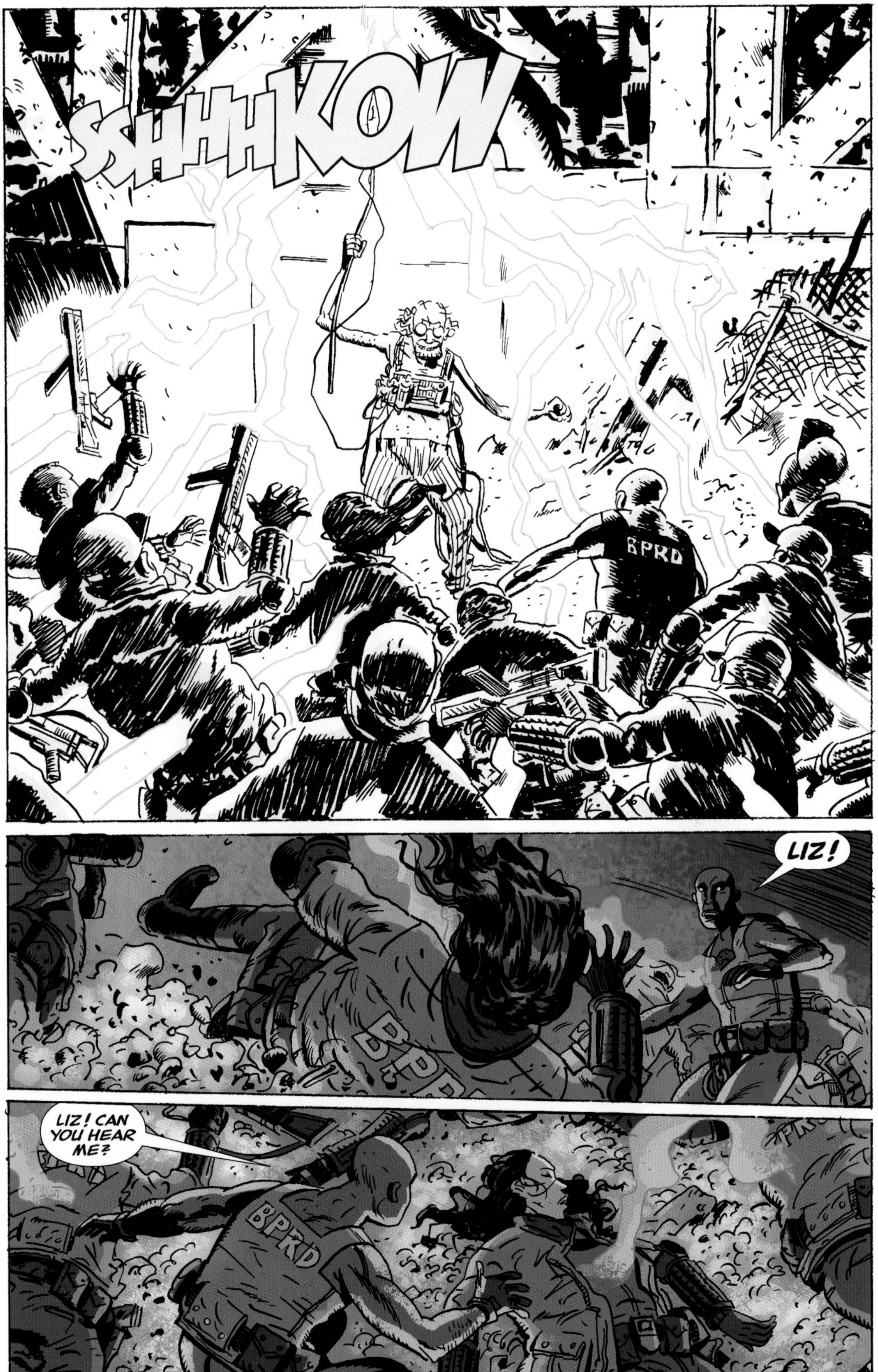
SSHHHKOW
BPRD
LIZ!
BPRD
LIZ! CAN YOU HEAR ME?
BPRD

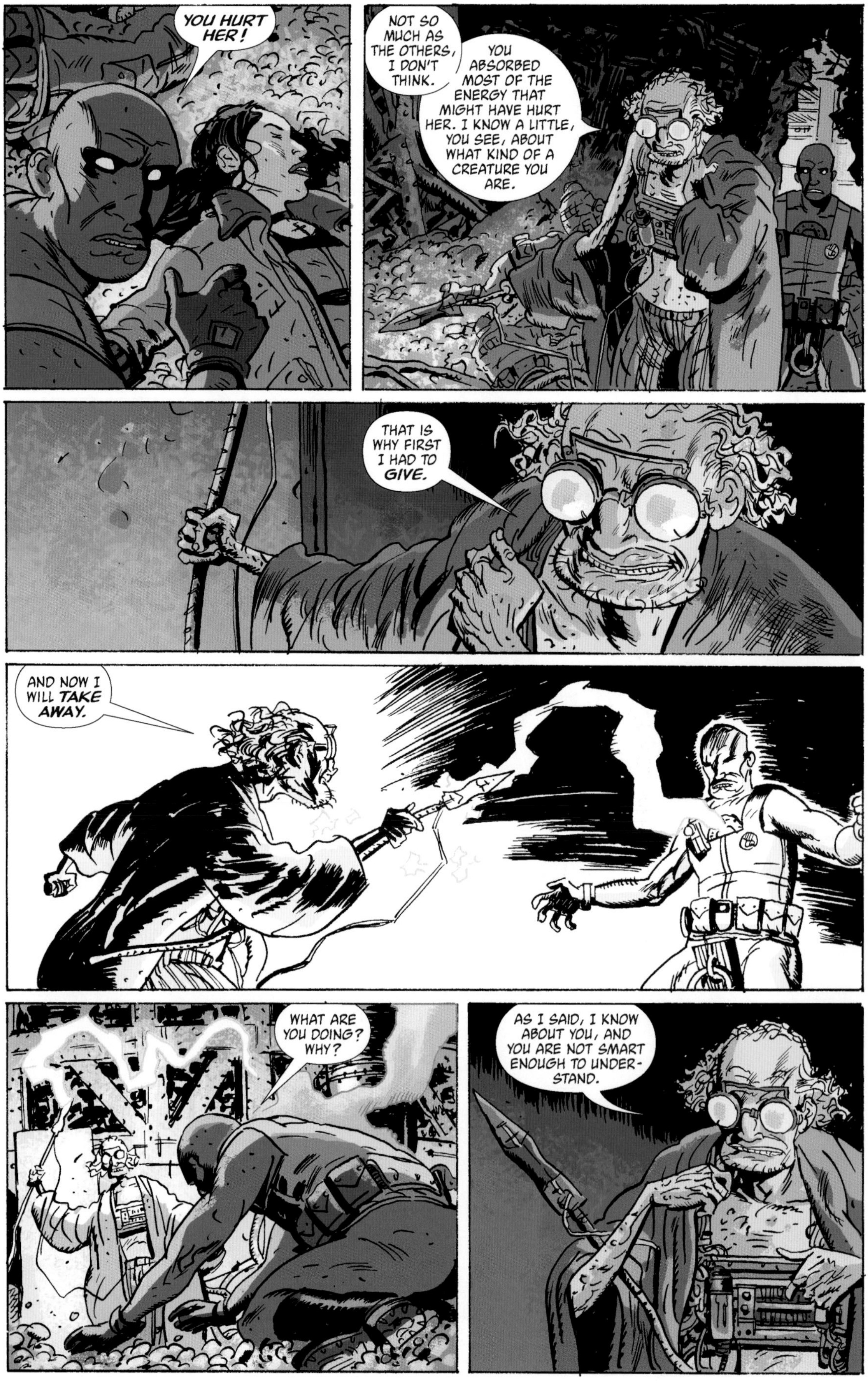
YOU HURT HER!
NOT SO MUCH AS THE OTHERS, I DON'T THINK.
YOU ABSORBED MOST OF THE ENERGY THAT MIGHT HAVE HURT HER. I KNOW A LITTLE, YOU SEE, ABOUT WHAT KIND OF A CREATURE YOU ARE.
THAT IS WHY FIRST I HAD TO GIVE.
AND NOW I WILL TAKE AWAY.
WHAT ARE YOU DOING? WHY?
AS I SAID, I KNOW ABOUT YOU, AND YOU ARE NOT SMART ENOUGH TO UNDER-STAND.

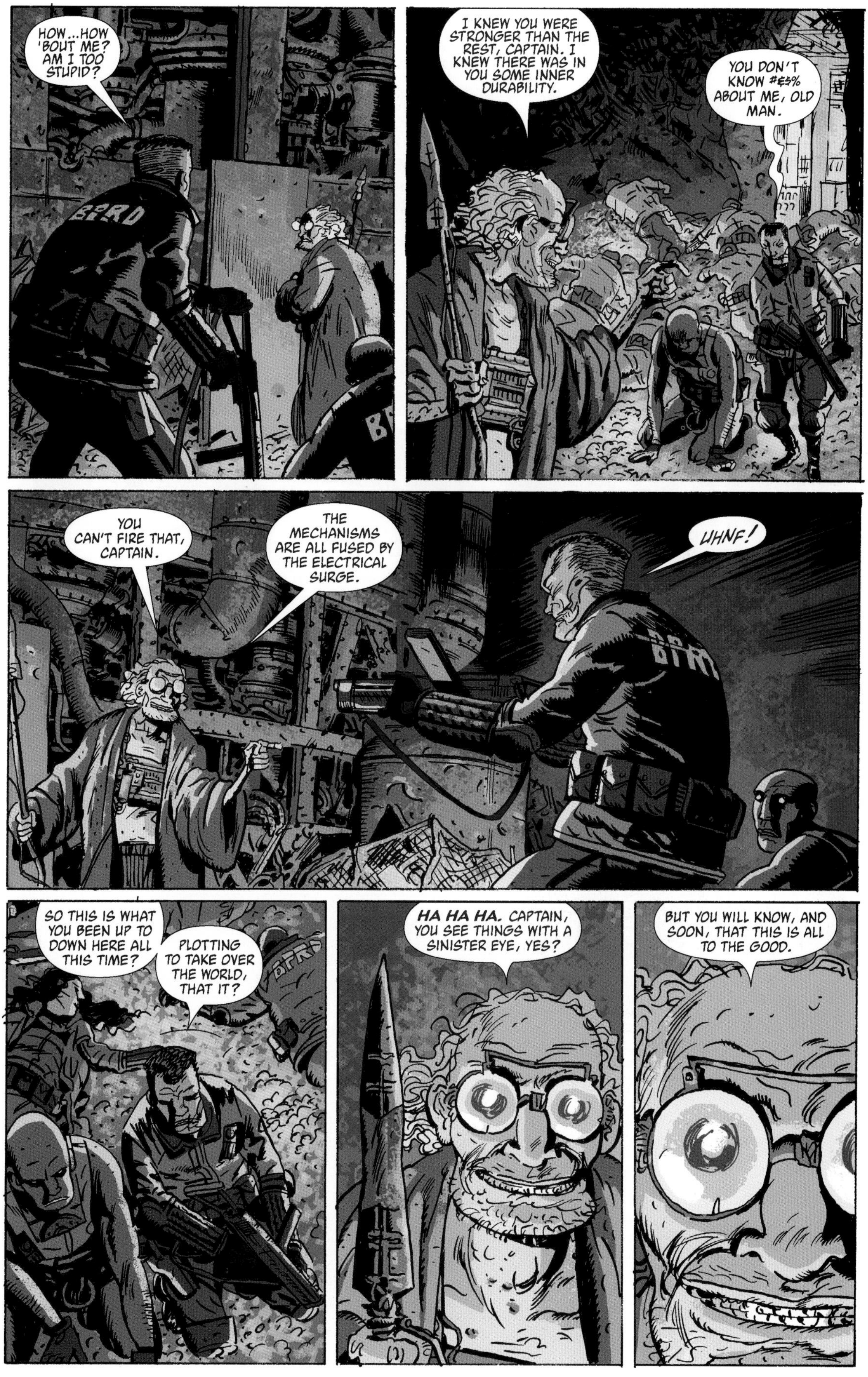
HOW...HOW 'BOUT ME? AM I TOO STUPID?
I KNEW YOU WERE STRONGER THAN THE REST, CAPTAIN. I KNEW THERE WAS IN YOU SOME INNER DURABILITY.
YOU DON'T KNOW #€$% ABOUT ME, OLD MAN.
YOU CAN'T FIRE THAT, CAPTAIN.
THE MECHANISMS ARE ALL FUSED BY THE ELECTRICAL SURGE.
UHNF!
SO THIS IS WHAT YOU BEEN UP TO DOWN HERE ALL THIS TIME?
PLOTTING TO TAKE OVER THE WORLD, THAT IT?
HA HA HA. CAPTAIN, YOU SEE THINGS WITH A SINISTER EYE, YES?
BUT YOU WILL KNOW, AND SOON, THAT THIS IS ALL TO THE GOOD.

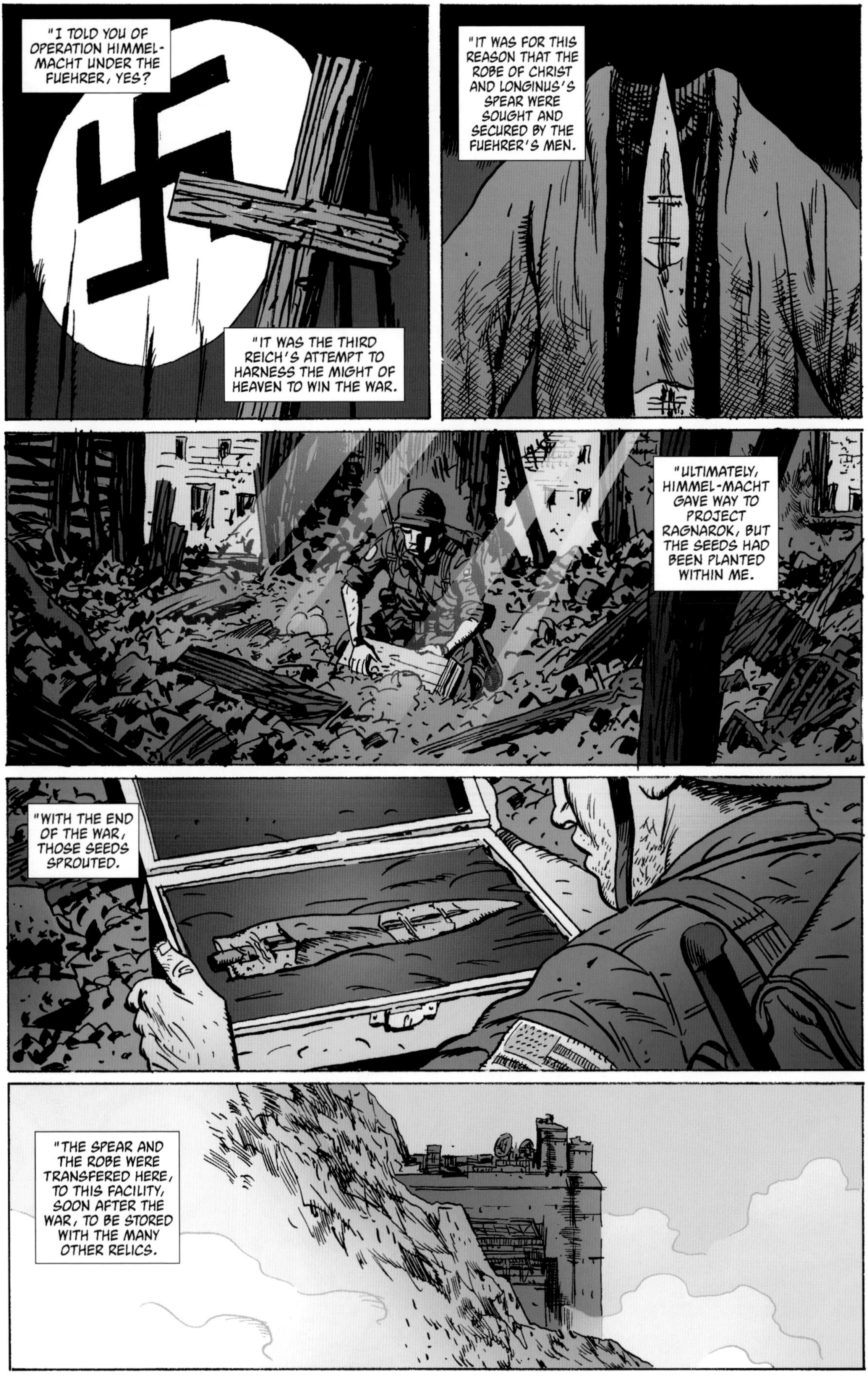
"I TOLD YOU OF OPERATION HIMMEL-MACHT UNDER THE FUEHRER, YES?
"IT WAS THE THIRD REICH'S ATTEMPT TO HARNESS THE MIGHT OF HEAVEN TO WIN THE WAR.
"IT WAS FOR THIS REASON THAT THE ROBE OF CHRIST AND LONGINUS'S SPEAR WERE SOUGHT AND SECURED BY THE FUEHRER'S MEN.
"ULTIMATELY, HIMMEL-MACHT GAVE WAY TO PROJECT RAGNAROK, BUT THE SEEDS HAD BEEN PLANTED WITHIN ME.
"WITH THE END OF THE WAR, THOSE SEEDS SPROUTED.
"THE SPEAR AND THE ROBE WERE TRANSFERED HERE, TO THIS FACILITY, SOON AFTER THE WAR, TO BE STORED WITH THE MANY OTHER RELICS.

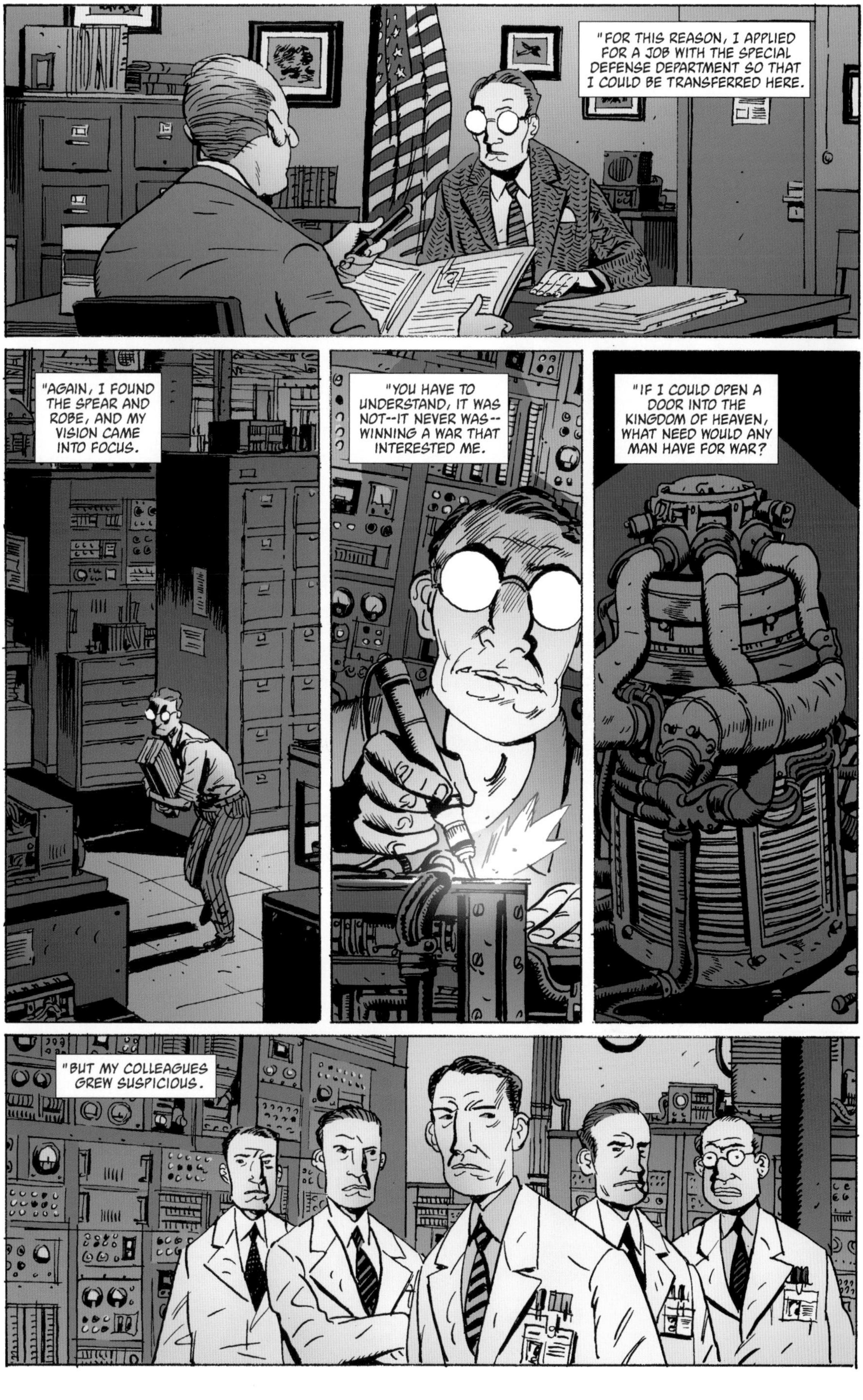
"FOR THIS REASON, I APPLIED FOR A JOB WITH THE SPECIAL DEFENSE DEPARTMENT SO THAT I COULD BE TRANSFERRED HERE.
"AGAIN, I FOUND THE SPEAR AND ROBE, AND MY VISION CAME INTO FOCUS.
"YOU HAVE TO UNDERSTAND, IT WAS NOT--IT NEVER WAS--WINNING A WAR THAT INTERESTED ME.
"IF I COULD OPEN A DOOR INTO THE KINGDOM OF HEAVEN, WHAT NEED WOULD ANY MAN HAVE FOR WAR?
"BUT MY COLLEAGUES GREW SUSPICIOUS.

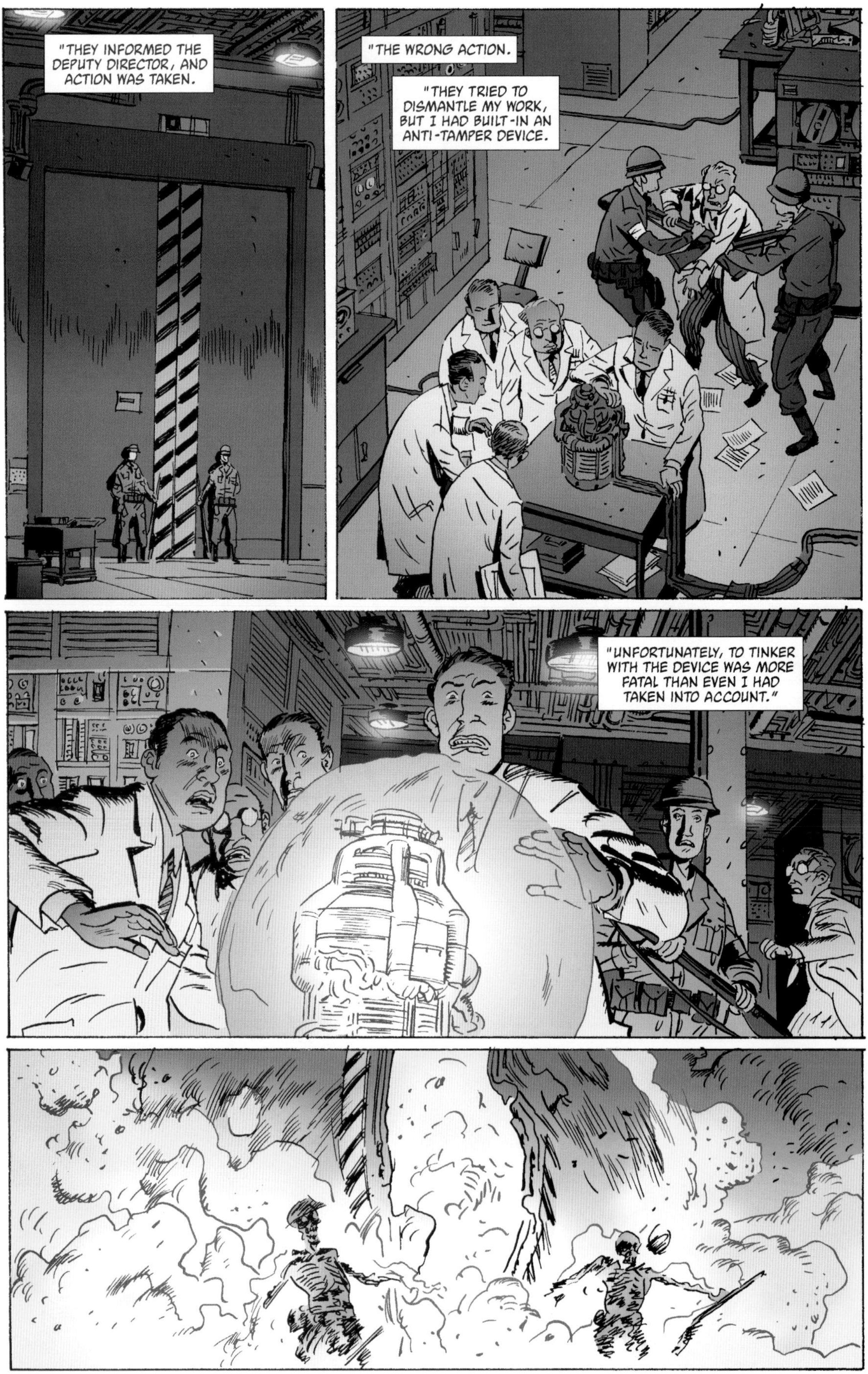
"THEY INFORMED THE DEPUTY DIRECTOR, AND ACTION WAS TAKEN.
"THE WRONG ACTION.
"THEY TRIED TO DISMANTLE MY WORK, BUT I HAD BUILT-IN AN ANTI-TAMPER DEVICE.
"UNFORTUNATELY, TO TINKER WITH THE DEVICE WAS MORE FATAL THAN EVEN I HAD TAKEN INTO ACCOUNT."

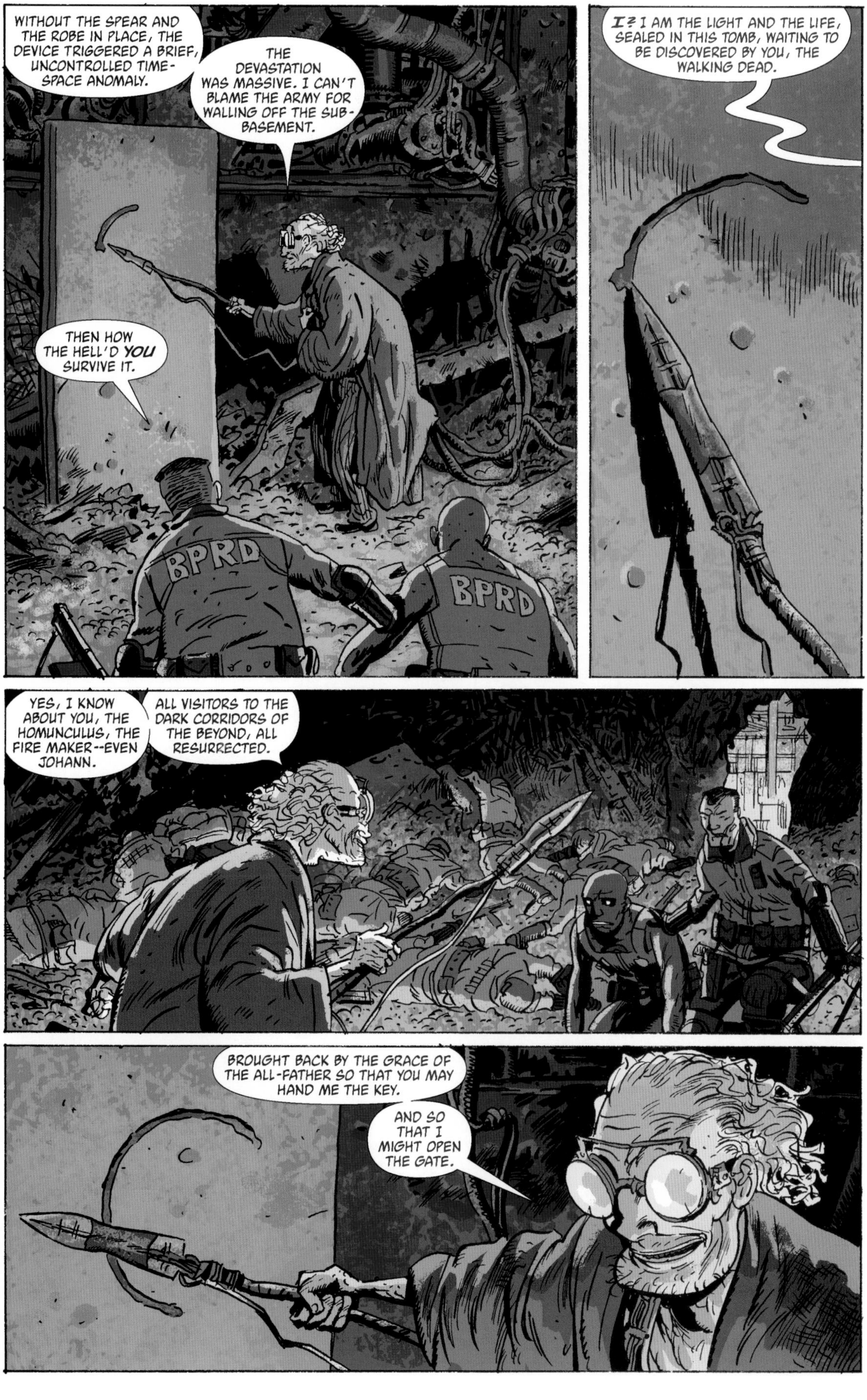
WITHOUT THE SPEAR AND THE ROBE IN PLACE, THE DEVICE TRIGGERED A BRIEF, UNCONTROLLED TIME-SPACE ANOMALY.
THE DEVASTATION WAS MASSIVE. I CAN'T BLAME THE ARMY FOR WALLING OFF THE SUB-BASEMENT.
THEN HOW THE HELL'D *YOU* SURVIVE IT.
BPRD
BPRD
I? I AM THE LIGHT AND THE LIFE, SEALED IN THIS TOMB, WAITING TO BE DISCOVERED BY YOU, THE WALKING DEAD.
YES, I KNOW ABOUT YOU, THE HOMUNCULUS, THE FIRE MAKER--EVEN JOHANN.
ALL VISITORS TO THE DARK CORRIDORS OF THE BEYOND, ALL RESURRECTED.
BROUGHT BACK BY THE GRACE OF THE ALL-FATHER SO THAT YOU MAY HAND ME THE KEY.
AND SO THAT I MIGHT OPEN THE GATE.

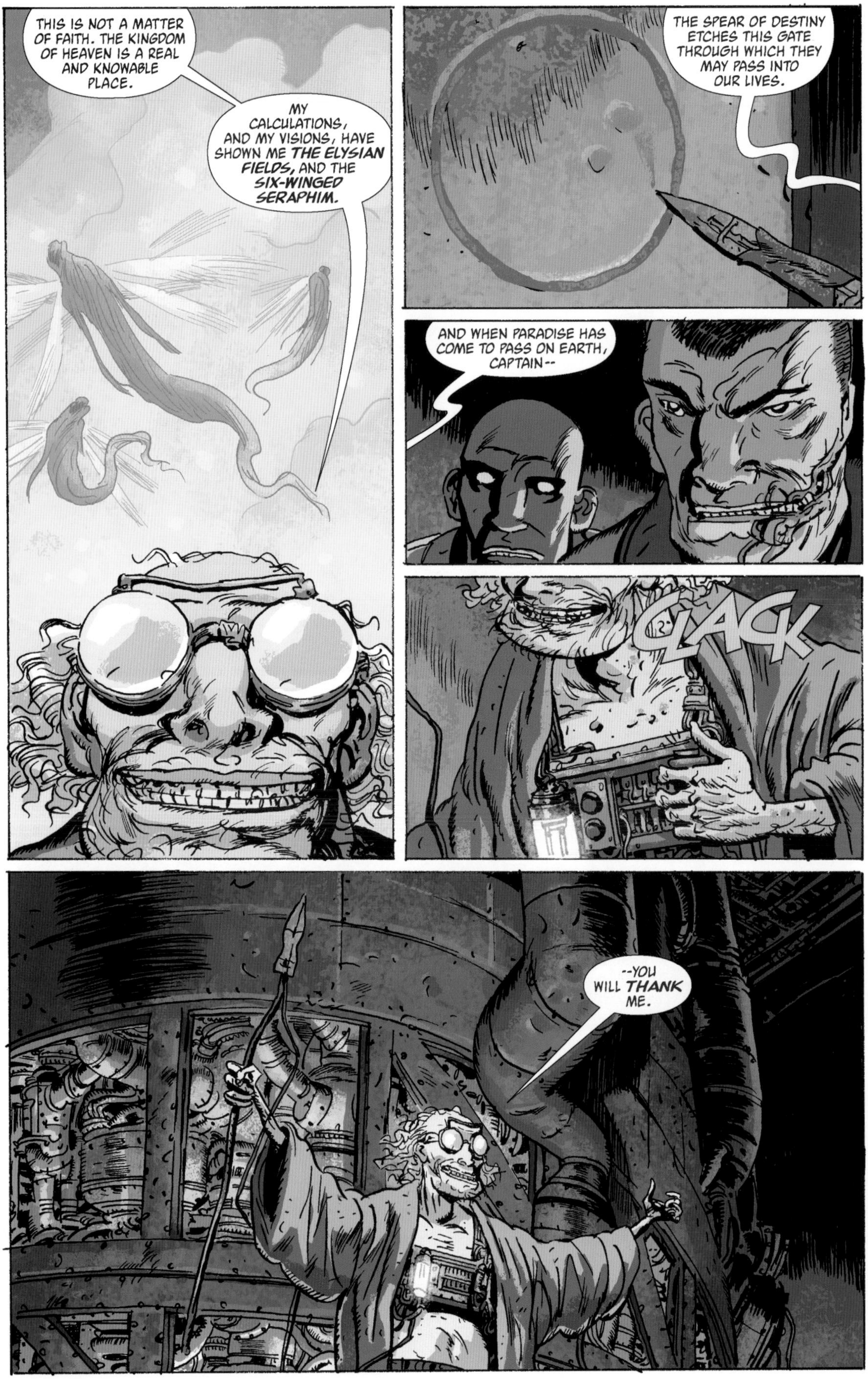
THIS IS NOT A MATTER OF FAITH. THE KINGDOM OF HEAVEN IS A REAL AND KNOWABLE PLACE.
MY CALCULATIONS, AND MY VISIONS, HAVE SHOWN ME THE ELYSIAN FIELDS, AND THE SIX-WINGED SERAPHIM.
THE SPEAR OF DESTINY ETCHES THIS GATE THROUGH WHICH THEY MAY PASS INTO OUR LIVES.
AND WHEN PARADISE HAS COME TO PASS ON EARTH, CAPTAIN--
CLACK
--YOU WILL THANK ME.

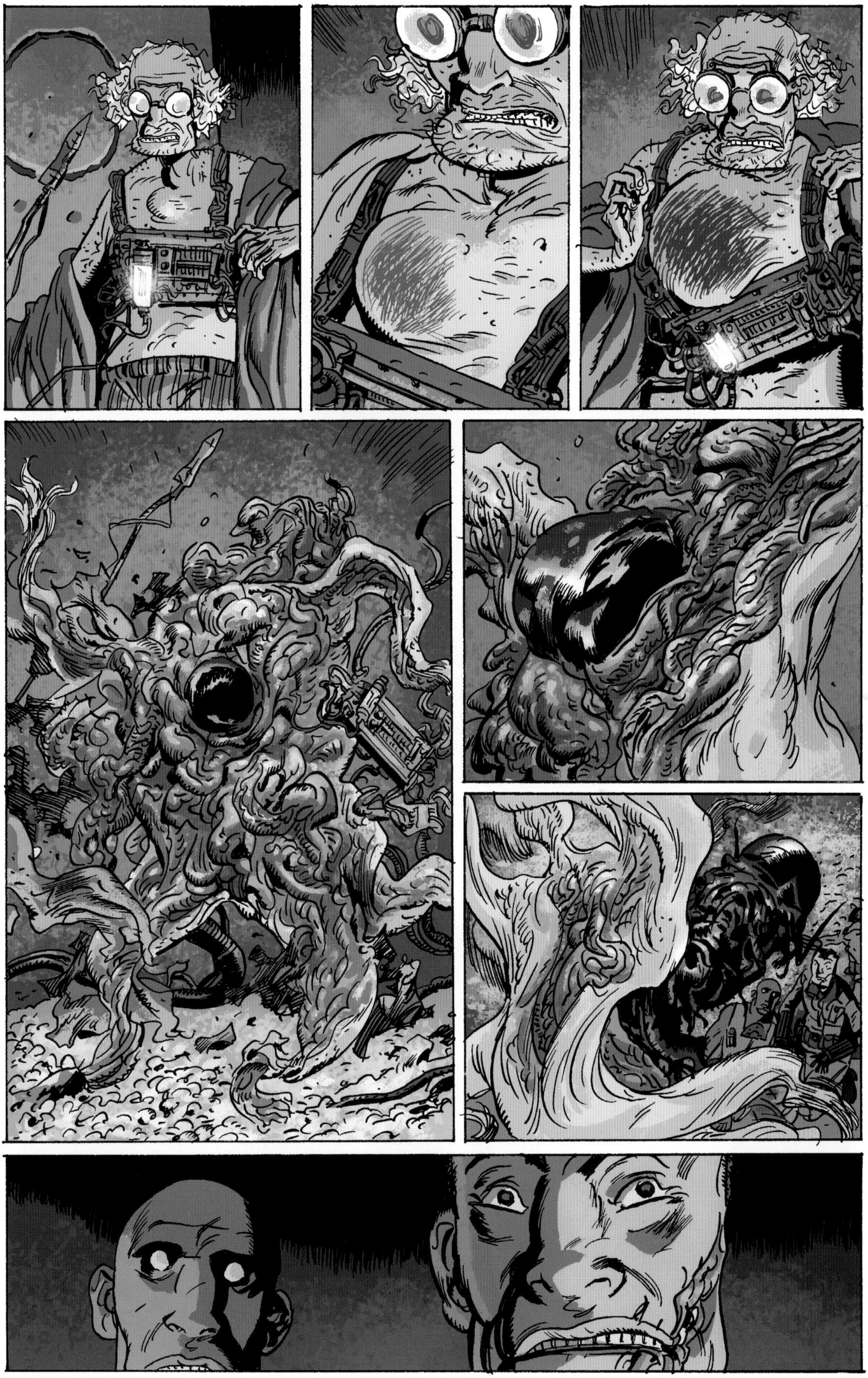

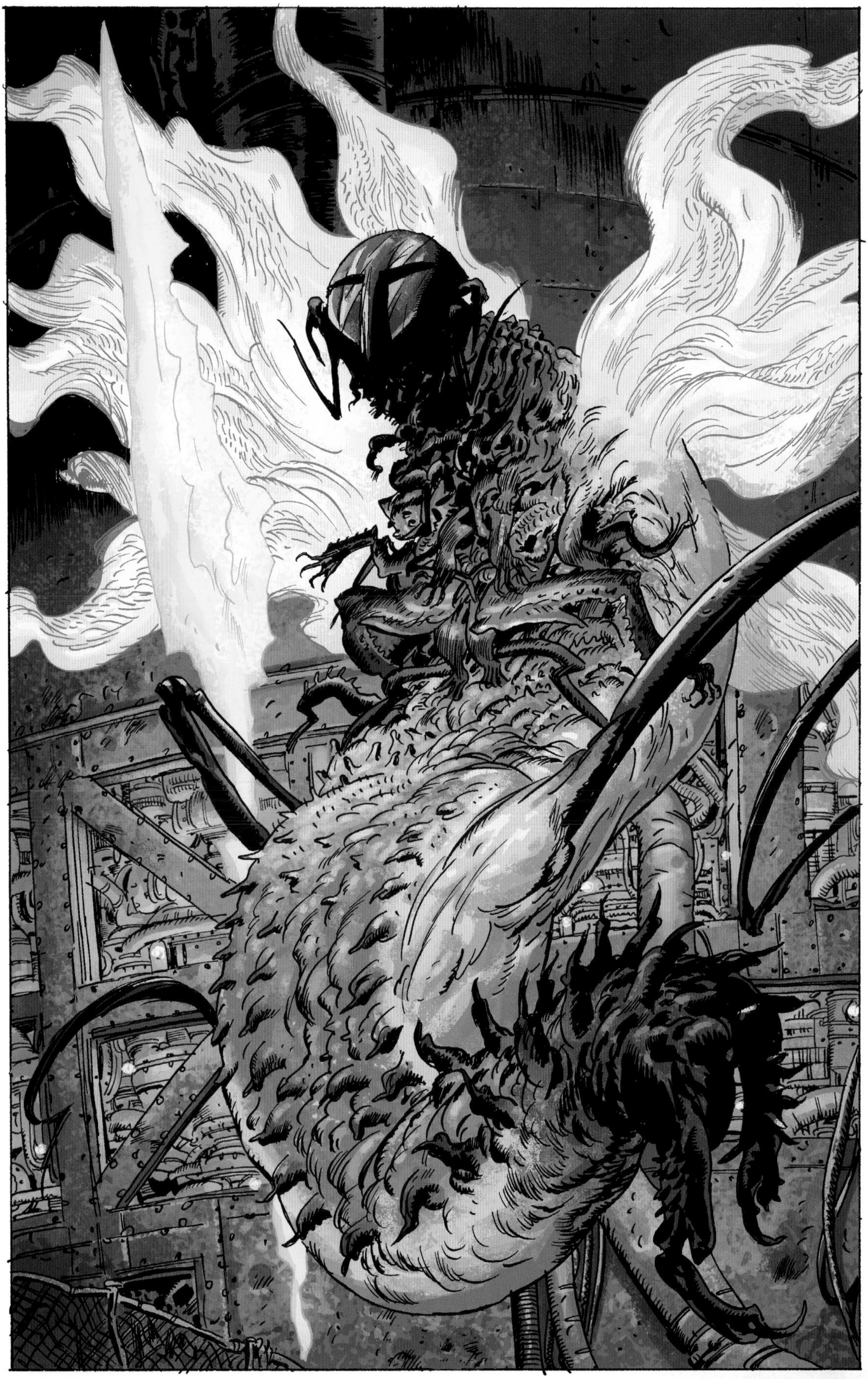

CHAPTER FIVE

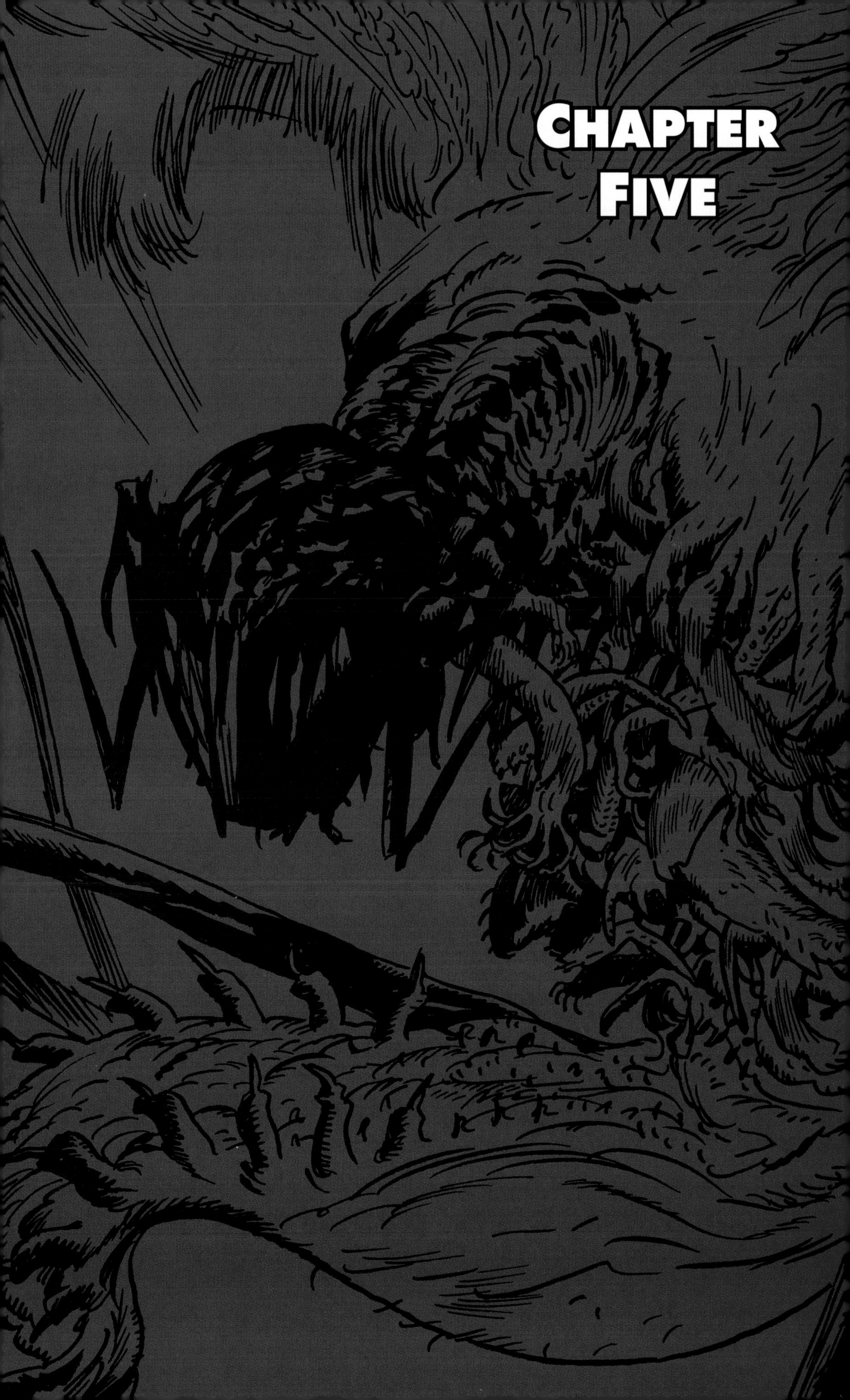

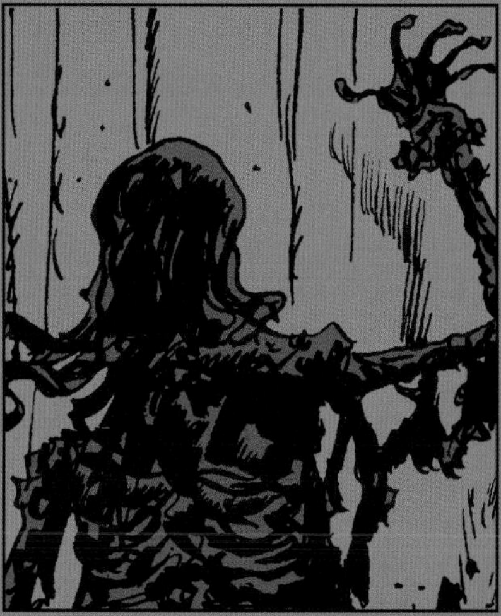

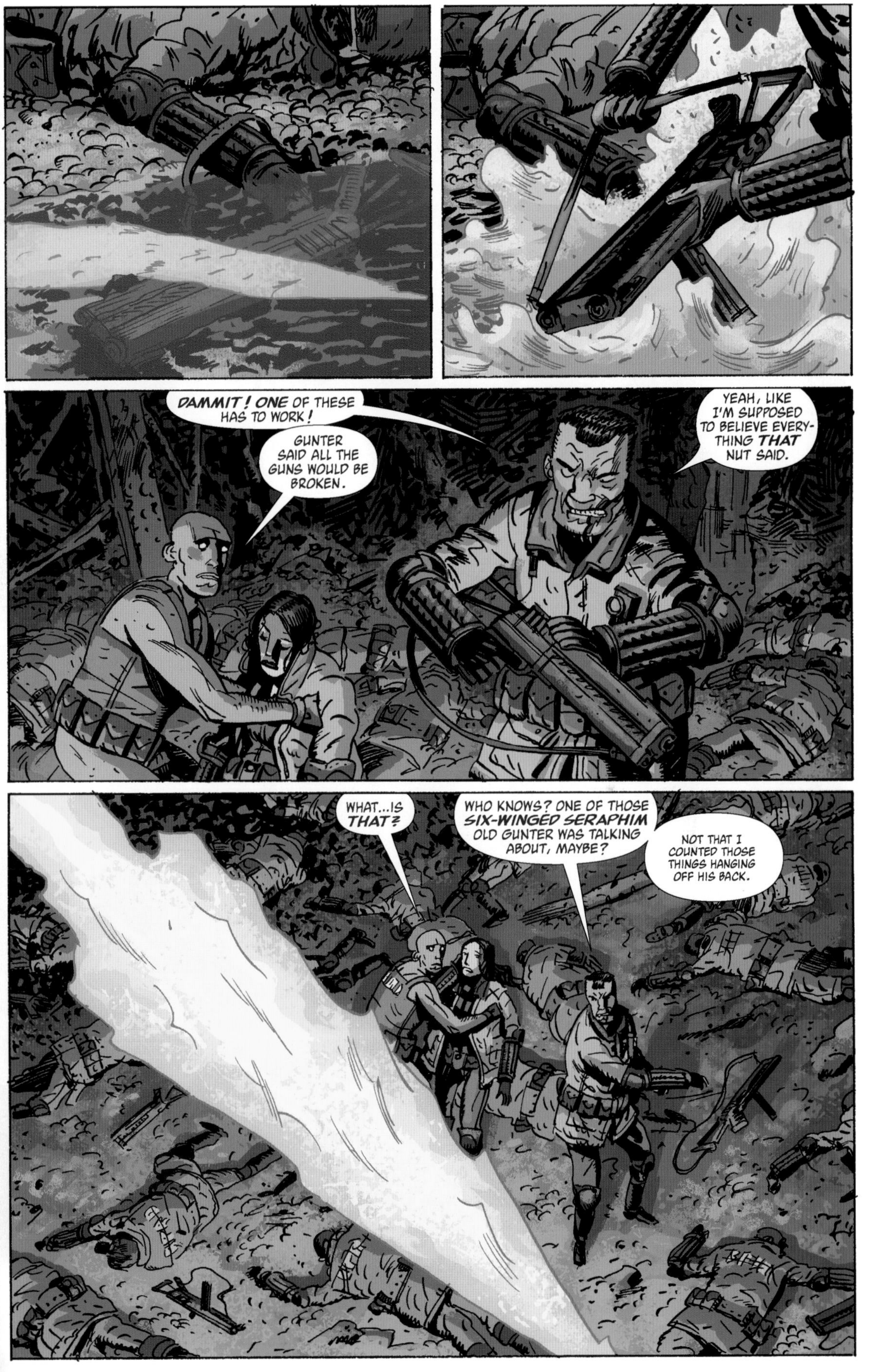
DAMMIT! ONE OF THESE HAS TO WORK!
GUNTER SAID ALL THE GUNS WOULD BE BROKEN.
YEAH, LIKE I'M SUPPOSED TO BELIEVE EVERY-THING THAT NUT SAID.
WHAT...IS THAT?
WHO KNOWS? ONE OF THOSE SIX-WINGED SERAPHIM OLD GUNTER WAS TALKING ABOUT, MAYBE?
NOT THAT I COUNTED THOSE THINGS HANGING OFF HIS BACK.

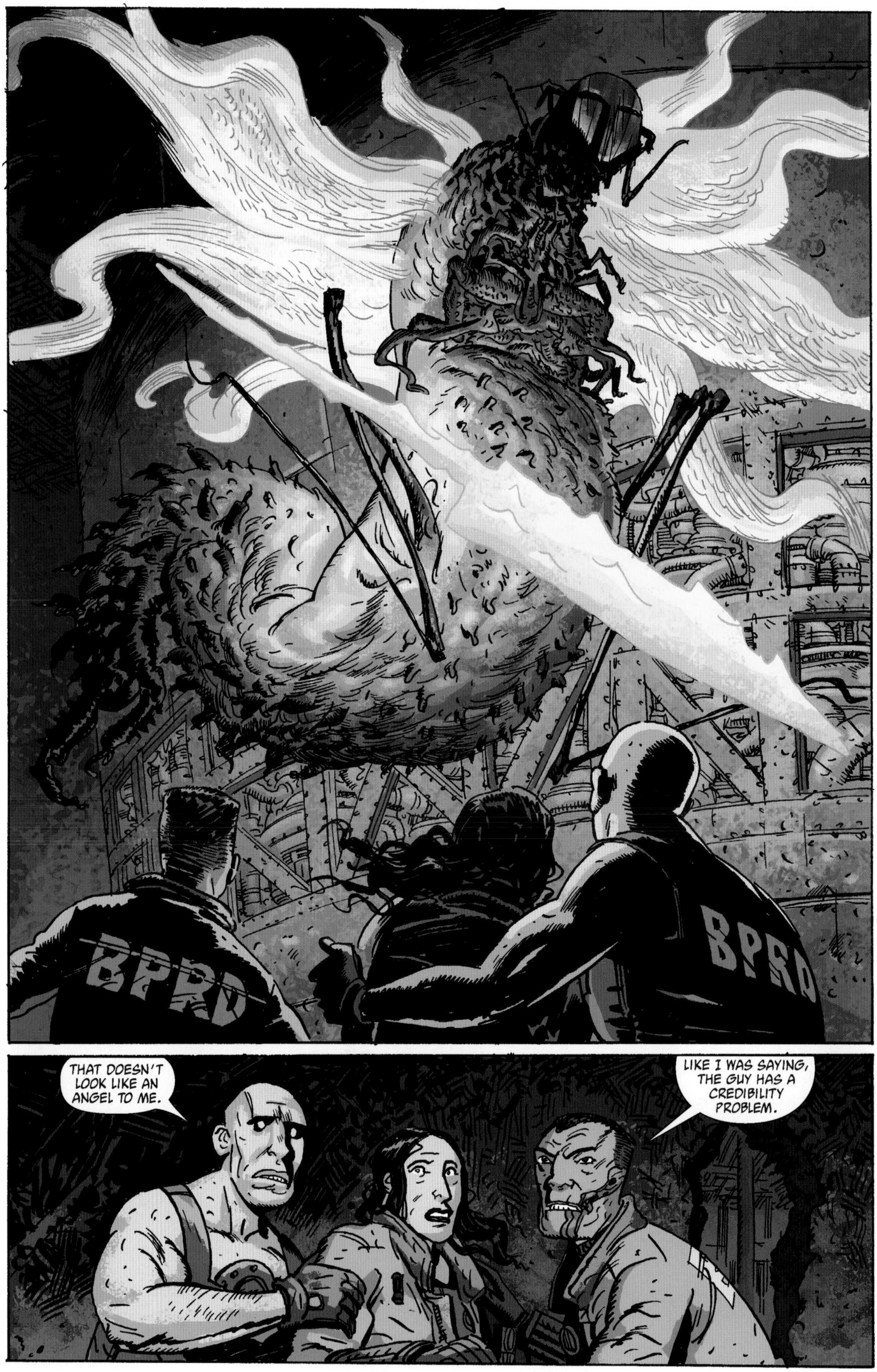
BPRD
BPRD
THAT DOESN'T LOOK LIKE AN ANGEL TO ME.
LIKE I WAS SAYING, THE GUY HAS A CREDIBILITY PROBLEM.

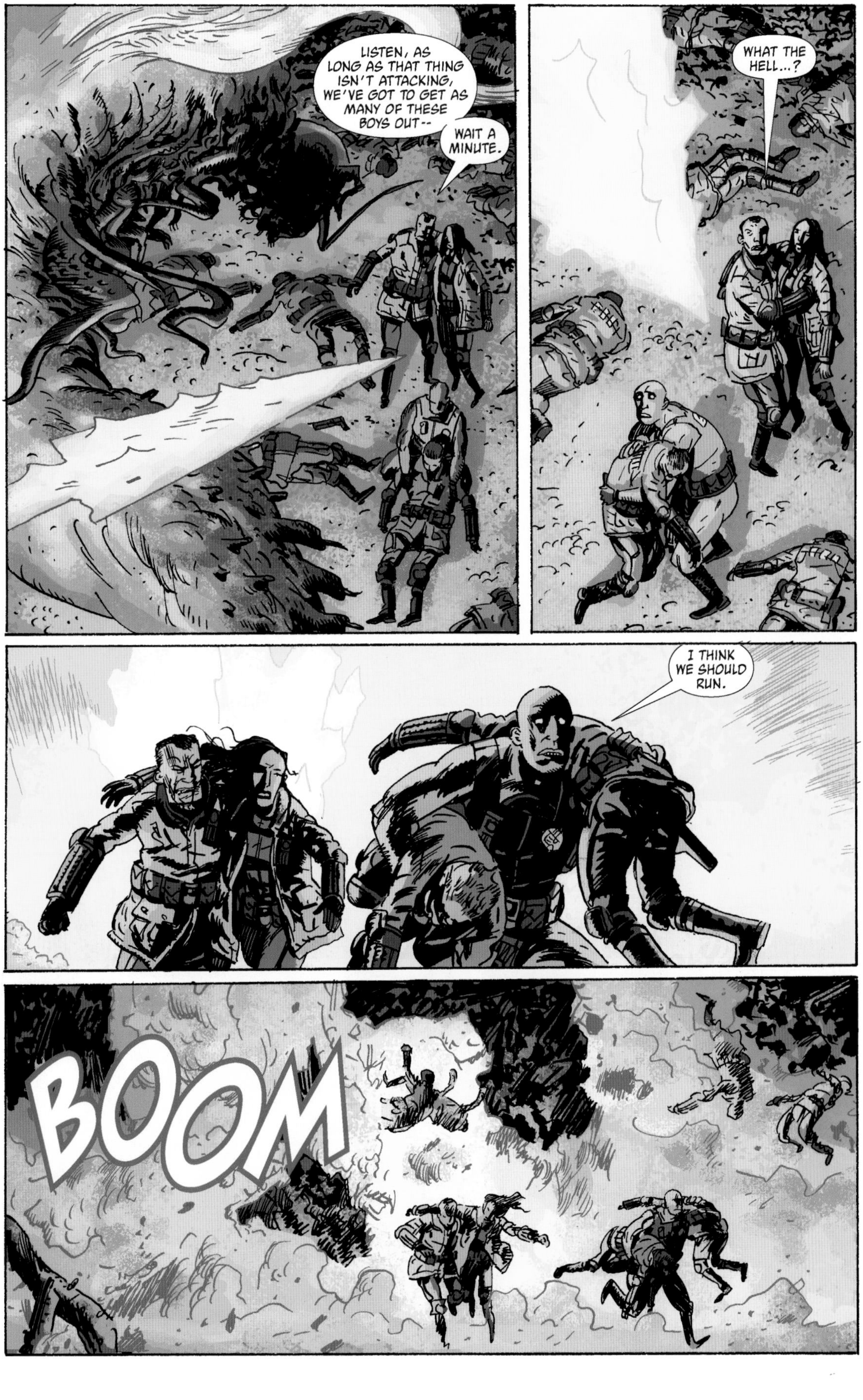
LISTEN, AS LONG AS THAT THING ISN'T ATTACKING, WE'VE GOT TO GET AS MANY OF THESE BOYS OUT--
WAIT A MINUTE.
WHAT THE HELL...?
I THINK WE SHOULD RUN.
BOOM

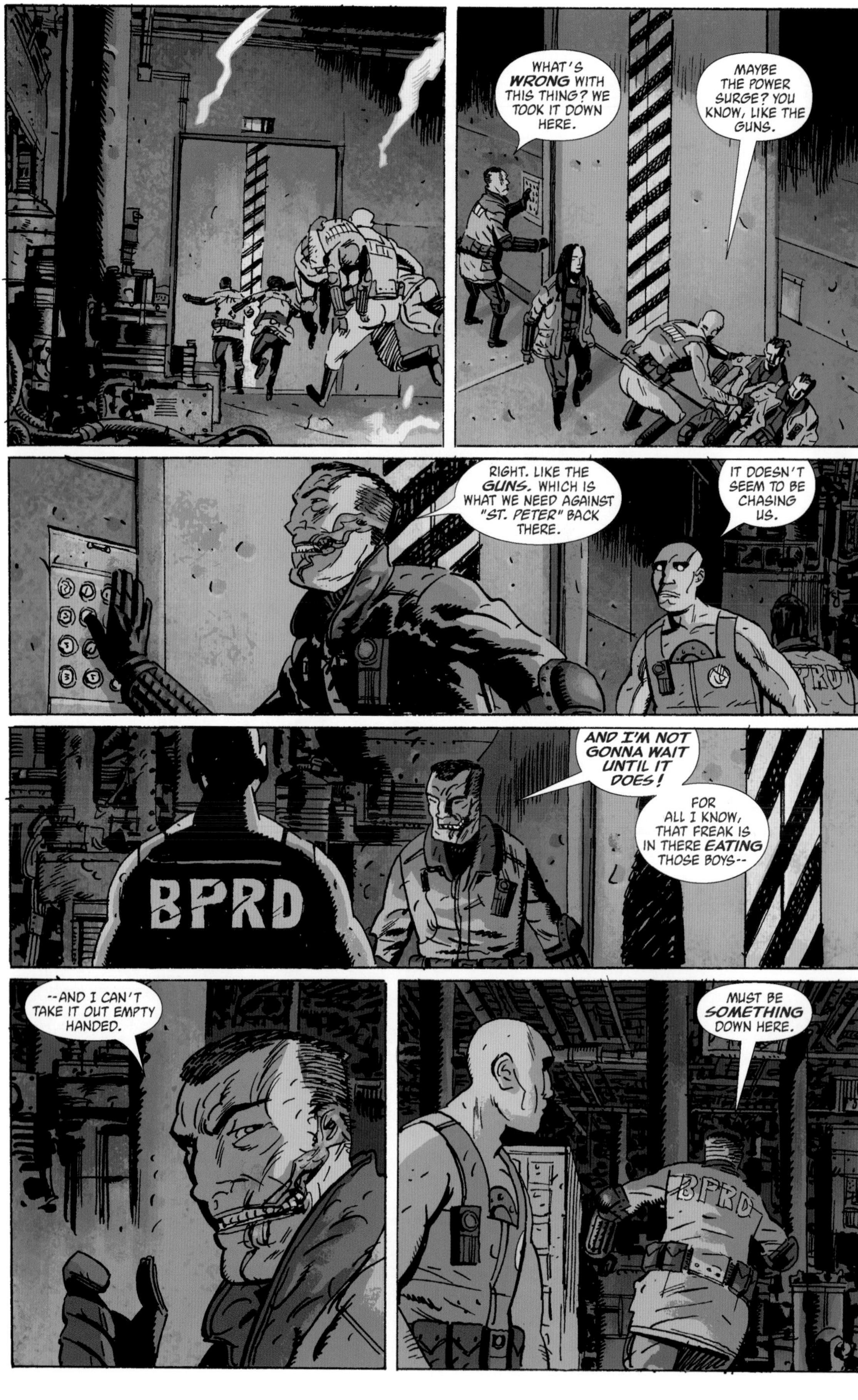
WHAT'S WRONG WITH THIS THING? WE TOOK IT DOWN HERE.
MAYBE THE POWER SURGE? YOU KNOW, LIKE THE GUNS.
RIGHT. LIKE THE GUNS. WHICH IS WHAT WE NEED AGAINST "ST. PETER" BACK THERE.
IT DOESN'T SEEM TO BE CHASING US.
BPRD
AND I'M NOT GONNA WAIT UNTIL IT DOES!
FOR ALL I KNOW, THAT FREAK IS IN THERE EATING THOSE BOYS--
--AND I CAN'T TAKE IT OUT EMPTY HANDED.
MUST BE SOMETHING DOWN HERE.
BPRD

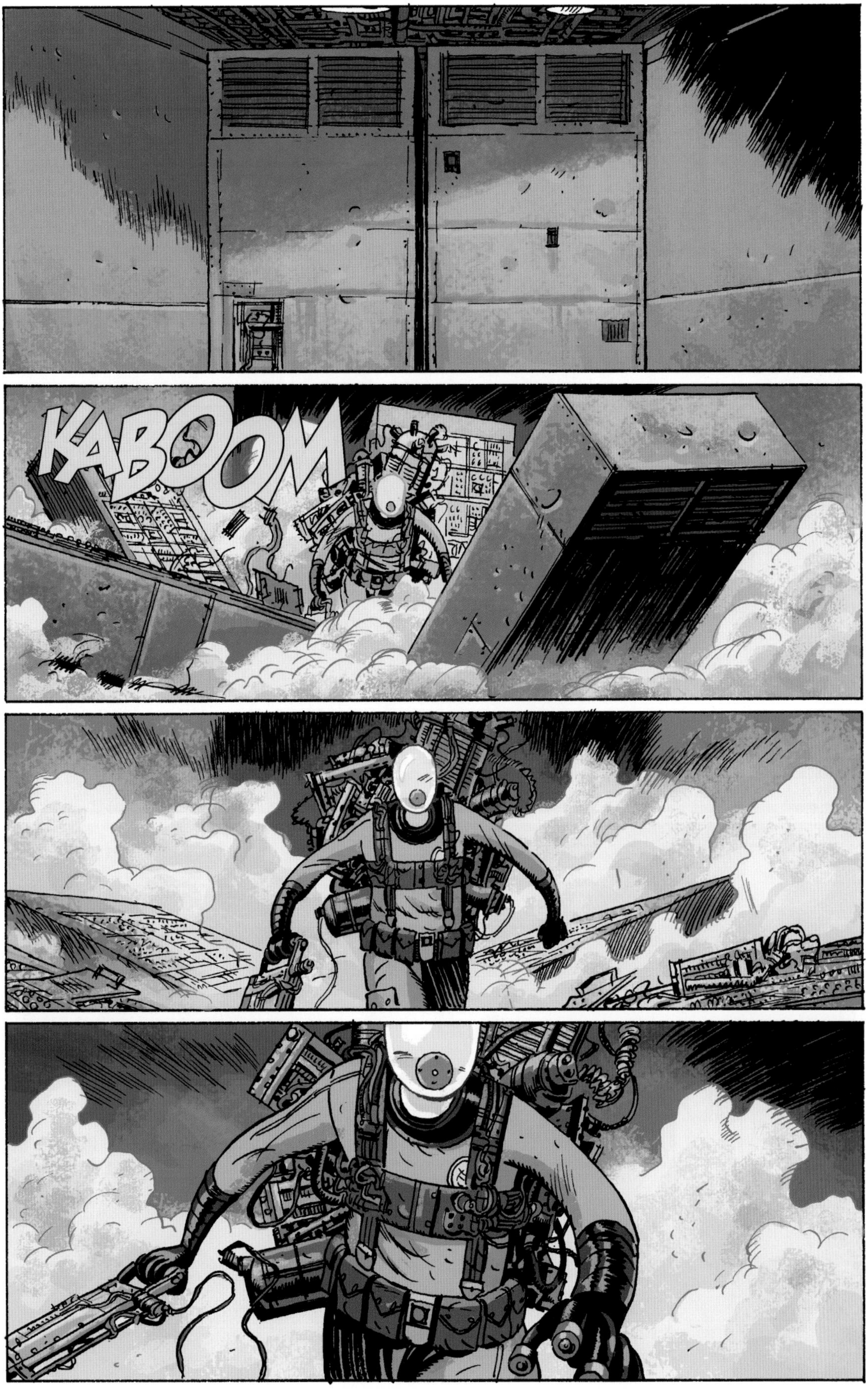
KABOOM

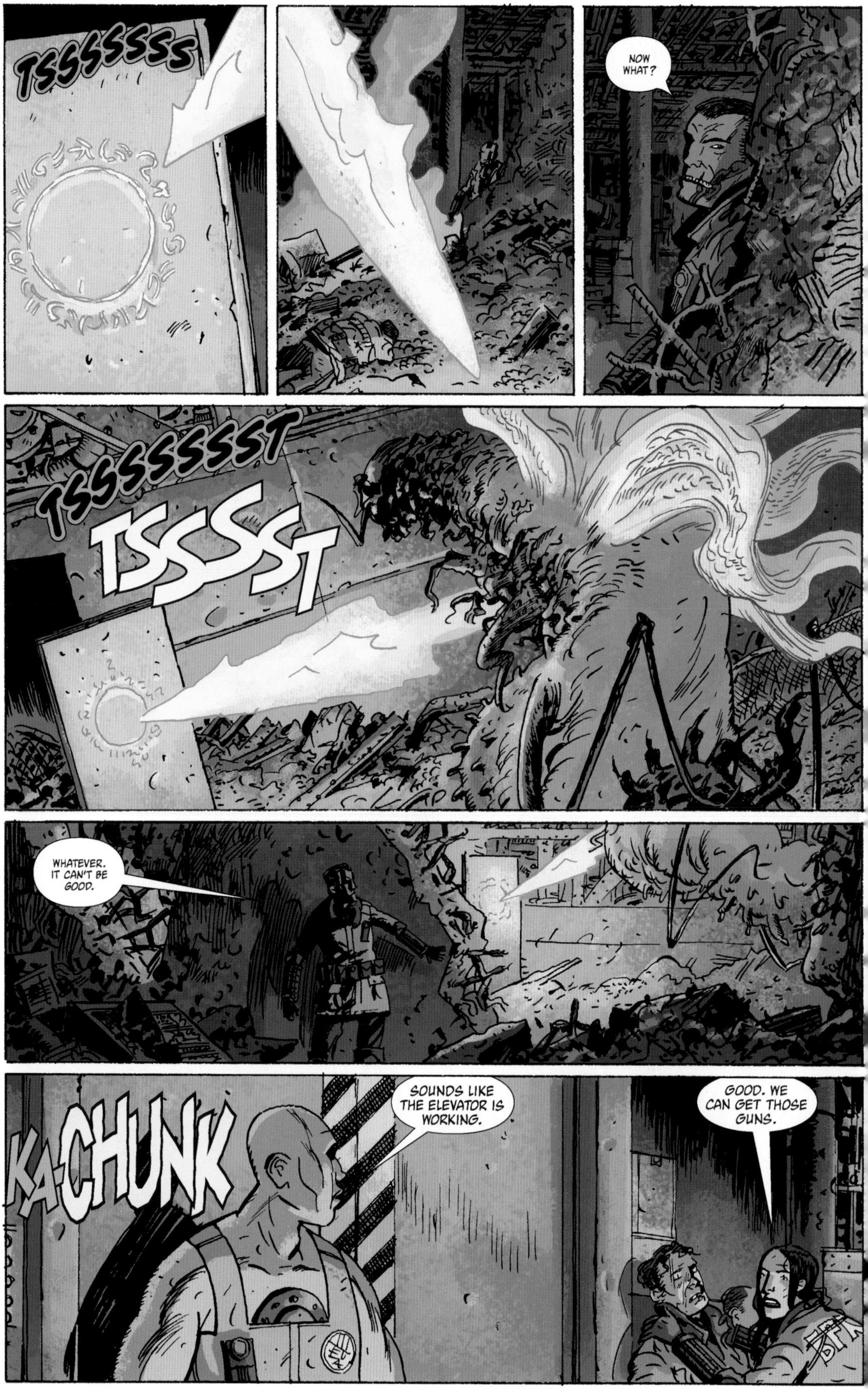
TSSSSSSS
NOW WHAT?
TSSSSSSST
TSSSST
WHATEVER. IT CAN'T BE GOOD.
KA-CHUNK
SOUNDS LIKE THE ELEVATOR IS WORKING.
GOOD. WE CAN GET THOSE GUNS.

DO WE REALLY NEED GUNS, THOUGH? WE HAVE *YOU.*

THAT THING ALREADY USES FIRE. DOESN'T SEEM LIKE I'D BE MUCH HELP.

ANYWAY, WHAT I DO WORKS BEST IN THE FIELD. DOWN HERE, ALL THESE MEN AND WOMEN...

RIGHT.

WELL, IF THE CAPTAIN SHOWS UP, TELL HIM I'LL BE BACK WITH SOME WEAPONS--

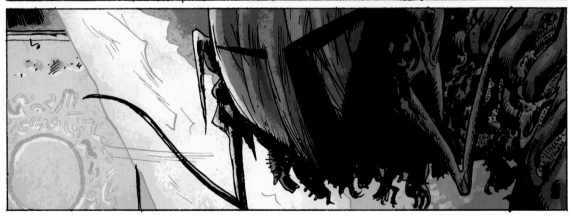

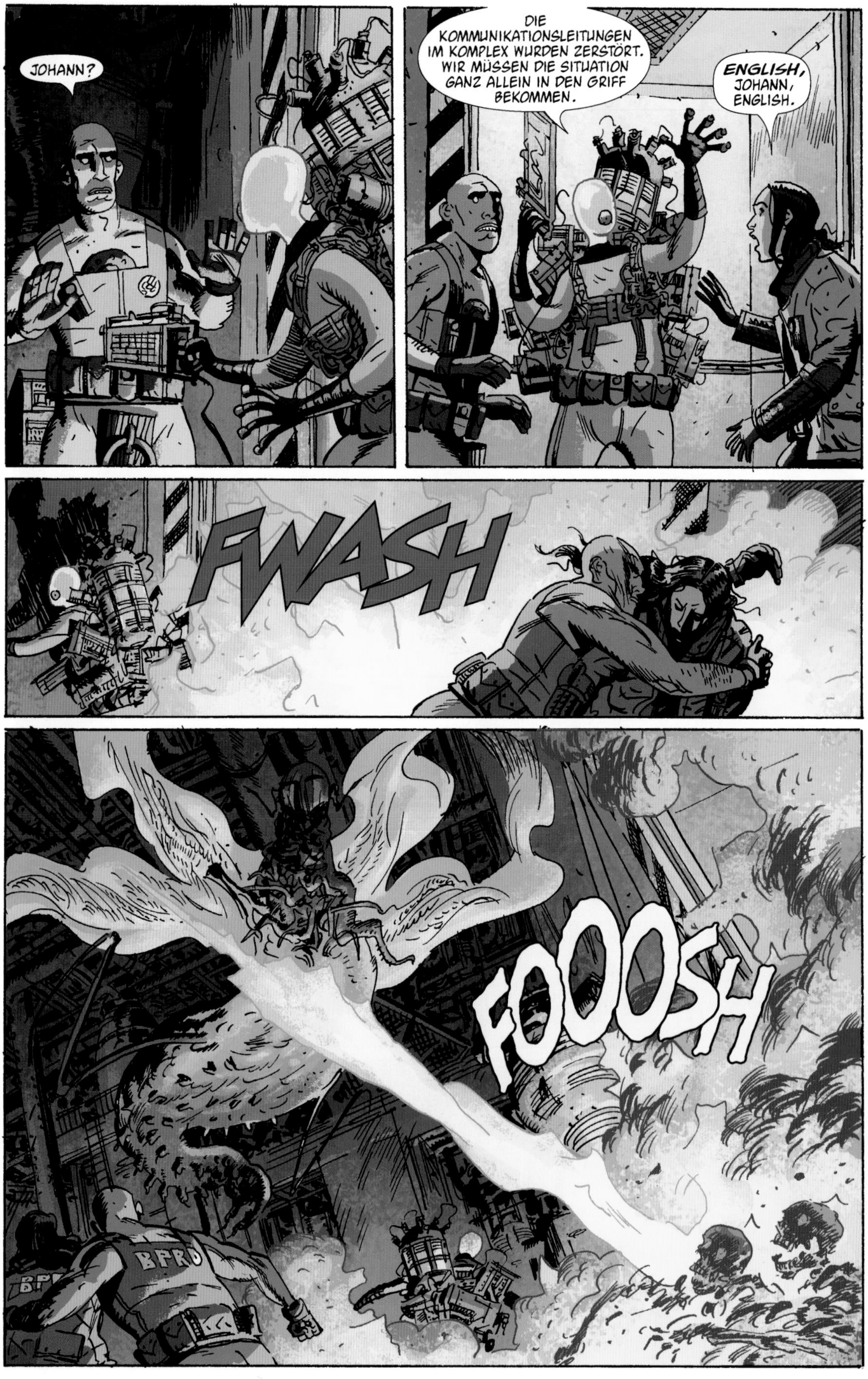
JOHANN?
DIE KOMMUNIKATIONSLEITUNGEN IM KOMPLEX WURDEN ZERSTÖRT. WIR MÜSSEN DIE SITUATION GANZ ALLEIN IN DEN GRIFF BEKOMMEN.
ENGLISH, JOHANN, ENGLISH.
FWASH
FOOOSH
BPRD

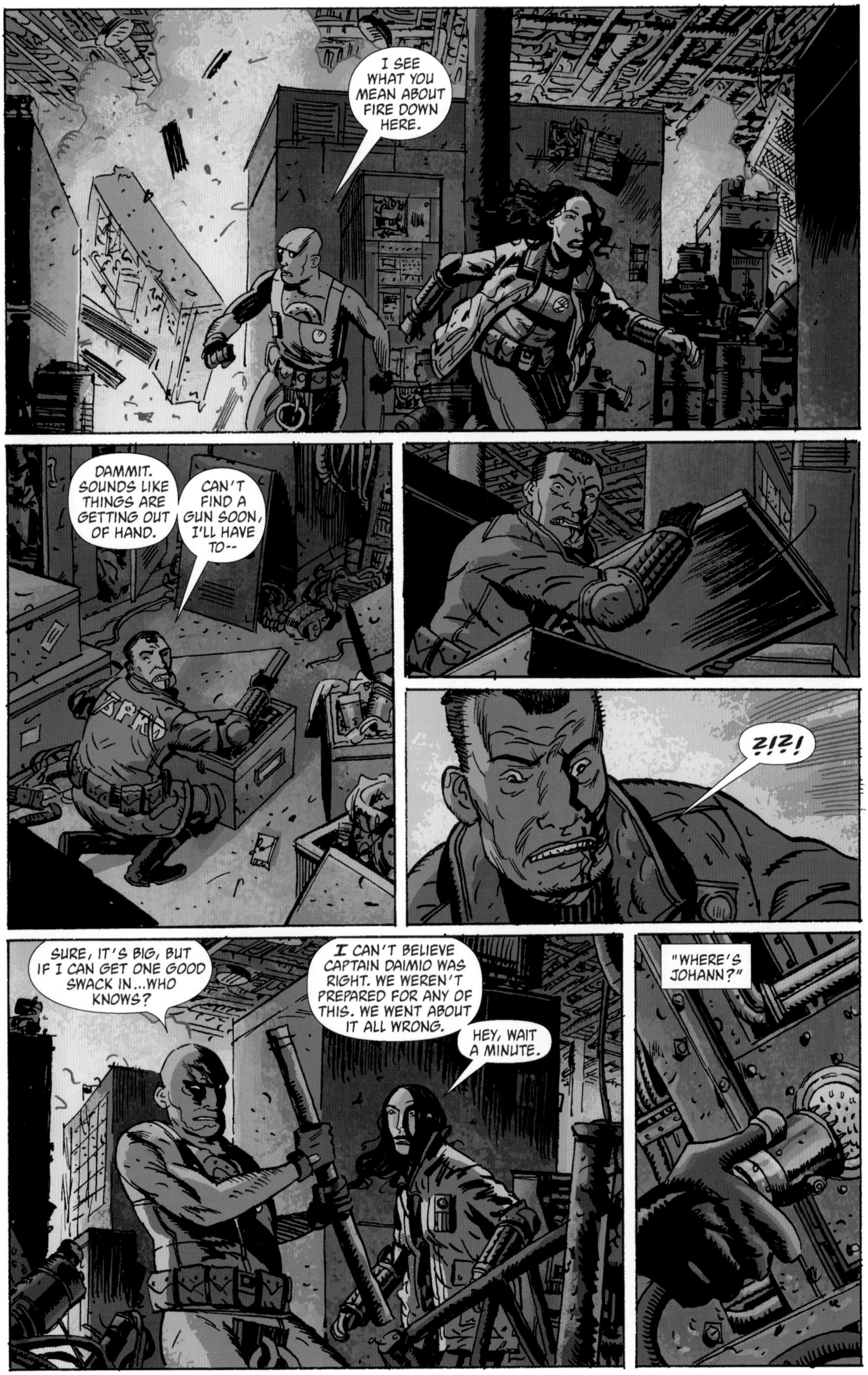
I SEE WHAT YOU MEAN ABOUT FIRE DOWN HERE.
DAMMIT. SOUNDS LIKE THINGS ARE GETTING OUT OF HAND.
CAN'T FIND A GUN SOON, I'LL HAVE TO--
?!?!
SURE, IT'S BIG, BUT IF I CAN GET ONE GOOD SWACK IN...WHO KNOWS?
I CAN'T BELIEVE CAPTAIN DAIMIO WAS RIGHT. WE WEREN'T PREPARED FOR ANY OF THIS. WE WENT ABOUT IT ALL WRONG.
HEY, WAIT A MINUTE.
"WHERE'S JOHANN?"

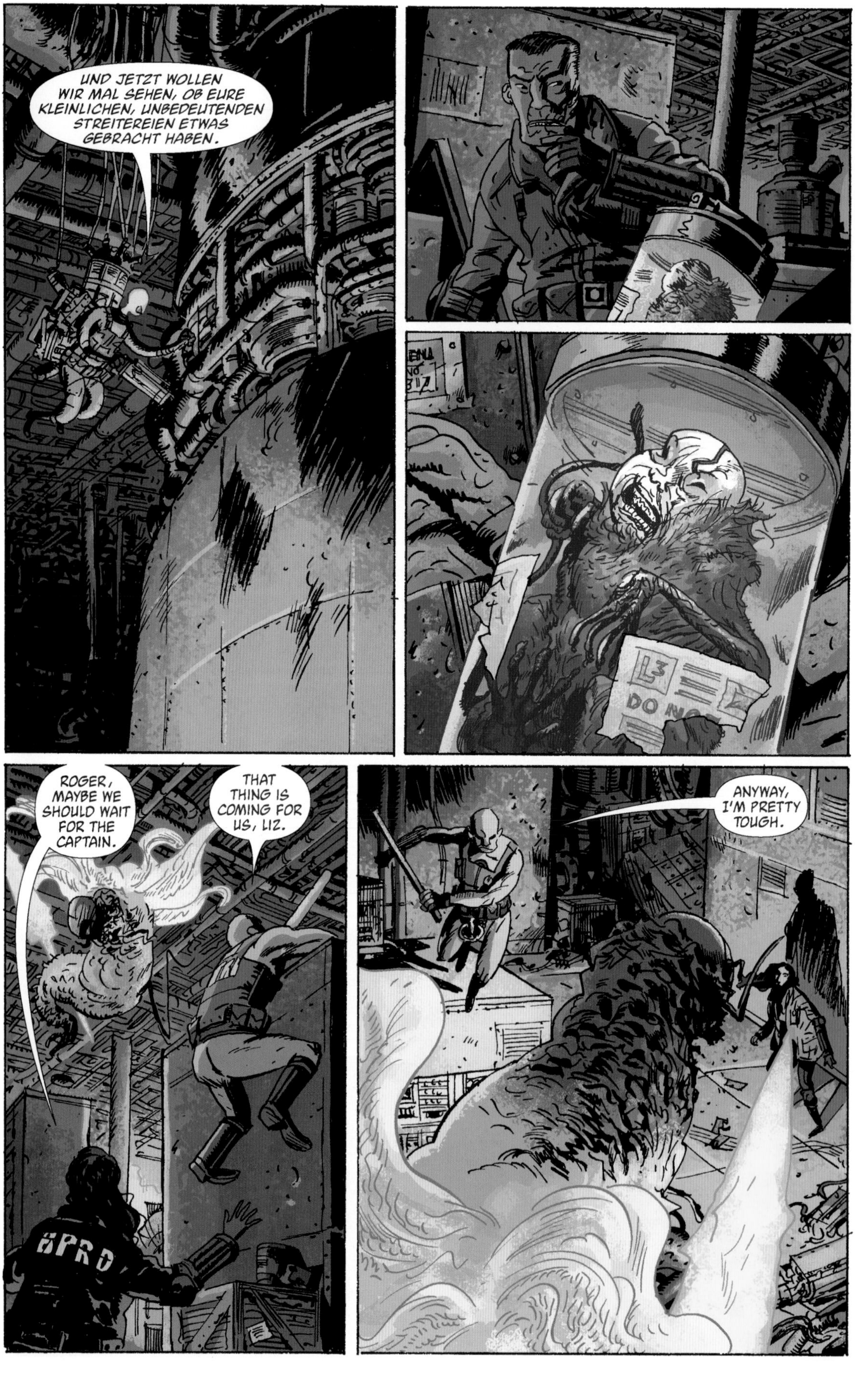
UND JETZT WOLLEN WIR MAL SEHEN, OB EURE KLEINLICHEN, UNBEDEUTENDEN STREITEREIEN ETWAS GEBRACHT HABEN.
ROGER, MAYBE WE SHOULD WAIT FOR THE CAPTAIN.
THAT THING IS COMING FOR US, LIZ.
ANYWAY, I'M PRETTY TOUGH.

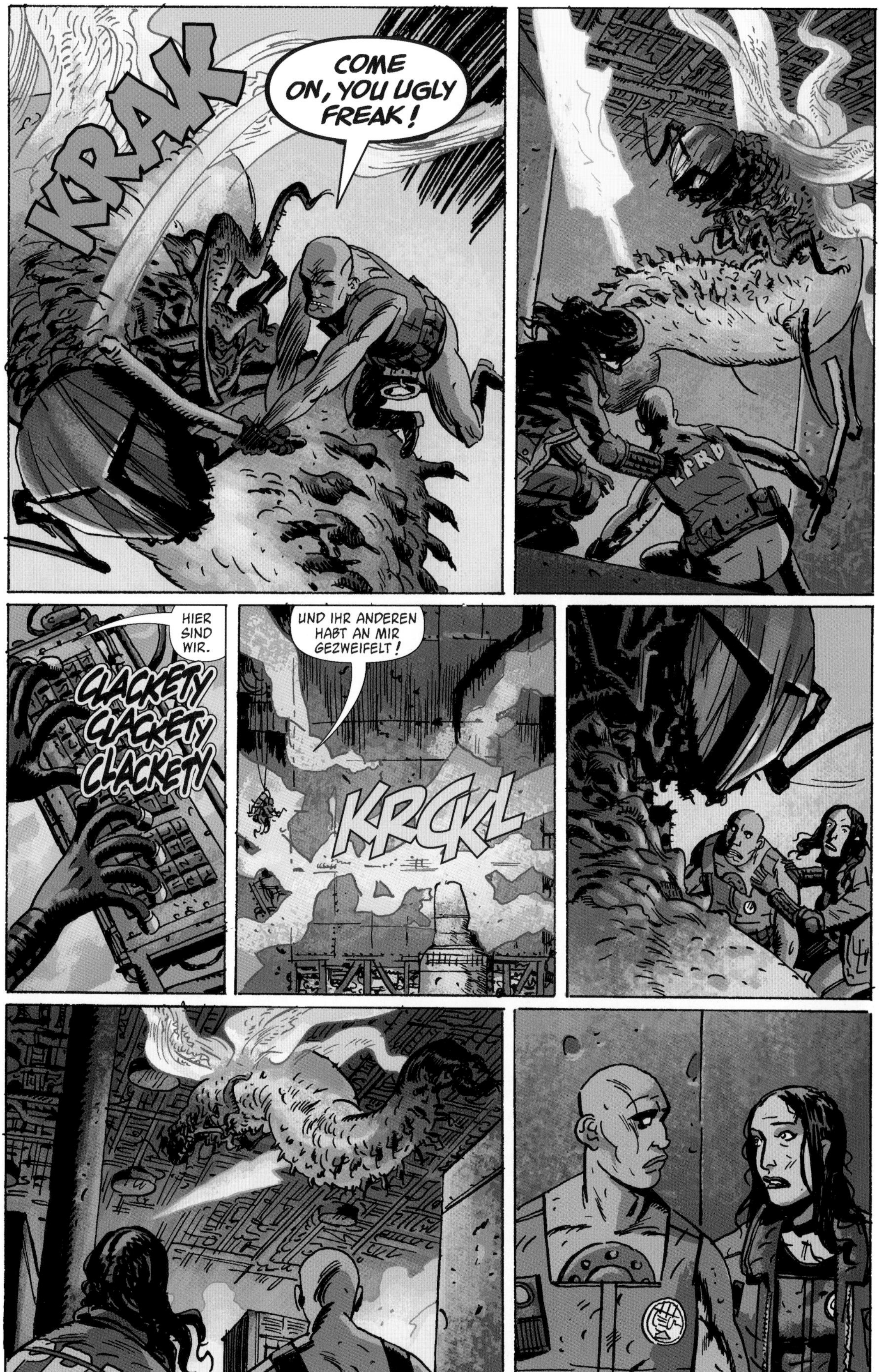
KRAK
COME ON, YOU UGLY FREAK!
BPRD
HIER SIND WIR.
CLACKETY CLACKETY CLACKETY
UND IHR ANDEREN HABT AN MIR GEZWEIFELT!
KRCKL

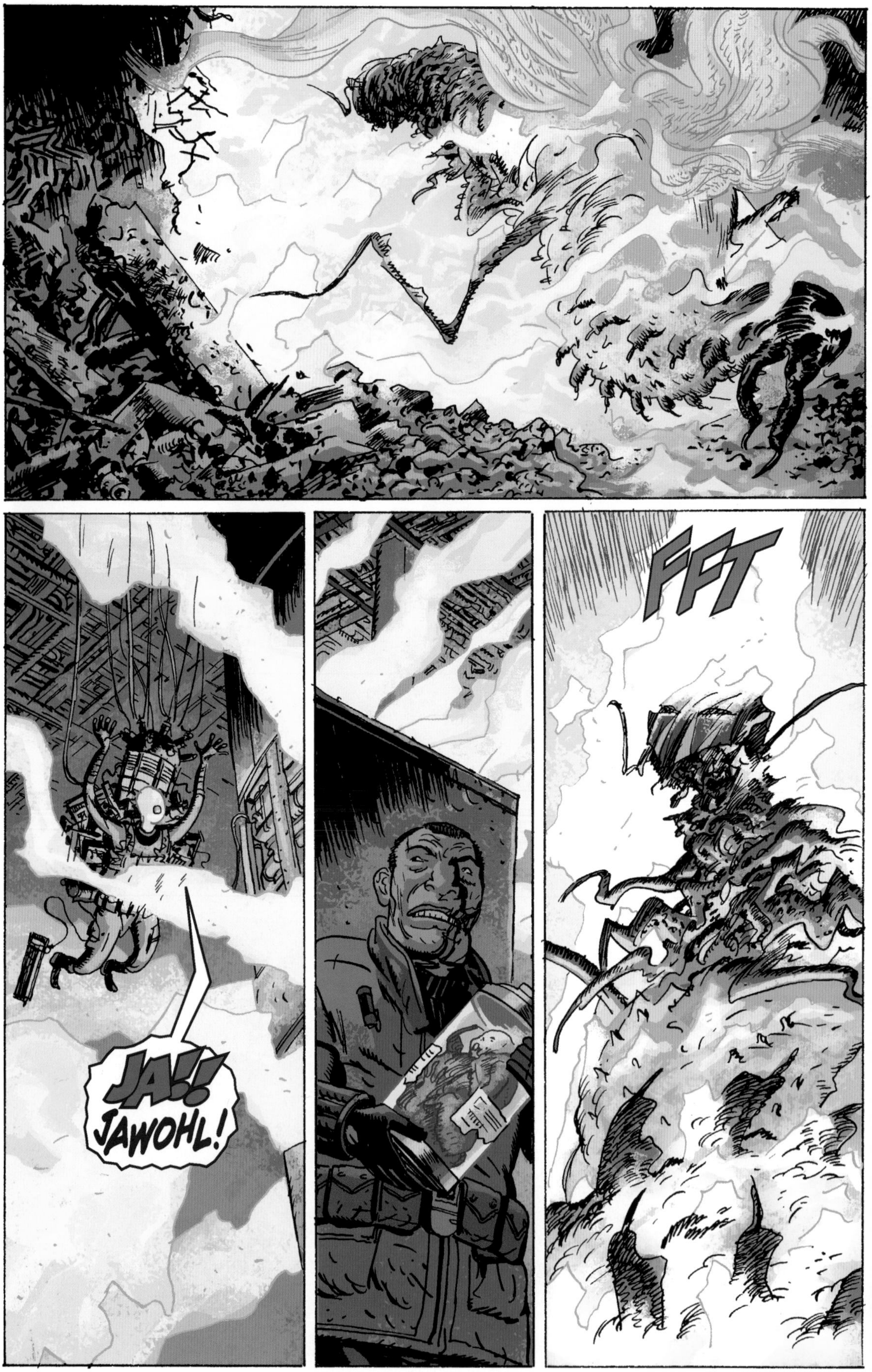
JA!! JAWOHL!
FFT

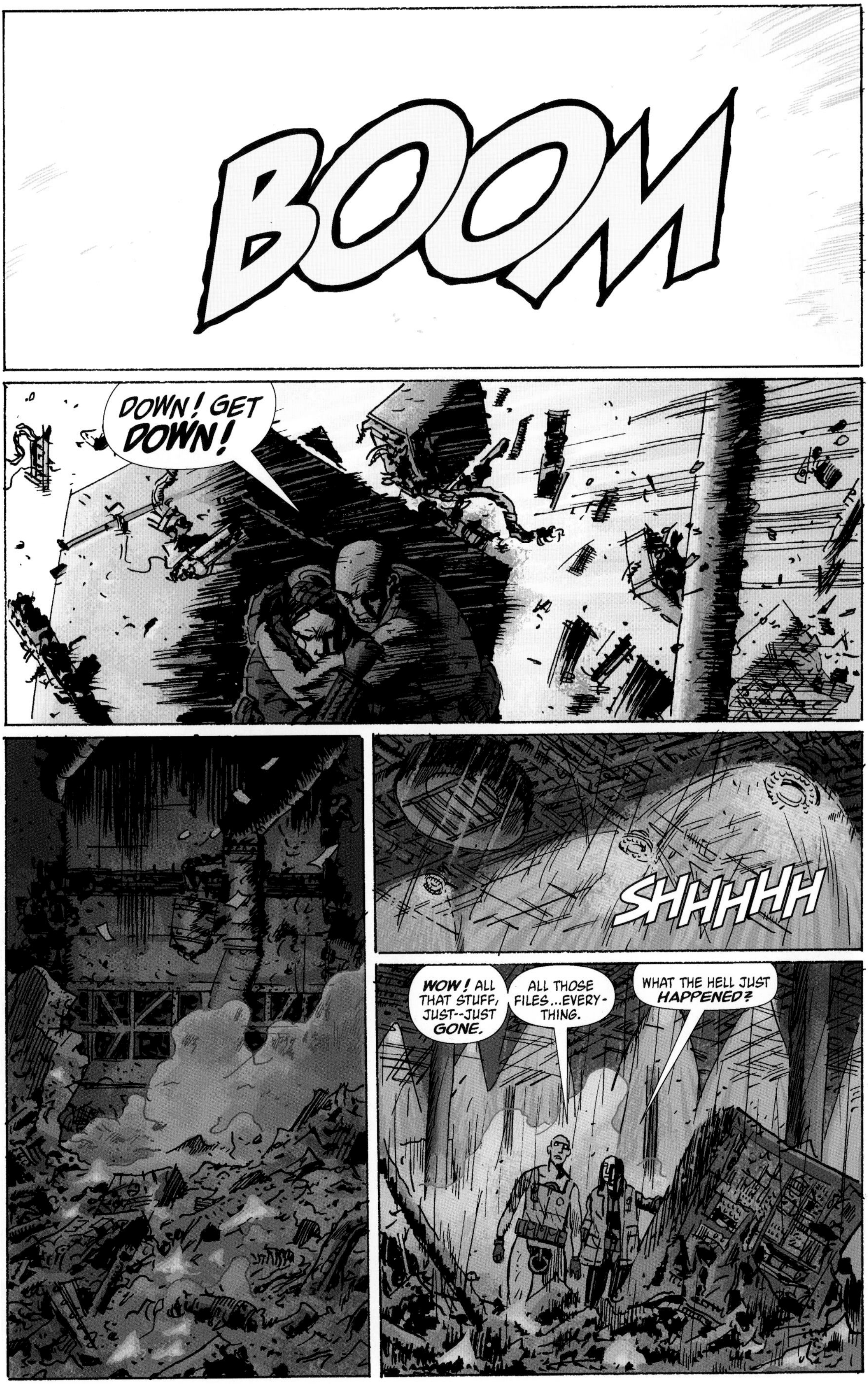
BOOM
DOWN! GET DOWN!
SHHHHH
WOW! ALL THAT STUFF, JUST--JUST GONE.
ALL THOSE FILES...EVERY-THING.
WHAT THE HELL JUST HAPPENED?

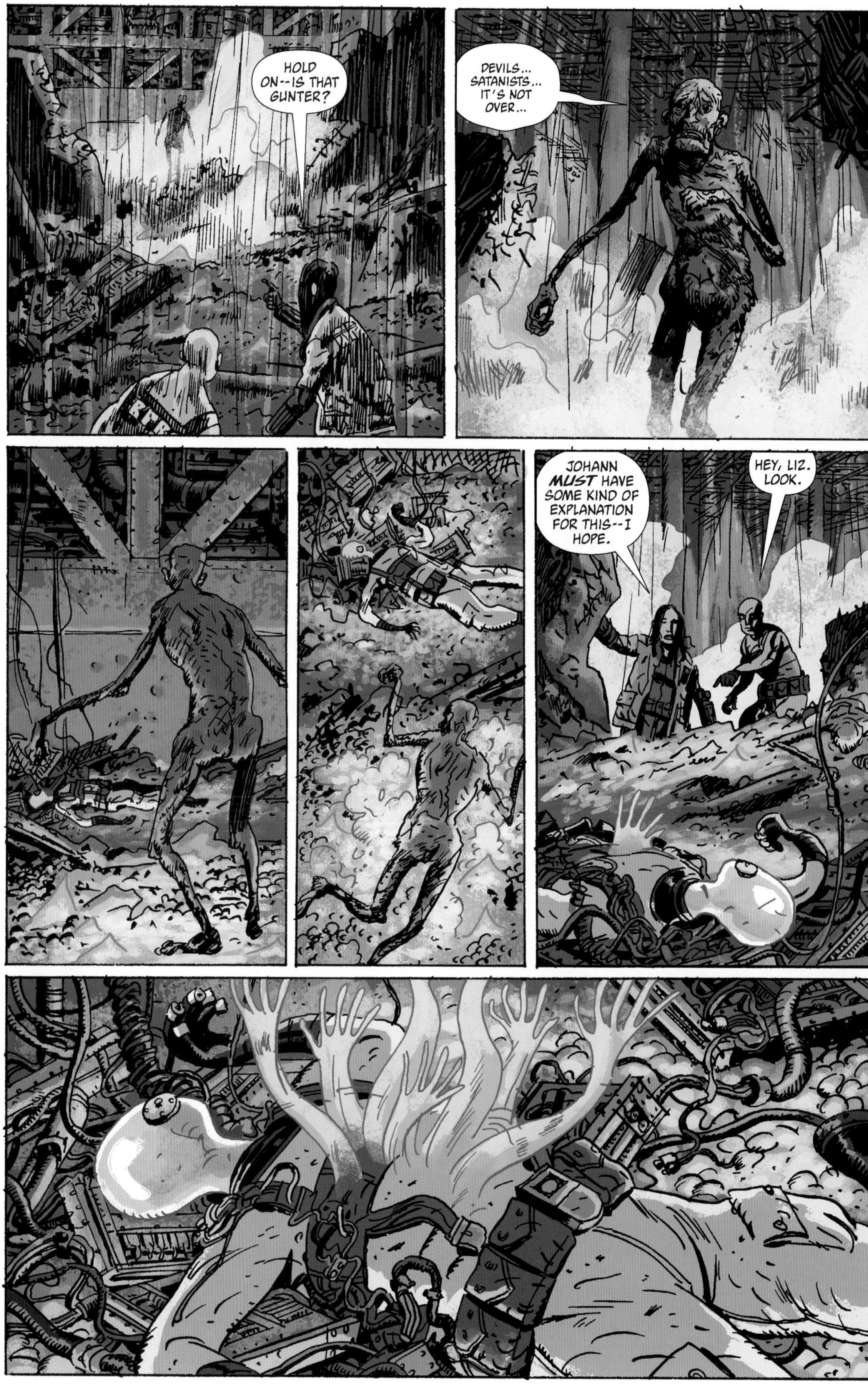
HOLD ON--IS THAT GUNTER?
DEVILS... SATANISTS... IT'S NOT OVER...
JOHANN MUST HAVE SOME KIND OF EXPLANATION FOR THIS--I HOPE.
HEY, LIZ. LOOK.

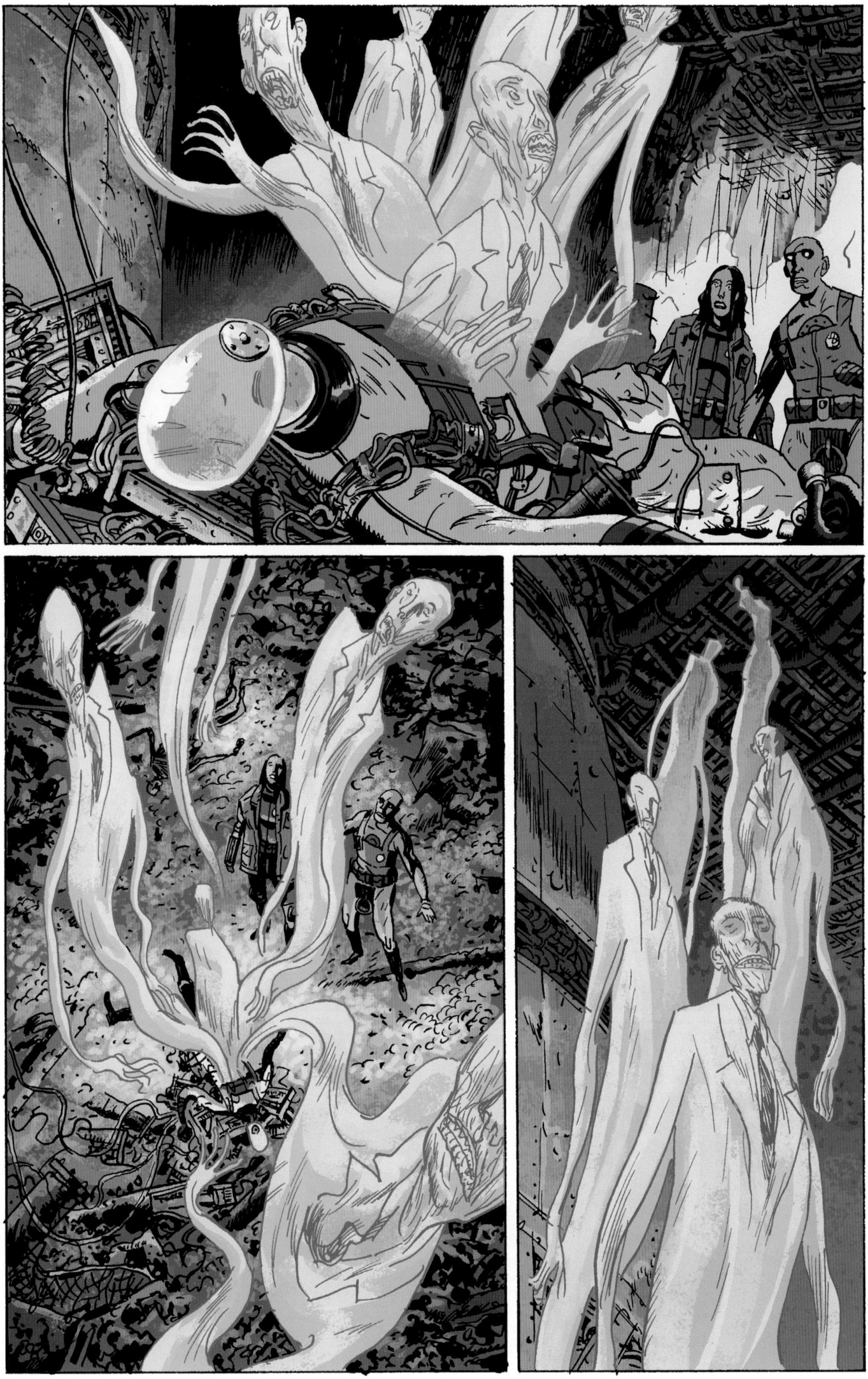

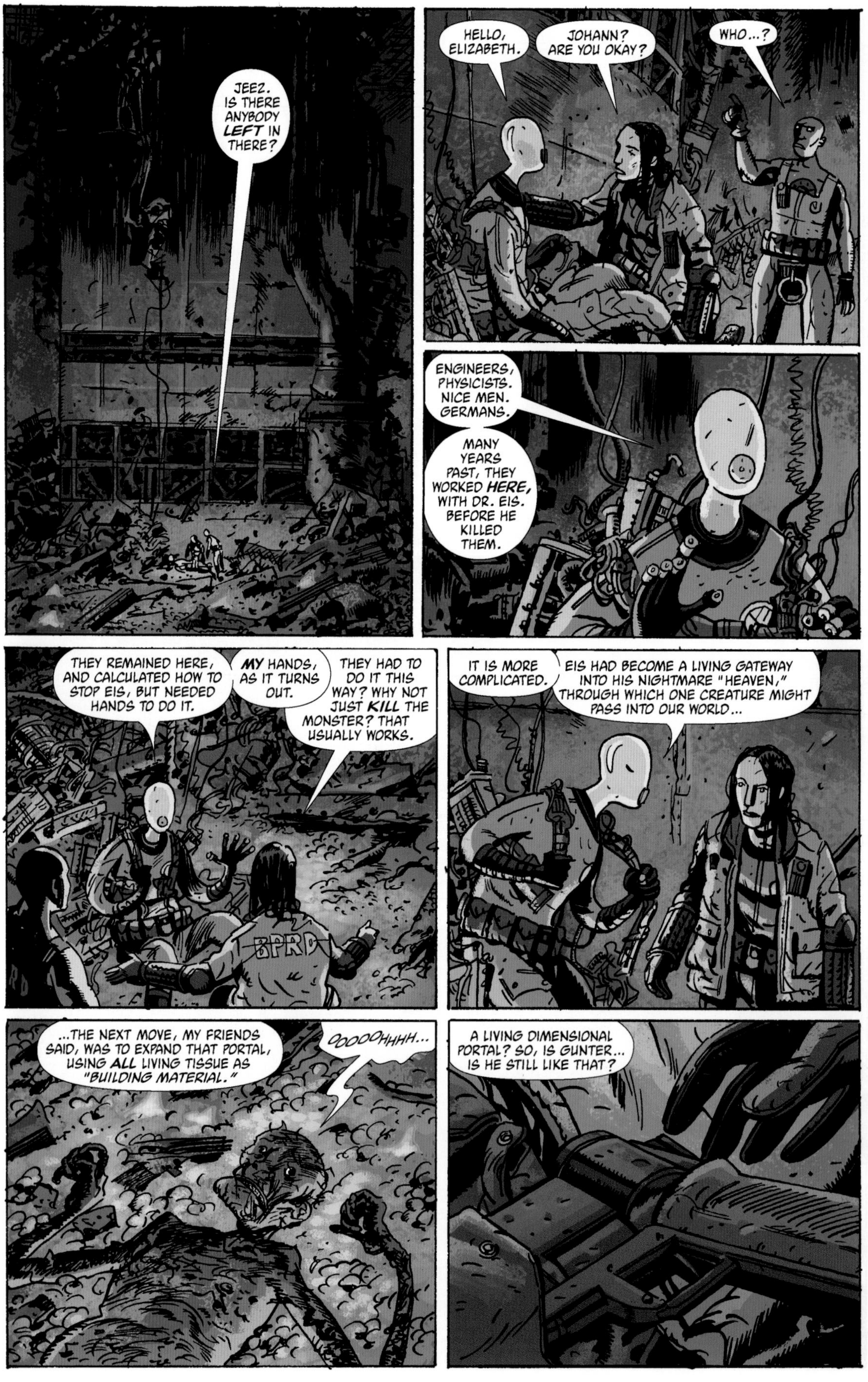
JEEZ. IS THERE ANYBODY LEFT IN THERE?
HELLO, ELIZABETH.
JOHANN? ARE YOU OKAY?
WHO...?
ENGINEERS, PHYSICISTS. NICE MEN. GERMANS.
MANY YEARS PAST, THEY WORKED HERE, WITH DR. EIS. BEFORE HE KILLED THEM.
THEY REMAINED HERE, AND CALCULATED HOW TO STOP EIS, BUT NEEDED HANDS TO DO IT.
MY HANDS, AS IT TURNS OUT.
THEY HAD TO DO IT THIS WAY? WHY NOT JUST KILL THE MONSTER? THAT USUALLY WORKS.
IT IS MORE COMPLICATED.
EIS HAD BECOME A LIVING GATEWAY INTO HIS NIGHTMARE "HEAVEN," THROUGH WHICH ONE CREATURE MIGHT PASS INTO OUR WORLD...
...THE NEXT MOVE, MY FRIENDS SAID, WAS TO EXPAND THAT PORTAL, USING ALL LIVING TISSUE AS "BUILDING MATERIAL."
OOOOOHHHH...
A LIVING DIMENSIONAL PORTAL? SO, IS GUNTER... IS HE STILL LIKE THAT?
BPRD

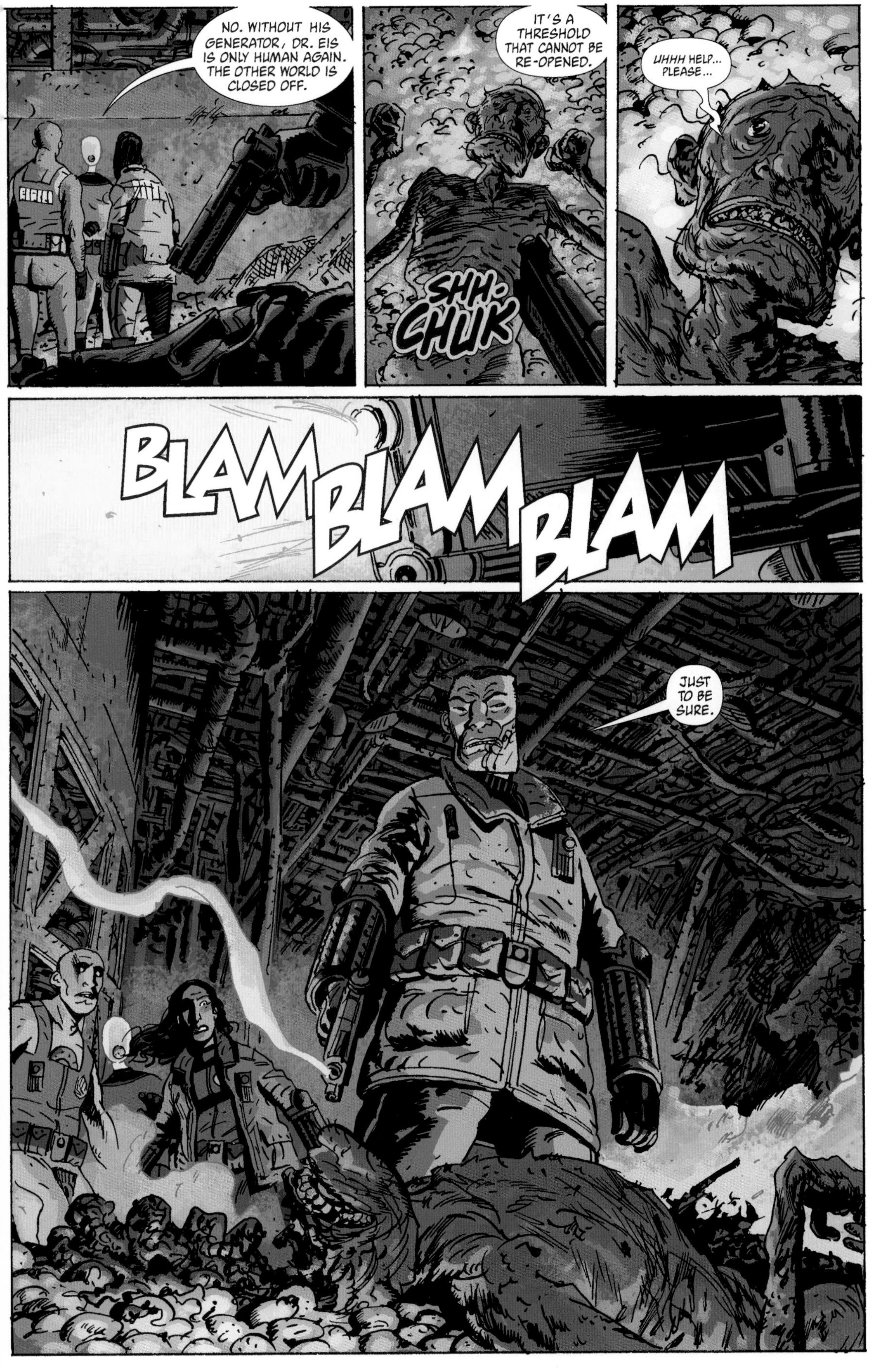
NO. WITHOUT HIS GENERATOR, DR. EIS IS ONLY HUMAN AGAIN. THE OTHER WORLD IS CLOSED OFF.
IT'S A THRESHOLD THAT CANNOT BE RE-OPENED.
SHH-CHUK
UHHH HELP... PLEASE...
BLAM BLAM BLAM
JUST TO BE SURE.

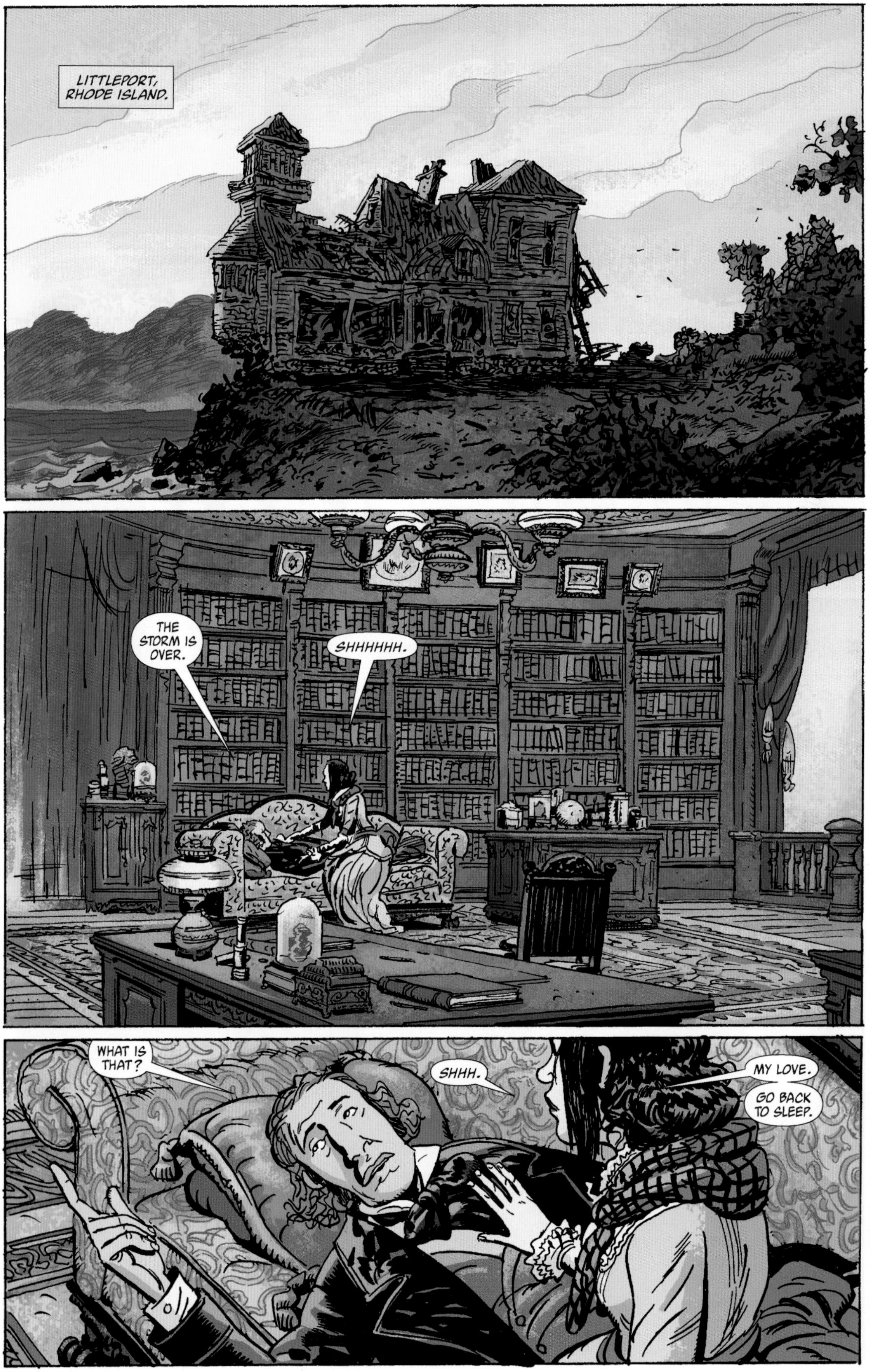
LITTLEPORT, RHODE ISLAND.
THE STORM IS OVER.
SHHHHHH.
WHAT IS THAT?
SHHH.
MY LOVE.
GO BACK TO SLEEP.

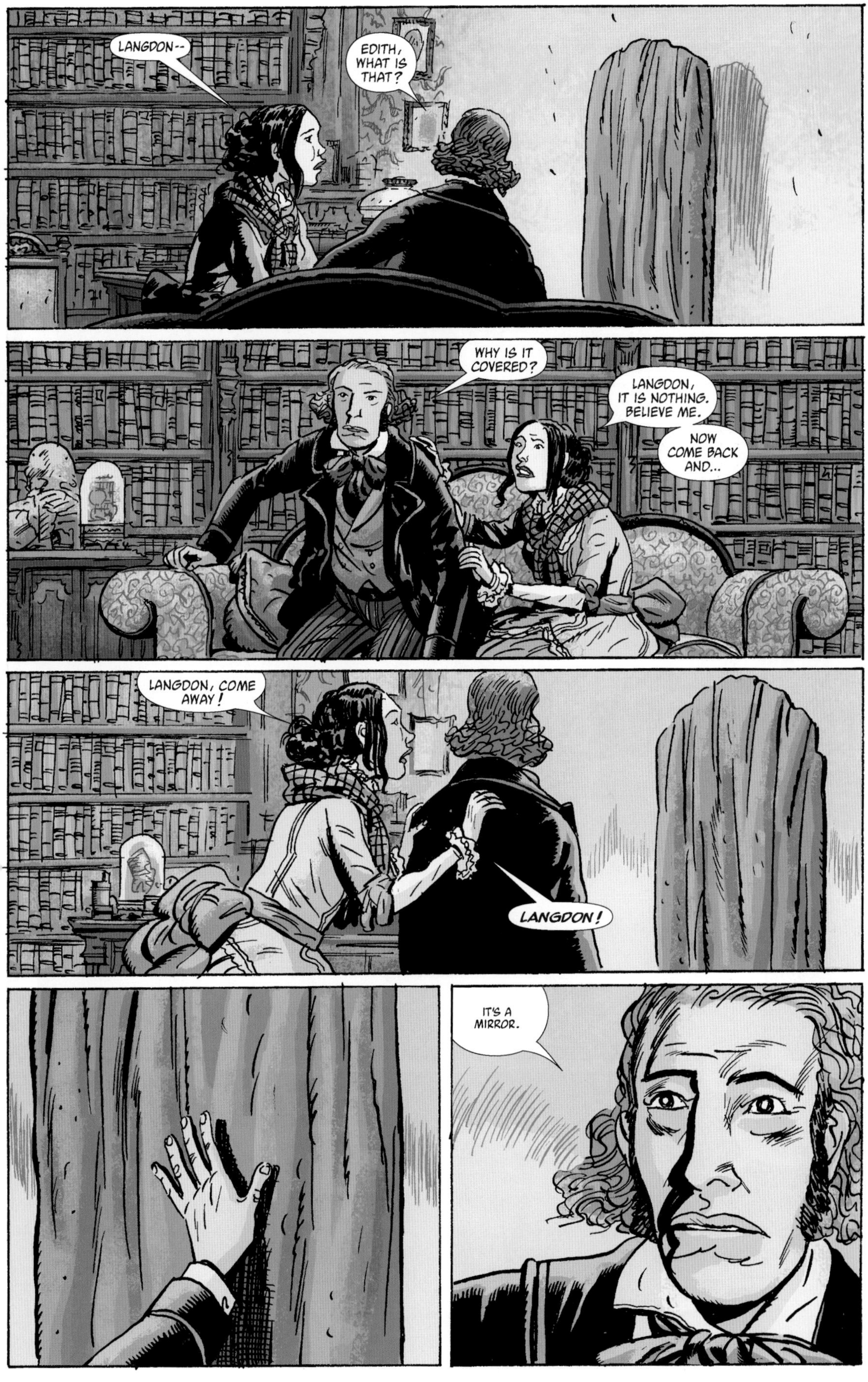
LANGDON--
EDITH, WHAT IS THAT?
WHY IS IT COVERED?
LANGDON, IT IS NOTHING. BELIEVE ME.
NOW COME BACK AND...
LANGDON, COME AWAY!
LANGDON!
IT'S A MIRROR.

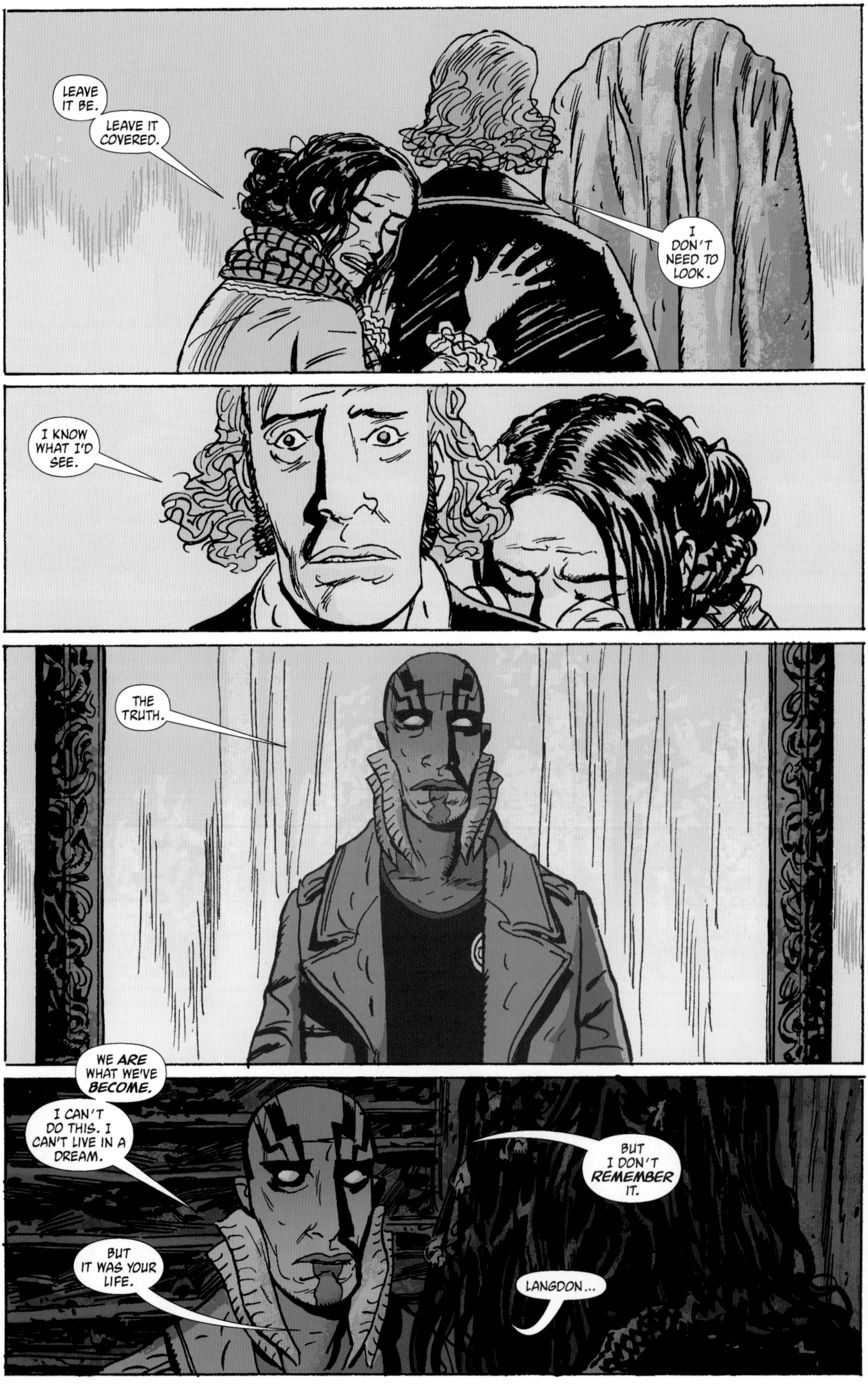
LEAVE IT BE.
LEAVE IT COVERED.
I DON'T NEED TO LOOK.
I KNOW WHAT I'D SEE.
THE TRUTH.
WE ARE WHAT WE'VE BECOME.
I CAN'T DO THIS. I CAN'T LIVE IN A DREAM.
BUT I DON'T REMEMBER IT.
BUT IT WAS YOUR LIFE.
LANGDON...

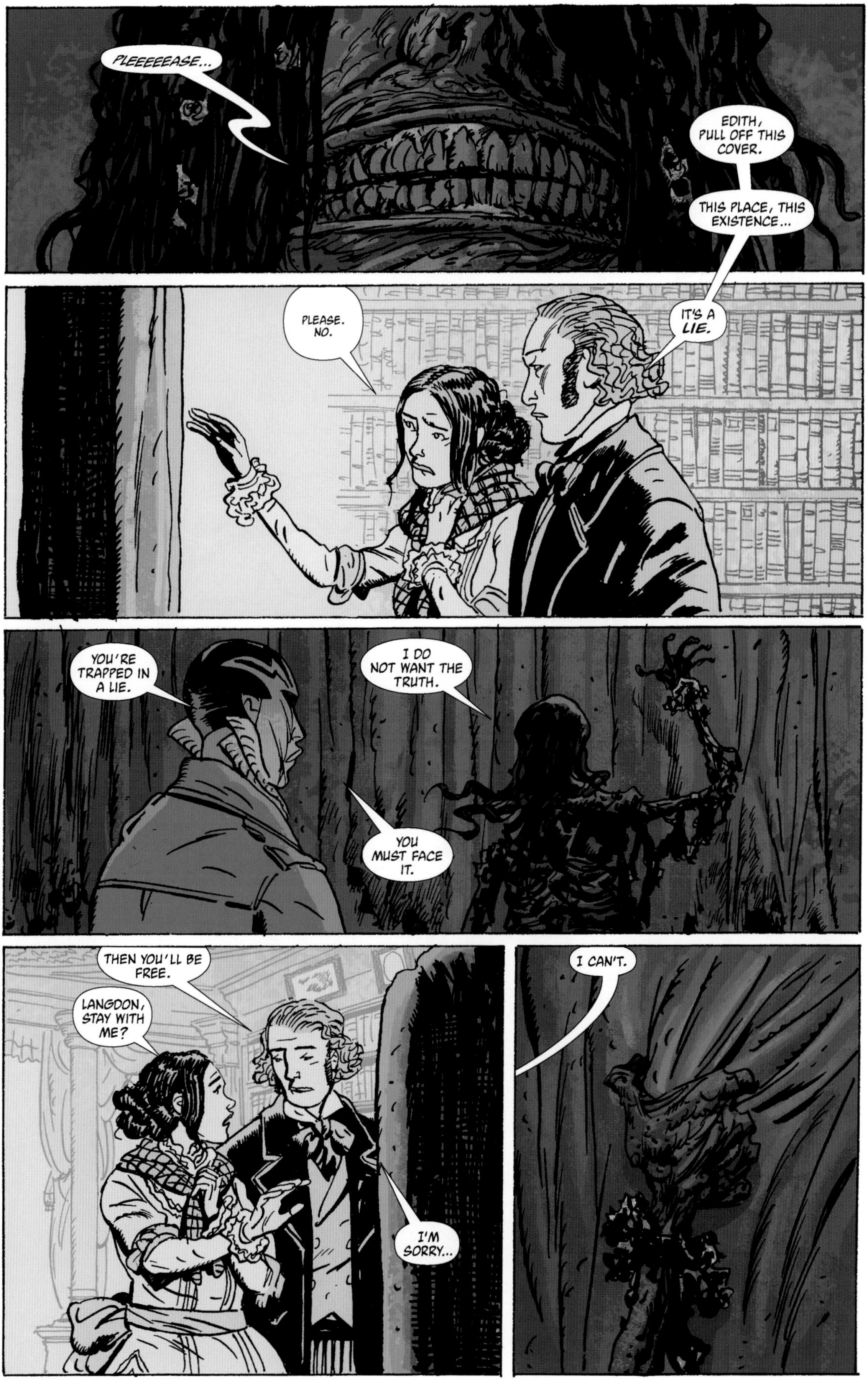
PLEEEEEASE...
EDITH, PULL OFF THIS COVER.
THIS PLACE, THIS EXISTENCE...
PLEASE. NO.
IT'S A LIE.
YOU'RE TRAPPED IN A LIE.
I DO NOT WANT THE TRUTH.
YOU MUST FACE IT.
THEN YOU'LL BE FREE.
LANGDON, STAY WITH ME?
I'M SORRY...
I CAN'T.

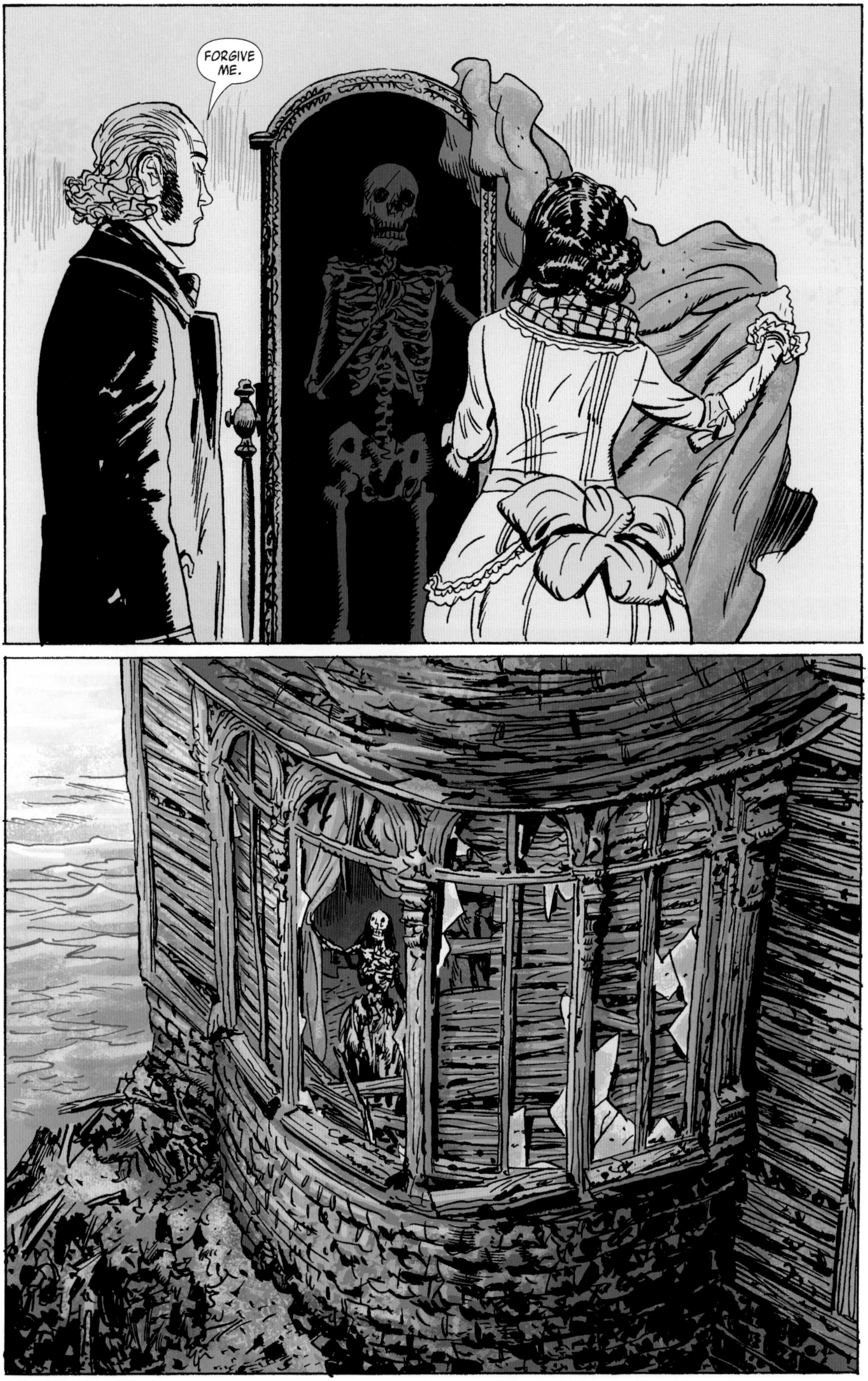
FORGIVE ME.

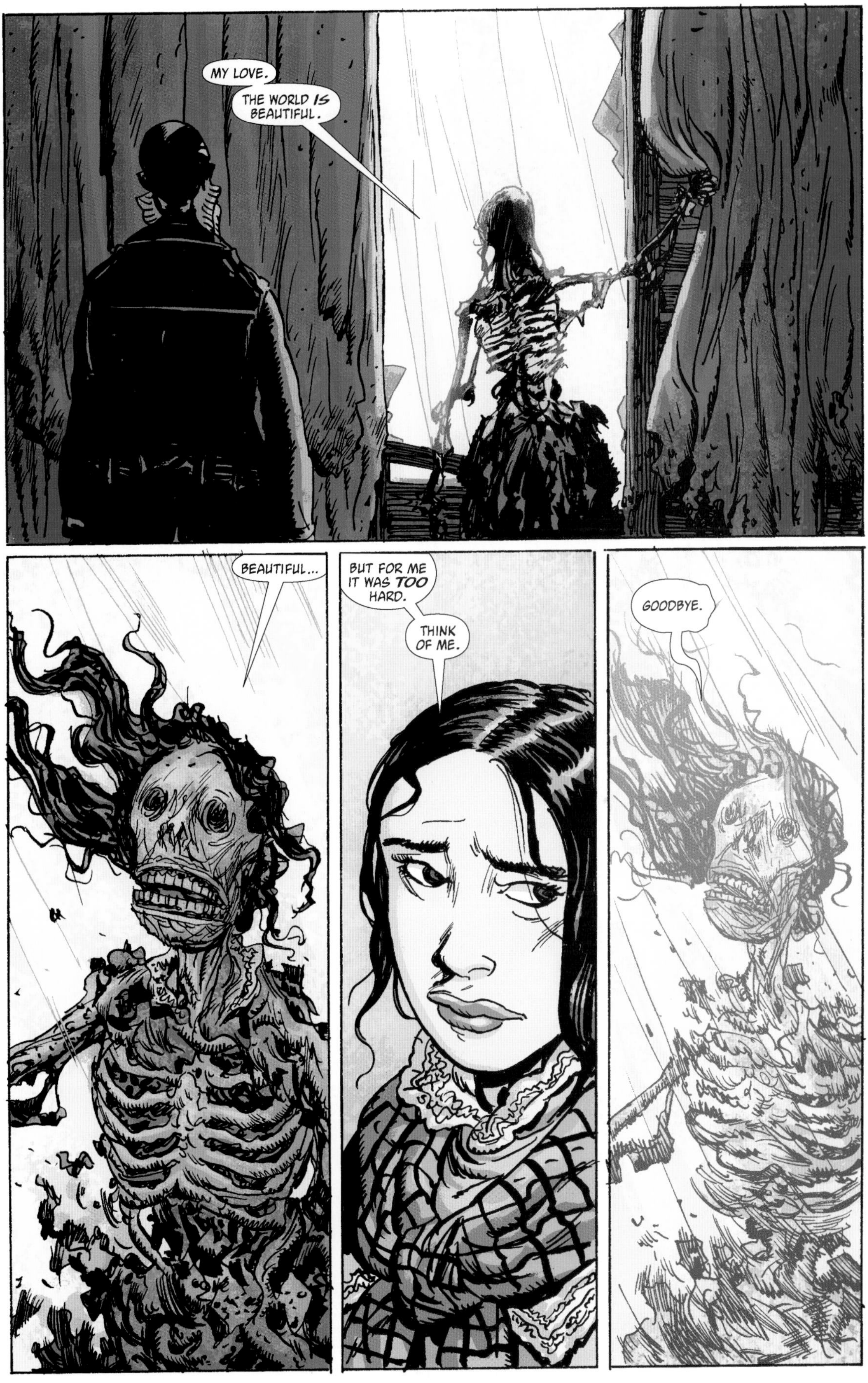
MY LOVE.
THE WORLD IS BEAUTIFUL.
BEAUTIFUL...
BUT FOR ME IT WAS TOO HARD.
THINK OF ME.
GOODBYE.

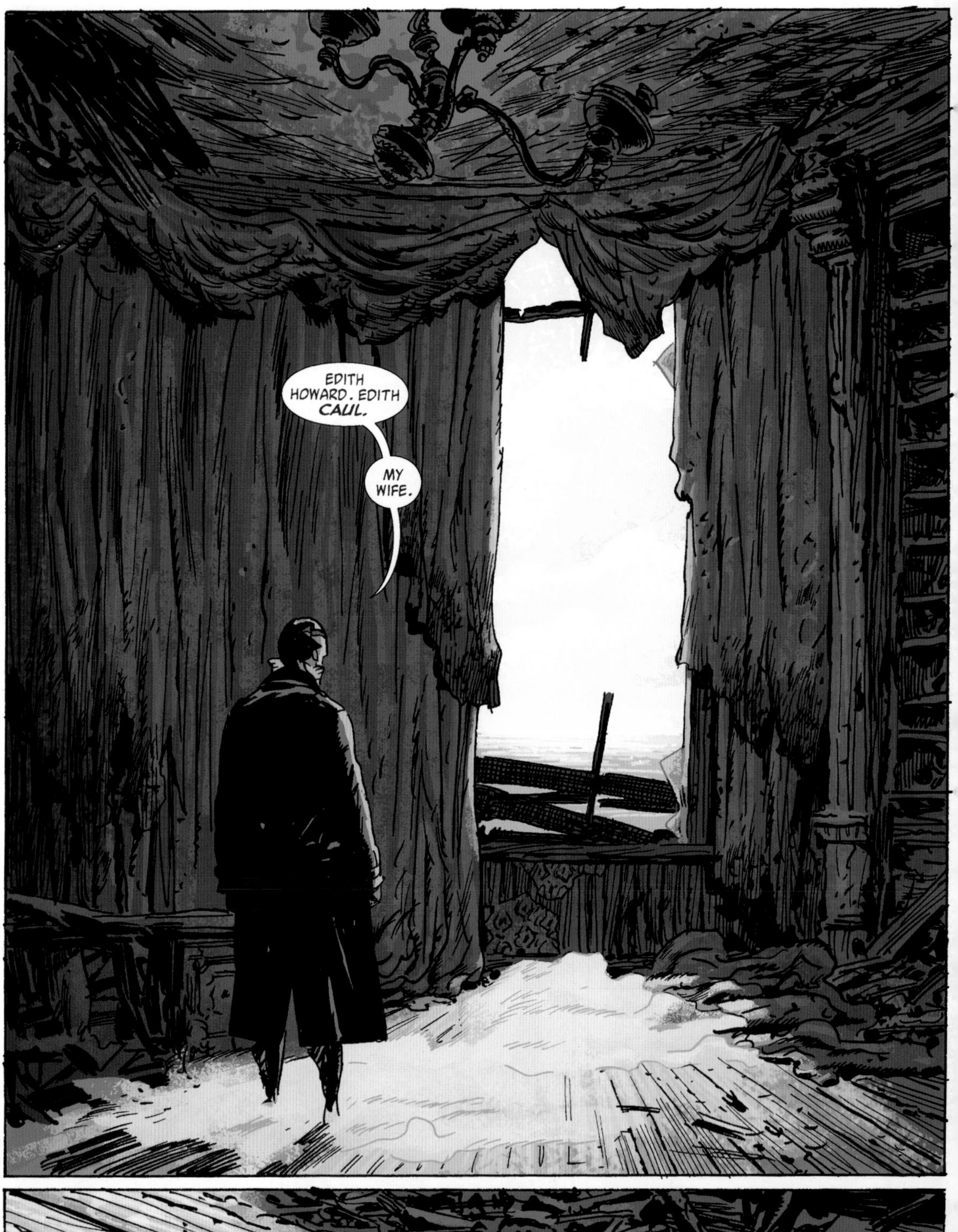
EDITH HOWARD. EDITH CAUL.
MY WIFE.
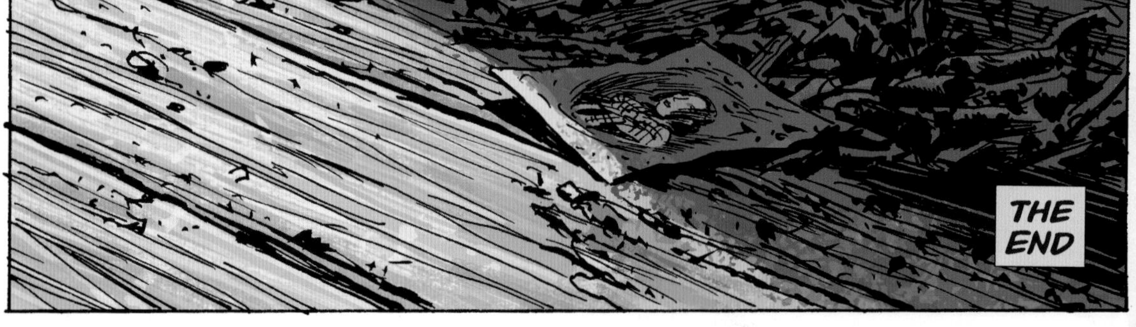
THE END

AFTERWORD

I guess I need to start by saying a few words about John Arcudi. I'm sure in his introduction he's written a whole bunch about himself, so there's not much left to say. I'll just say this (in case he forgot to mention it)—John's a great writer, and he's a master at working that fine line between humor and horror. When it comes to old comics and monsters, we speak the same language (though he knows much bigger words than I do), and we are both in awe of the weird genius of Guy Davis. When I decided that I wanted someone to co-write *B.P.R.D.* with me, John was the only name on my list, and if he'd said no … Well, I don't like to think about that.

After writing *Plague of Frogs*, I knew I wanted to write the B.P.R.D. in a new direction. I wanted to relocate them into a mountain and, as is so often the case when you move into a mountain, I knew something bad would happen there. I also wanted to introduce a new, hard-ass, formerly dead, military-type character. Over a couple of lunches and a lot of phone calls, John and I hammered out a story. The way I remember it, John came in with most of what went on in the new headquarters, and he and Guy created all those new (old) World War II-era villains. The stuff with Abe and his dead wife was all me.

The scene with the dead woman, the mirror, and the window has actually been knocking around in my head for years. For a while, I was going to build a Hellboy story around it. I'm glad I didn't. I'm glad I saved it for Abe. It was inspired by a great story by Nathaniel Hawthorne, "Feathertop," in which a scarecrow is turned into a man, but his reflection in a mirror reveals his true self. Ultimately he decides he cannot live with the illusion of humanity, and chooses to be nothing. Very creepy and very sad. If you haven't read it, I suggest you do so at once.

My thanks to Guy and John, and a *special* thanks to Dave Stewart, who, I think, outdid himself this time. And, finally, thanks to Scott Allie, who must certainly have a few gray hairs by now.

There you go …

MIKE MIGNOLA

New York City

B.P.R.D.™

SKETCHBOOK

While most of the design work for the B.P.R.D. was already done before I started on the *Plague of Frogs* story line, *The Dead* would bring a lot of new designs for the B.P.R.D. team. But first there were the sketches for the short story "Born Again"—below are some early drawings for the living fossil.

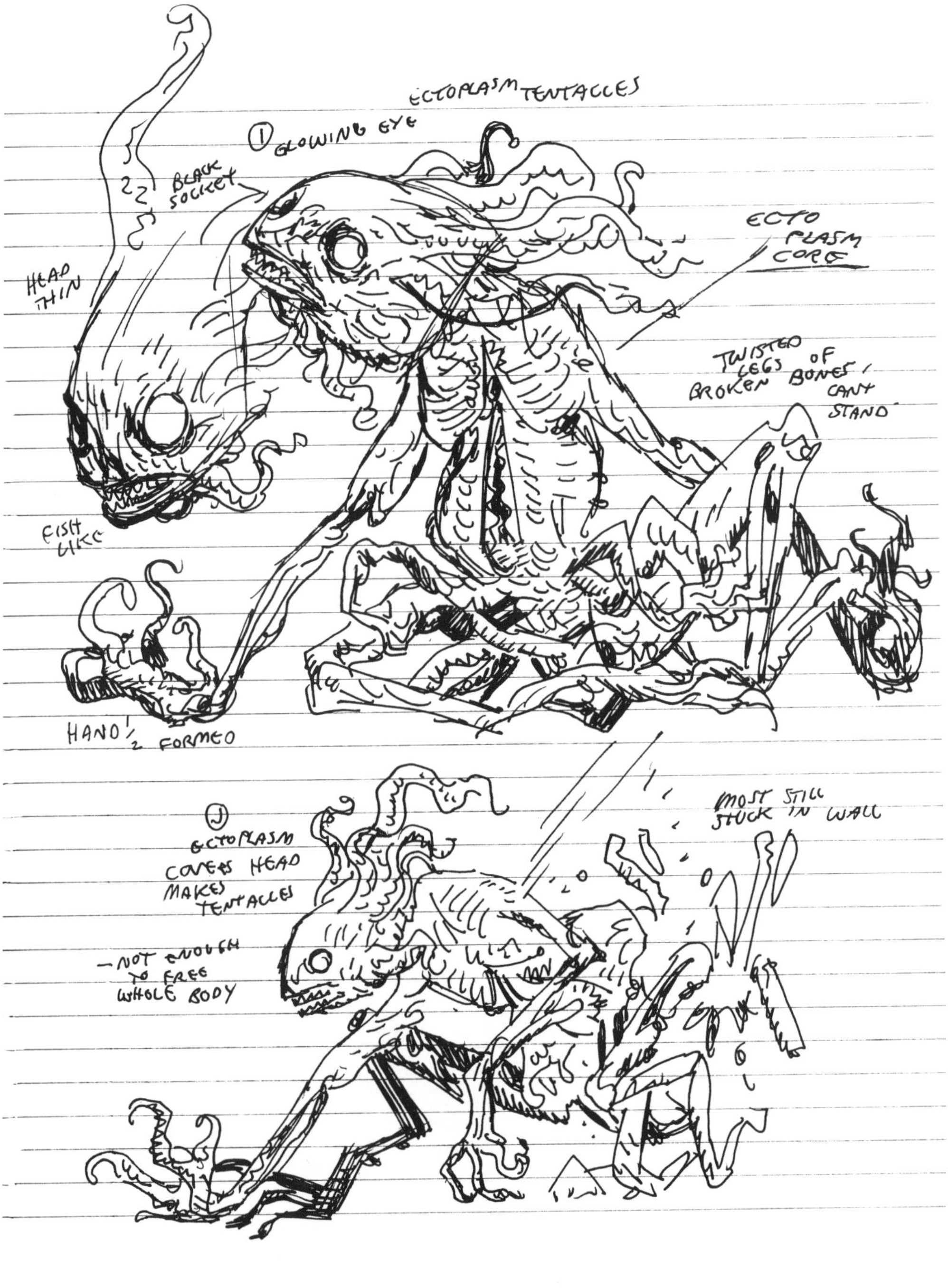
ECTOPLASM TENTACLES
1 GLOWING EYE
BLACK SOCKET
ECTO PLASM CORE
HEAD THIN
TWISTED LEGS OF BROKEN BONES / CANT STAND
FISH LIKE
HAND ½ FORMED
2 ECTOPLASM COVERS HEAD MAKES TENTACLES
MOST STILL STUCK IN WALL
—NOT ENOUGH TO FREE WHOLE BODY

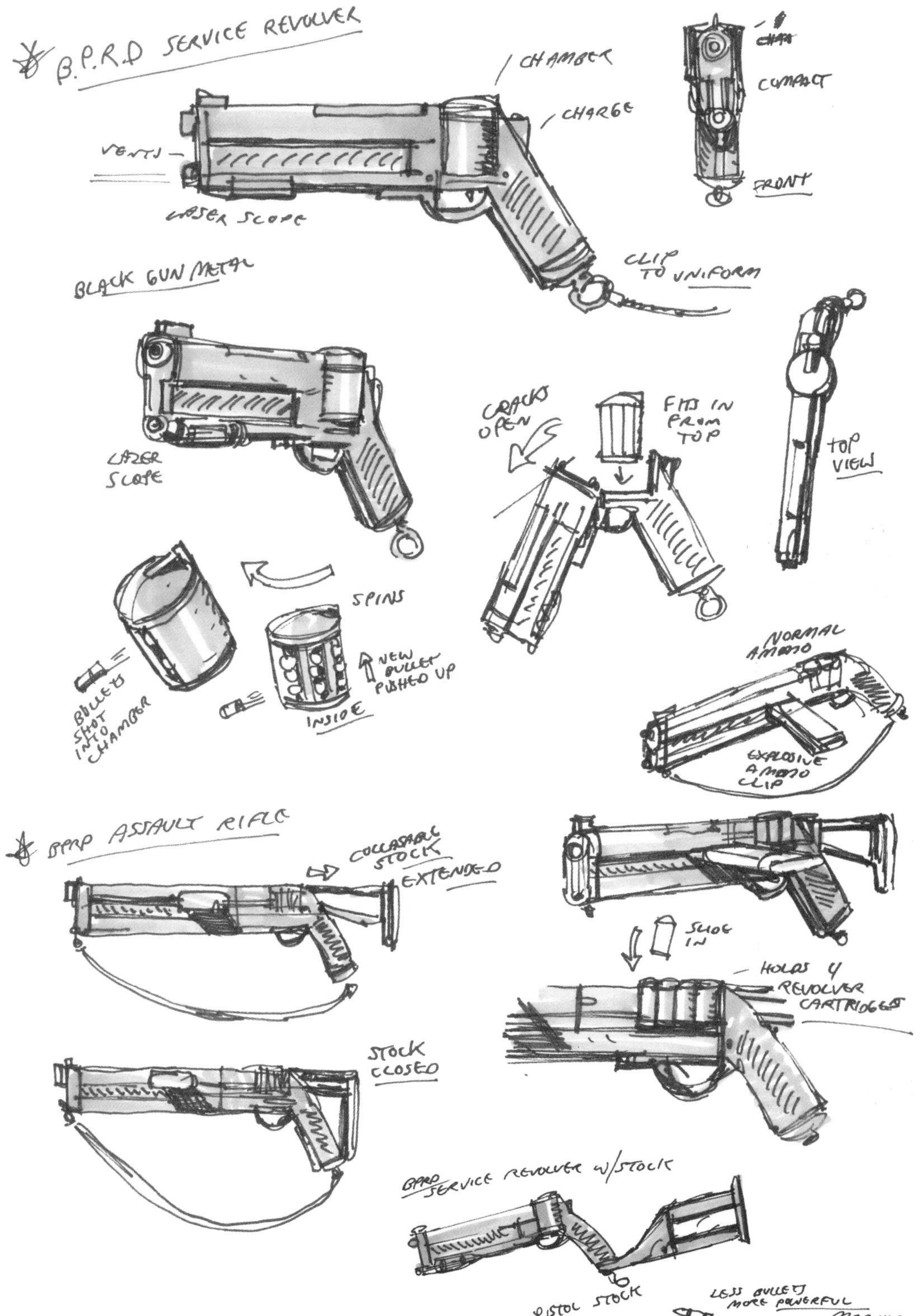
B.P.R.D SERVICE REVOLVER
CHAMBER
CHARGE
VENTS
LASER SCOPE
COMPACT
FRONT
CLIP TO UNIFORM
BLACK GUN METAL
LAZER SCOPE
CRACKS OPEN
FITS IN FROM TOP
TOP VIEW
SPINS
BULLETS SHOT INTO CHAMBER
NEW BULLET PUSHED UP
INSIDE
NORMAL AMMO
EXPLOSIVE AMMO CLIP
BPRD ASSAULT RIFLE
COLLASABLE STOCK
EXTENDED
SLIDE IN
HOLDS 4 REVOLVER CARTRIDGES
STOCK CLOSED
BPRD SERVICE REVOLVER W/STOCK
PISTOL STOCK

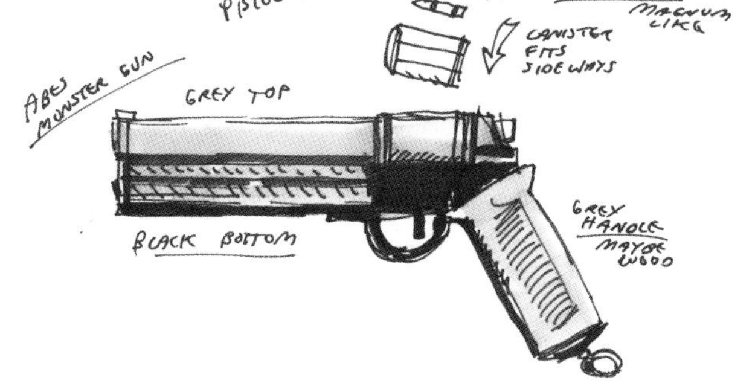
LESS BULLETS MORE POWERFUL
MAGNUM LIKE
CANISTER FITS SIDEWAYS
ABES MONSTER GUN
GREY TOP
BLACK BOTTOM
GREY HANDLE
MAYBE WOOD

Mike reworked the new uniforms of the B.P.R.D. team to reflect a more organized utilitarian feel and I wanted the guns to match that.

B.P.R.D MOUNTAIN

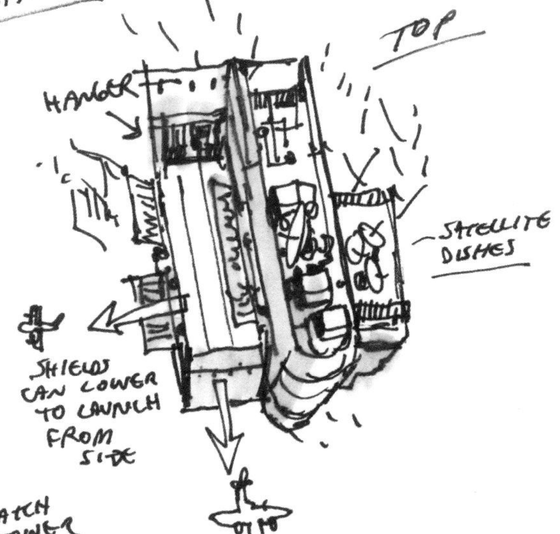
TOP
HANGER
SATELLITE DISHES
SHIELDS CAN LOWER TO LAUNCH FROM SIDE

With the majority of the B.P.R.D. H.Q. resting inside the mountain itself, I modeled the command post that juts out of the mountainside after a submarine's conning tower. I also liked the idea that planes would launch and land far inside the mountain only using the outside runway like a jump point.

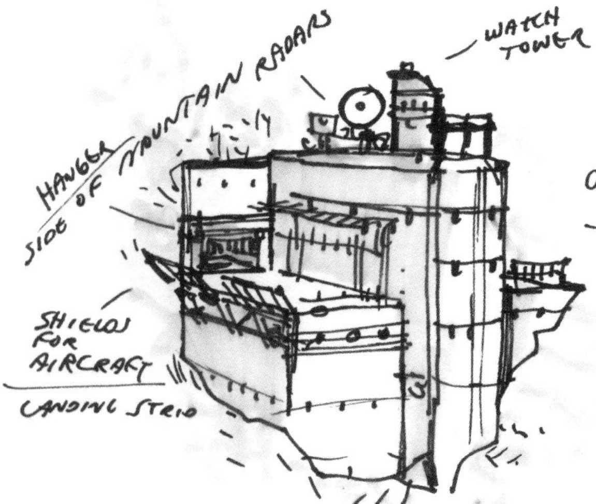
WATCH TOWER
SIDE OF MOUNTAIN RADARS
HANGER
SHIELDS FOR AIRCRAFT
LANDING STRIP

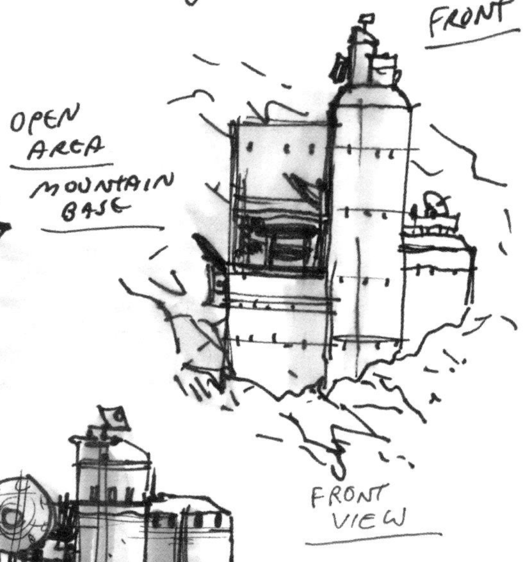
FRONT
OPEN AREA
MOUNTAIN BASE
FRONT VIEW

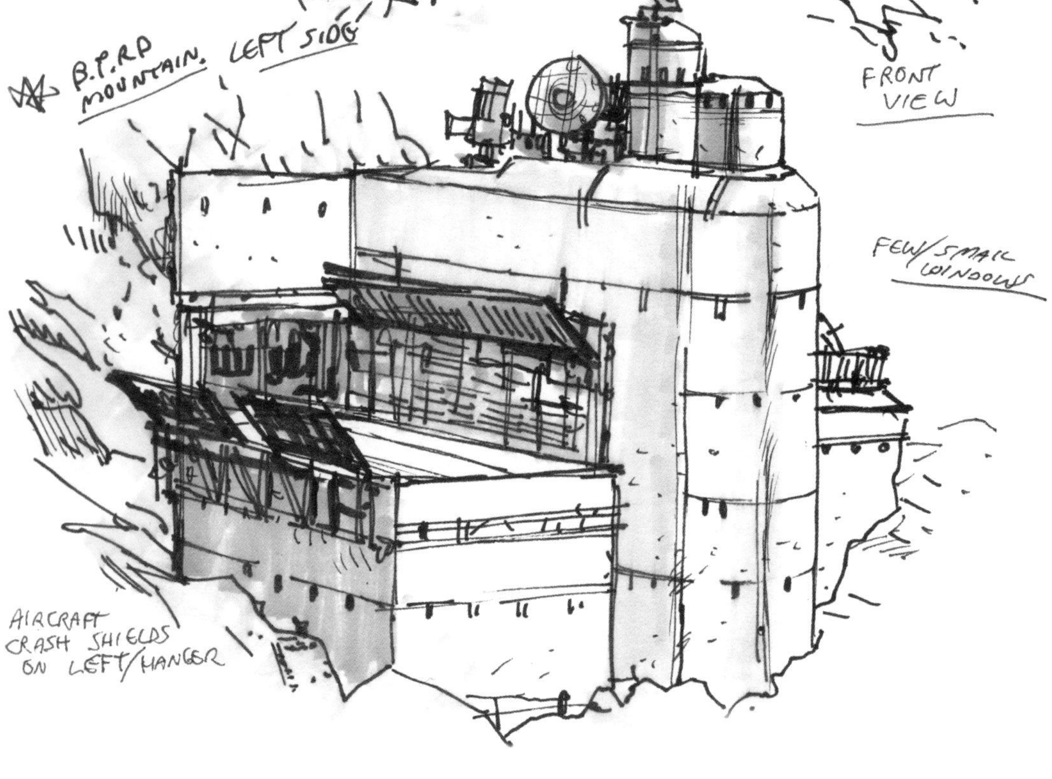
B.P.R.D MOUNTAIN, LEFT SIDE
FEW/SMALL WINDOWS
AIRCRAFT CRASH SHIELDS ON LEFT/HANGER

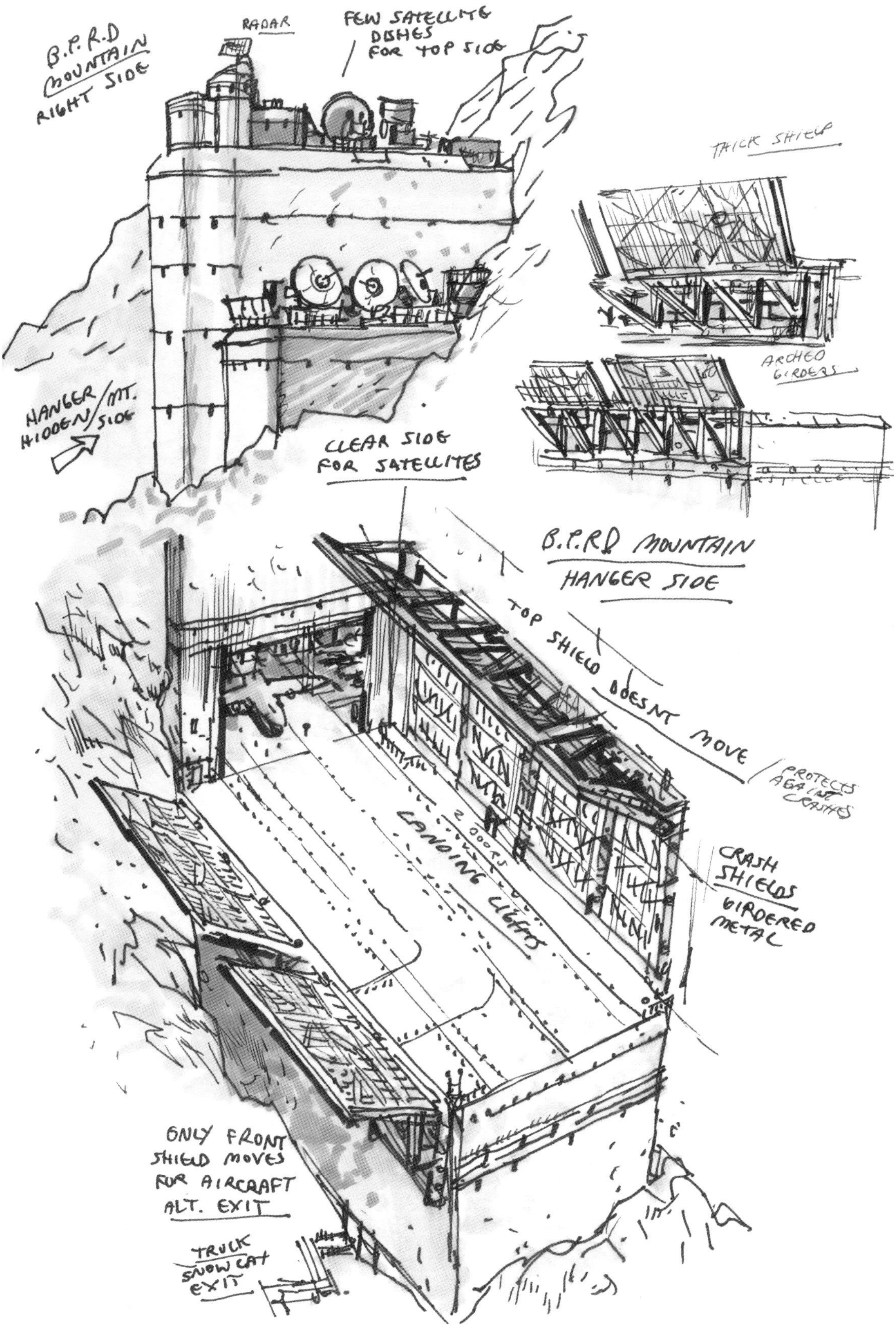
B.P.R.D MOUNTAIN
RIGHT SIDE
RADAR
FEW SATELLITE DISHES FOR TOP SIDE
THICK SHIELD
ARCHED GIRDERS
HANGER/MT. HIDDEN SIDE
CLEAR SIDE FOR SATELLITES
B.P.R.D MOUNTAIN
HANGER SIDE
TOP SHIELD DOESNT MOVE
PROTECTS AGAINST CRASHES
CRASH SHIELDS
GIRDERED METAL
2 DOORS
LANDING LIGHTS
ONLY FRONT SHIELD MOVES FOR AIRCRAFT
ALT. EXIT
TRUCK
SNOW CAT EXIT

A lot of times designs come out as first imagined after reading the script—
Abe's corpse wife was one of them. I wanted her to be a dark mass of hair
and gunk, almost a silhouette until seen close.

ABE WIFE
SEA HAG

TEETH
ALWAYS
SHOW

HAIR IN
FRONT OF
EYES

MUCKY
TORN
CLOTHES

BARNACLES/GROWTHS
ON HAIR/FACE

LONG
BONG
FINGERS

EYES
NEVER
SHOW

HIGH DOLLAR
ROTTED ORES

JAGGED
POINTY HANDS
LIKE CRAB LEGS

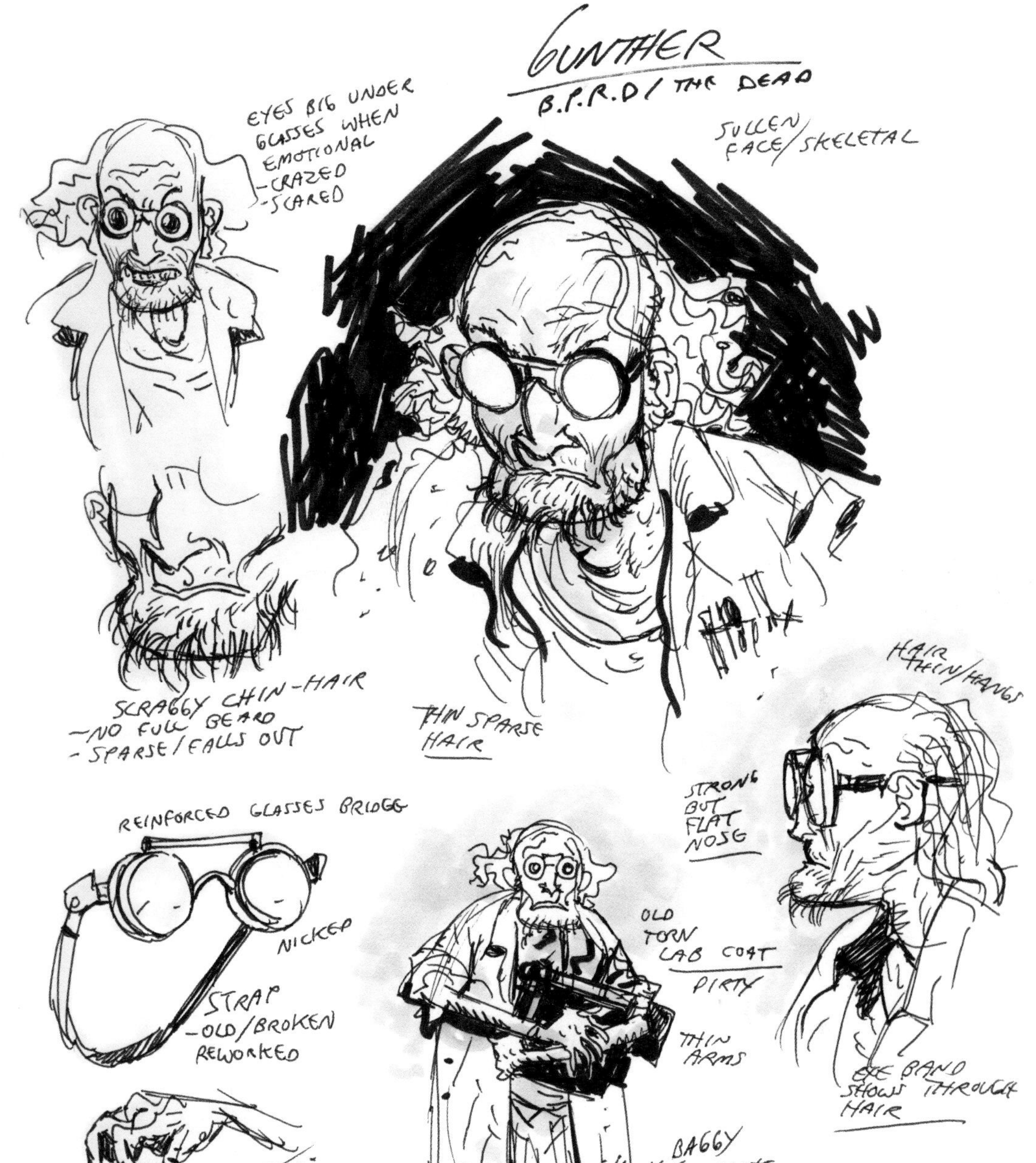
GUNTHER
B.P.R.D / THE DEAD
EYES BIG UNDER GLASSES WHEN EMOTIONAL -CRAZED -SCARED
SULLEN FACE / SKELETAL
SCRAGGY CHIN-HAIR -NO FULL BEARD -SPARSE / FALLS OUT
THIN SPARSE HAIR
HAIR THIN / HANGS
STRONG BUT FLAT NOSE
REINFORCED GLASSES BRIDGE
NICKED
STRAP -OLD / BROKEN REWORKED
OLD TORN LAB COAT
DIRTY
THIN ARMS
EYE BAND SHOWS THROUGH HAIR
BAGGY 40'S PANTS
STRIPED
OLD SHOES
HANDS TWISTED ARTHRITIC
KNOBBY WARTED HANDS
LIKE OLD JOHN CARRADINE
TYPES TOO MUCH!

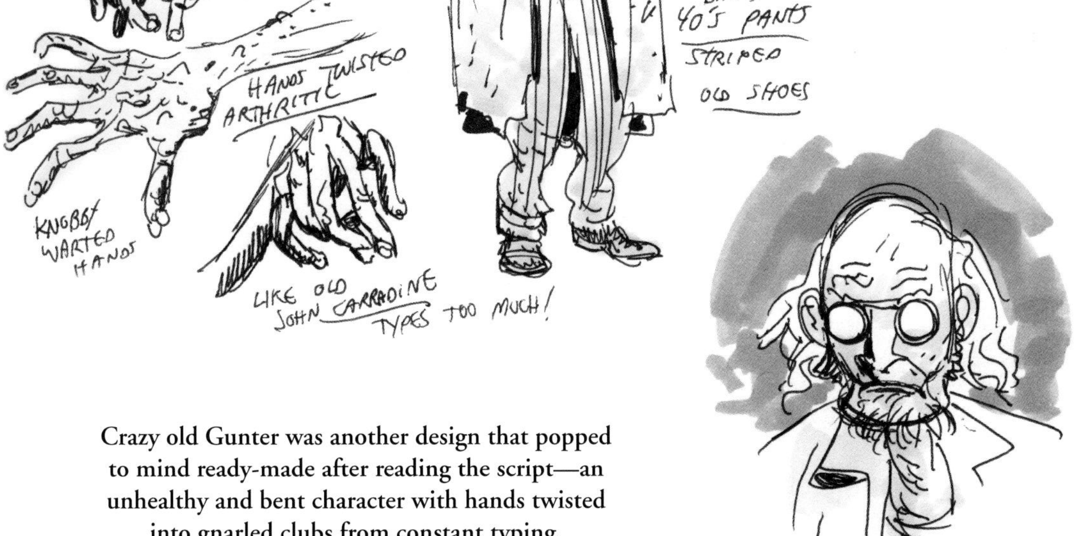

Crazy old Gunter was another design that popped to mind ready-made after reading the script—an unhealthy and bent character with hands twisted into gnarled clubs from constant typing.

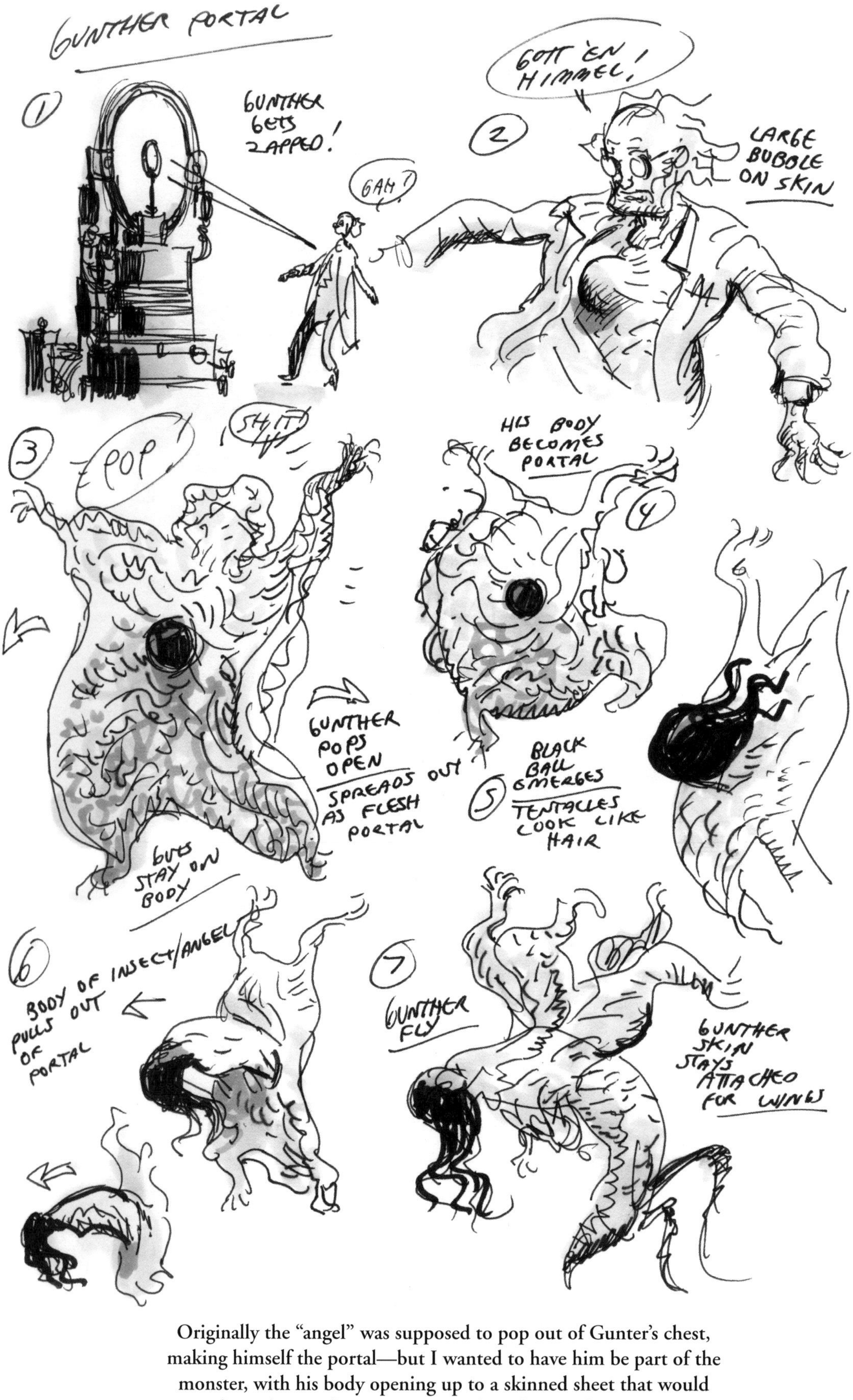
GUNTHER PORTAL
1
GUNTHER GETS ZAPPED!
GAH?
GOTT 'EN HIMMEL!
2
LARGE BUBBLE ON SKIN
3
POP
SHIT
GUNTHER POPS OPEN
SPREADS OUT AS FLESH PORTAL
GUTS STAY ON BODY
HIS BODY BECOMES PORTAL
4
BLACK BALL EMERGES
5
TENTACLES LOOK LIKE HAIR
6
BODY OF INSECT/ANGEL PULLS OUT OF PORTAL
7
GUNTHER FLY
GUNTHER SKIN STAYS ATTACHED FOR WINGS

Originally the "angel" was supposed to pop out of Gunter's chest, making himself the portal—but I wanted to have him be part of the monster, with his body opening up to a skinned sheet that would form the angel's wings as a nice horrific transformation.

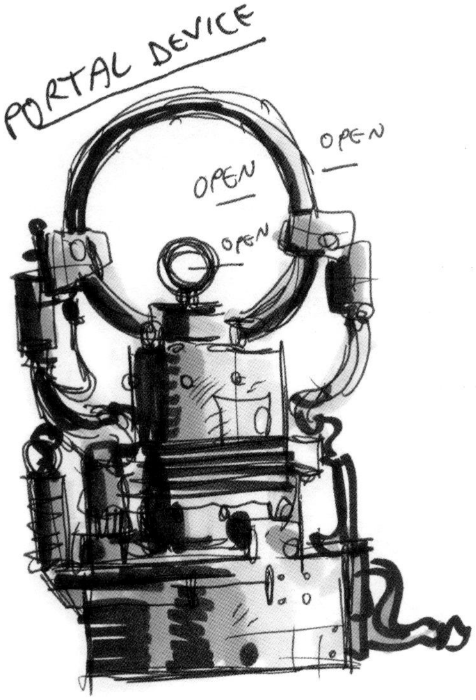
PORTAL DEVICE
OPEN
OPEN
OPEN

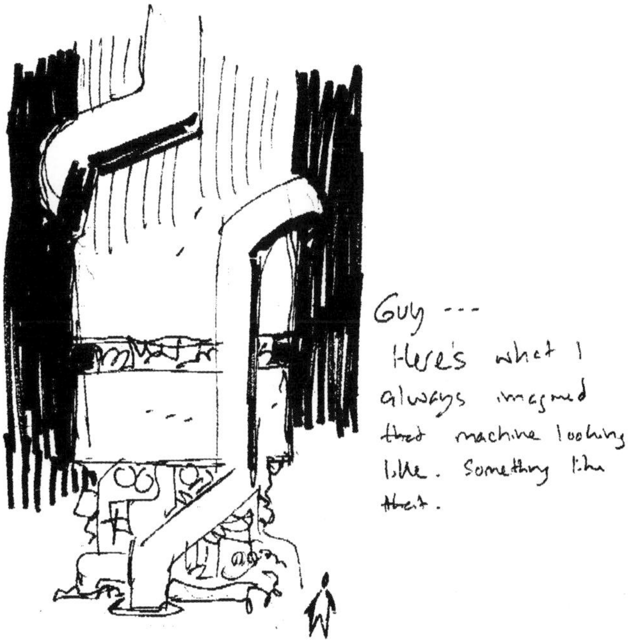
Guy ---
Here's what I always imagined that machine looking like. Something like that.

Above, the first design of the portal machine was too close in design to the "Hell-hole generator" from the *Hellboy* movie. Upper right is Mike's sketch of a blast-furnace-type design that I redrew into the final version, below.

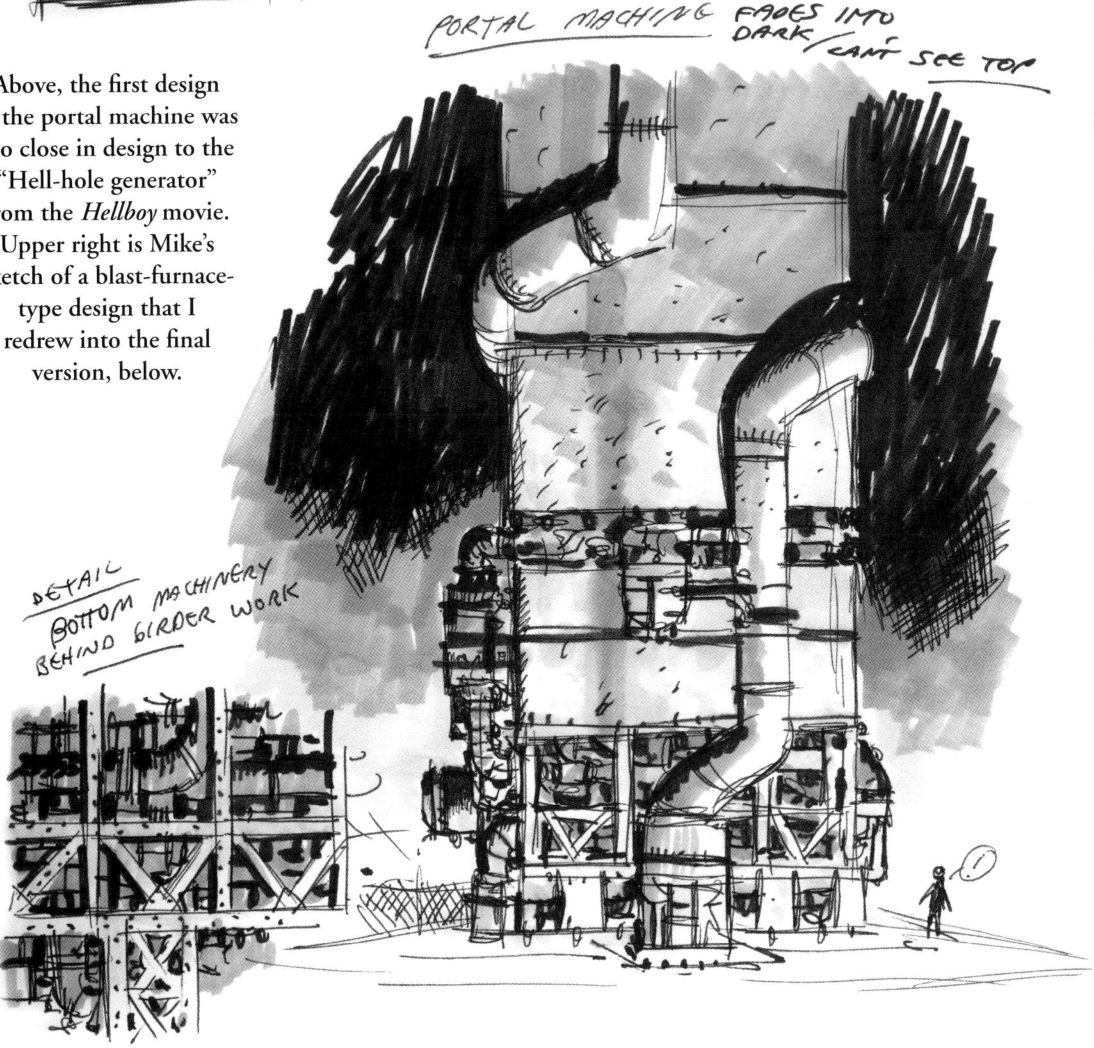
PORTAL MACHINE FADES INTO DARK/CAN'T SEE TOP
DETAIL
BOTTOM MACHINERY BEHIND GIRDER WORK

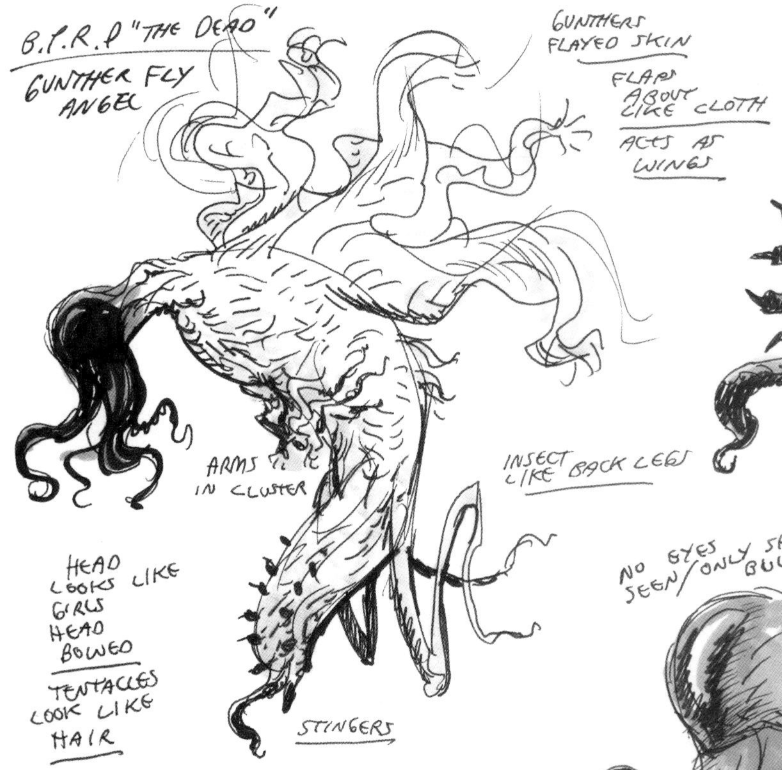
B.P.R.D "THE DEAD"
GUNTHER FLY ANGEL
GUNTHERS FLAYED SKIN
FLAPS ABOUT LIKE CLOTH
ACTS AS WINGS
ARMS IN CLUSTER
INSECT LIKE BACK LEGS
HEAD LOOKS LIKE GIRLS HEAD BOWED
TENTACLES LOOK LIKE HAIR
STINGERS

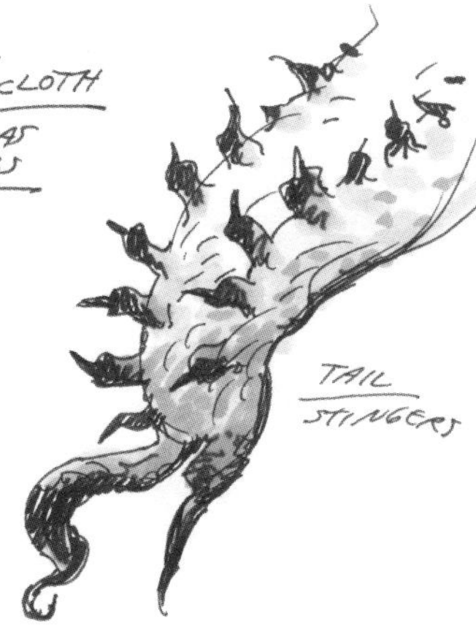
TAIL STINGERS

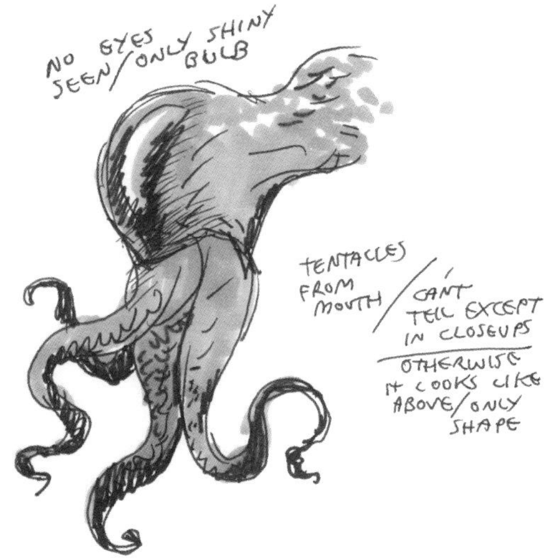
NO EYES SEEN/ONLY SHINY BULB
TENTACLES FROM MOUTH / CAN'T TELL EXCEPT IN CLOSEUPS
OTHERWISE IT LOOKS LIKE ABOVE/ONLY SHAPE

The "angel" was the one design in this series that went through the most reworking—while the basic body shape remained the same, the head went through a lot of redesigns. Originally it was a black mass of tentacles, but that was considered too close in feel to the design for Abe's wife, with her matted black hair.

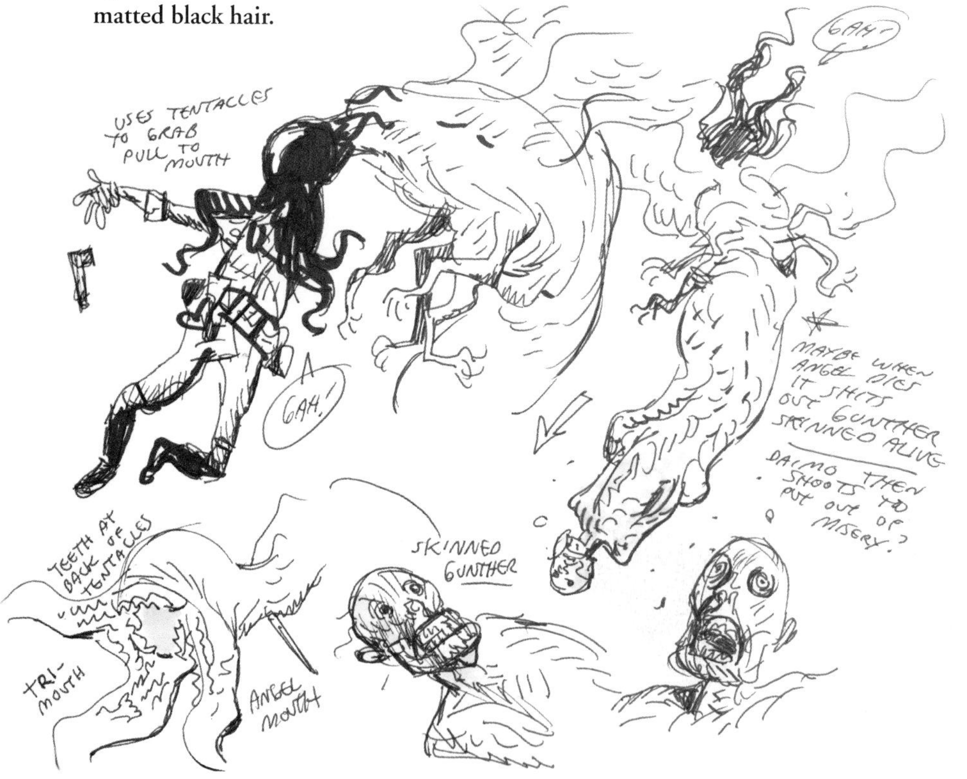
GAH!
USES TENTACLES TO GRAB PULL TO MOUTH
GAH!
MAYBE WHEN ANGEL DIES IT SHITS OUT GUNTHER SKINNED ALIVE
DAIMO THEN SHOOTS TO PUT OUT OF MISERY?
TEETH AT BACK OF TENTACLES
TRI-MOUTH
ANGEL MOUTH
SKINNED GUNTHER

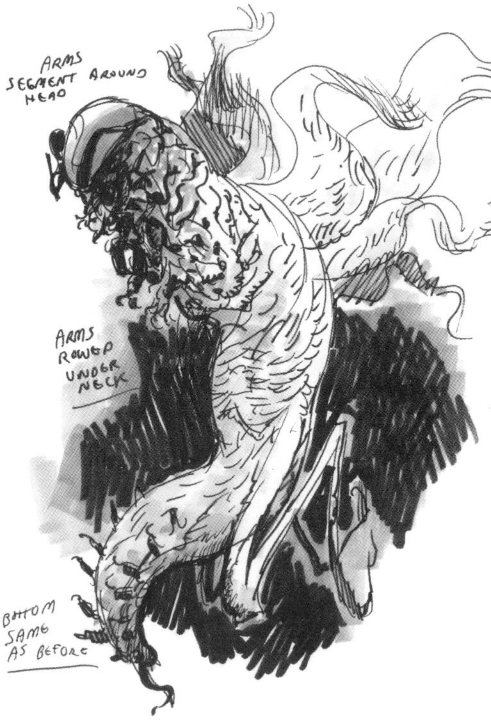
ARMS SEGMENT AROUND HEAD
ARMS ROWED UNDER NECK
BOTTOM SAME AS BEFORE

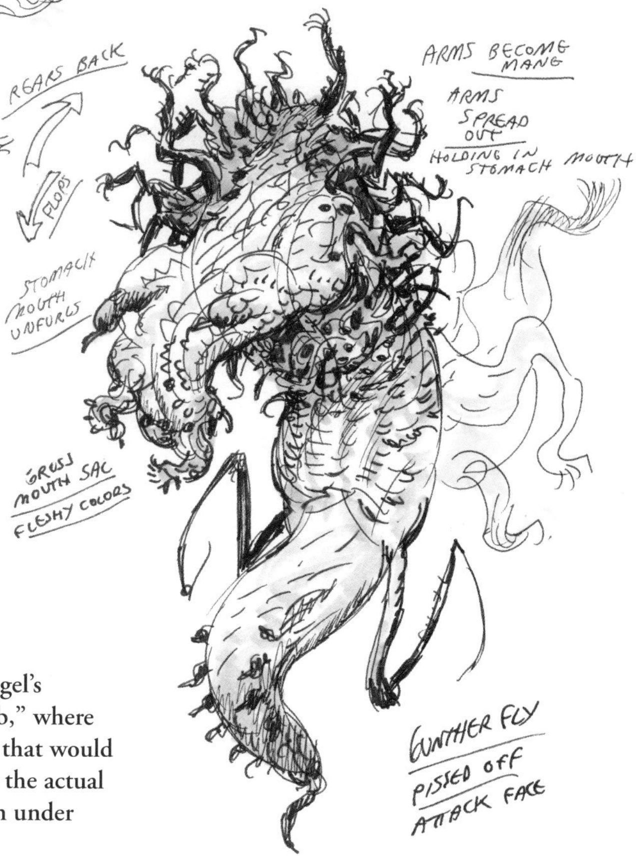
REARS BACK
FLOPS
STOMACH MOUTH UNFURLS
ARMS BECOME MANG
ARMS SPREAD OUT
HOLDING IN STOMACH MOUTH
GROSS MOUTH SAC
FLESHY COLORS
GUNTHER FLY
PISSED OFF
ATTACK FACE

The final direction for the angel's head was inspired by a "Heike crab," where the top of the head would be a shell that would resemble a stylized tribal face while the actual mouth and face would be hidden under the mass of arms.

—Guy Davis
Crab Point, MI

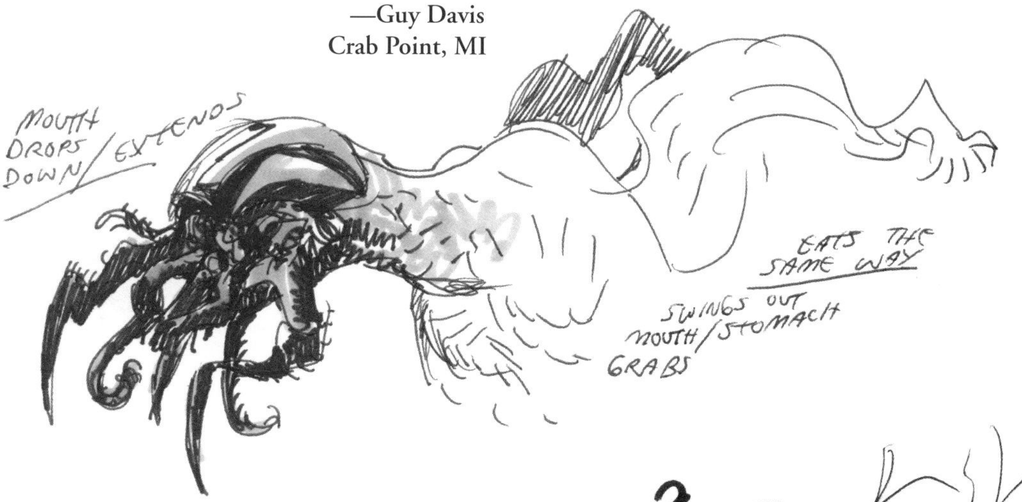
MOUTH DROPS DOWN/ EXTENDS
EATS THE SAME WAY
SWINGS OUT MOUTH/STOMACH
GRABS

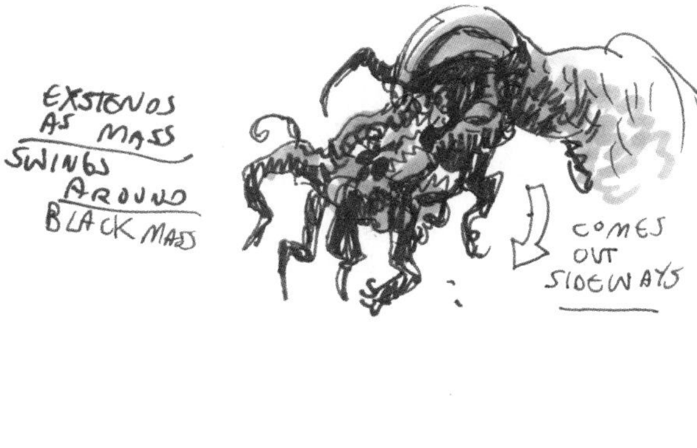
EXSTENDS AS MASS
SWINGS AROUND
BLACK MASS
COMES OUT SIDEWAYS

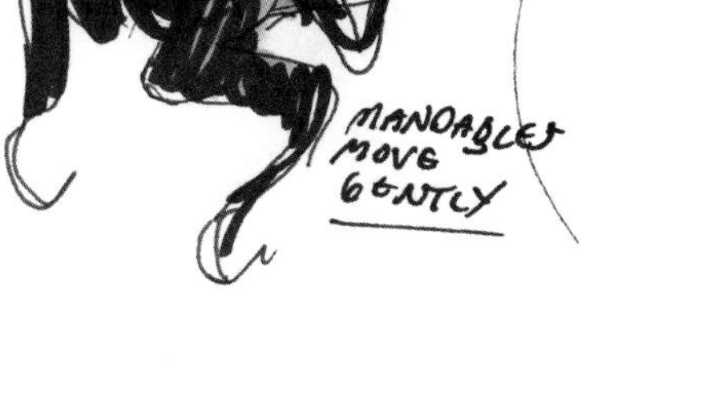
MANDABLES MOVE GENTLY

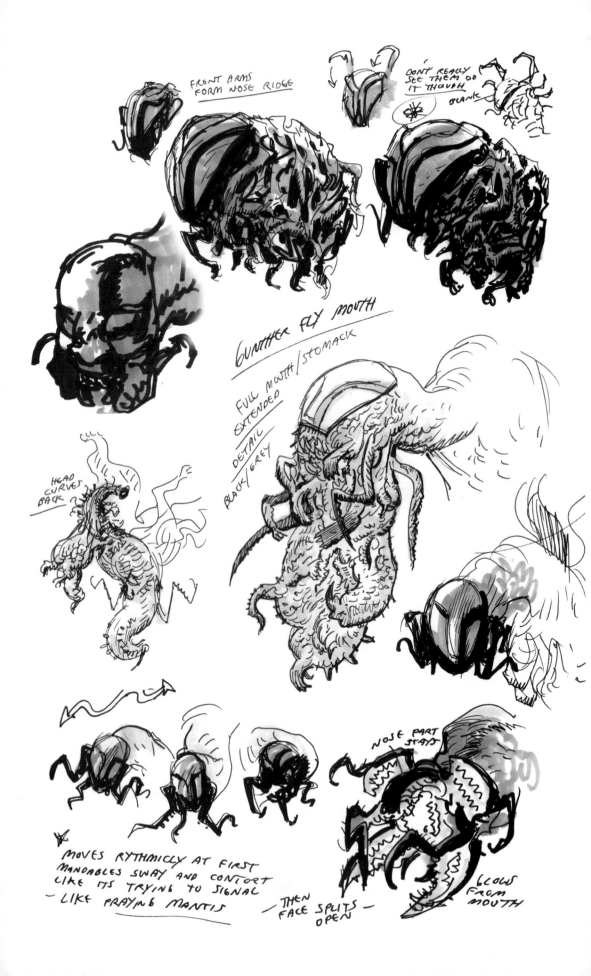

FRONT ARMS
FORM NOSE RIDGE

DON'T REALLY
SEE THEM DO
IT THOUGH

BLANK

GUNTHER FLY MOUTH

FULL MOUTH / STOMACK
EXTENDED

DETAIL

BLACK / GREY

HEAD
CURVES
BACK

NOSE PART
STAYS

MOVES RYTHMICLY AT FIRST
MANDABLES SWAY AND CONTORT
LIKE ITS TRYING TO SIGNAL
— LIKE PRAYING MANTIS

— THEN
FACE SPLITS
OPEN

GLOWS
FROM
MOUTH

ALSO FROM DARK HORSE BOOKS!

Mike Mignola
Jill Thompson
Evan Dorkin
Kelley Jones
Eric Powell
Gary Gianni
and others
The Dark Horse
BOOK OF THE DEAD

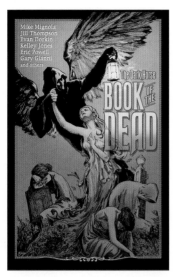

THE DARK HORSE BOOK OF THE DEAD

Mike Mignola, Guy Davis, Jill Thompson, Evan Dorkin, Kelley Jones, Gary Gianni, and others

Mike Mignola presents a *Hellboy* yarn combining Shakespeare and graverobbing, Guy Davis draws a tale of ill-fated love in ancient Japan, and Gary Gianni illustrates a rare story by *Conan* creator Robert E. Howard. And that's just a taste of the tales inside this hardcover horror anthology featuring the finest talents in comics.

$14.95, ISBN: 1-59307-281-3

"BREAKNECK STORYTELLING" — Wizard
"A GENUINELY FUN COMIC" — Keith Giffen
THE NEVERMEN
STREETS OF BLOOD
PHIL AMARA
GUY DAVIS

NEVERMEN: STREETS OF BLOOD

Phil Amara and Guy Davis

The Nevermen are a trio of trenchcoated punch-monkeys in fashionable eyewear that protect a dirty burg called Midnight City from Lovecraftian thugs. Yet far below the city streets, an even greater threat is brewing. He calls himself Winterbone, and he has something catastrophic in store for the city's goggled gangbusters.

$9.95, ISBN: 1-56971-823-7

THE GOON
HEAPS OF RUINATION
by Eric Powell

THE GOON VOLUME 3: HEAPS OF RUINATION

Eric Powell

Beware all undead minions and other variegated doers of badness! Start russlin' up trouble with the honest folks of Lonely Street and the Goon'll serve you up a fist sandwich but quick—as evidenced by the fine tales collected here, including a guest appearance by Hellboy, courtesy of artist extraordinairé Mike Mignola!

$12.95, ISBN: 1-59307-292-9

THE FOG

THE FOG

Scott Allie, Todd Herman, Andy Owens and Dave Stewart. Cover by Mike Mignola

An ancient curse has followed a group of Shanghai traders to America. But what does this weird fog have to do with a pyromaniac refugee from the Civil War, the disappearance of one of the traders' sons, or the terrible change coming over the Americans in this small seaside town?

$6.95, ISBN: 1-59307-423-9

AVAILABLE AT YOUR LOCAL COMICS SHOP OR BOOKSTORE

To find a comics shop in your area, call 1-888-266-4226

For more information or to order direct visit darkhorse.com or call 1-800-862-0052 • Mon.-Sat. 9 A.M. to 5 P.M. Pacific Time

***Prices and availability subject to change without notice**

DARK HORSE COMICS™ *drawing on your nightmares*
darkhorse.com

HELLBOY™

by MIKE MIGNOLA

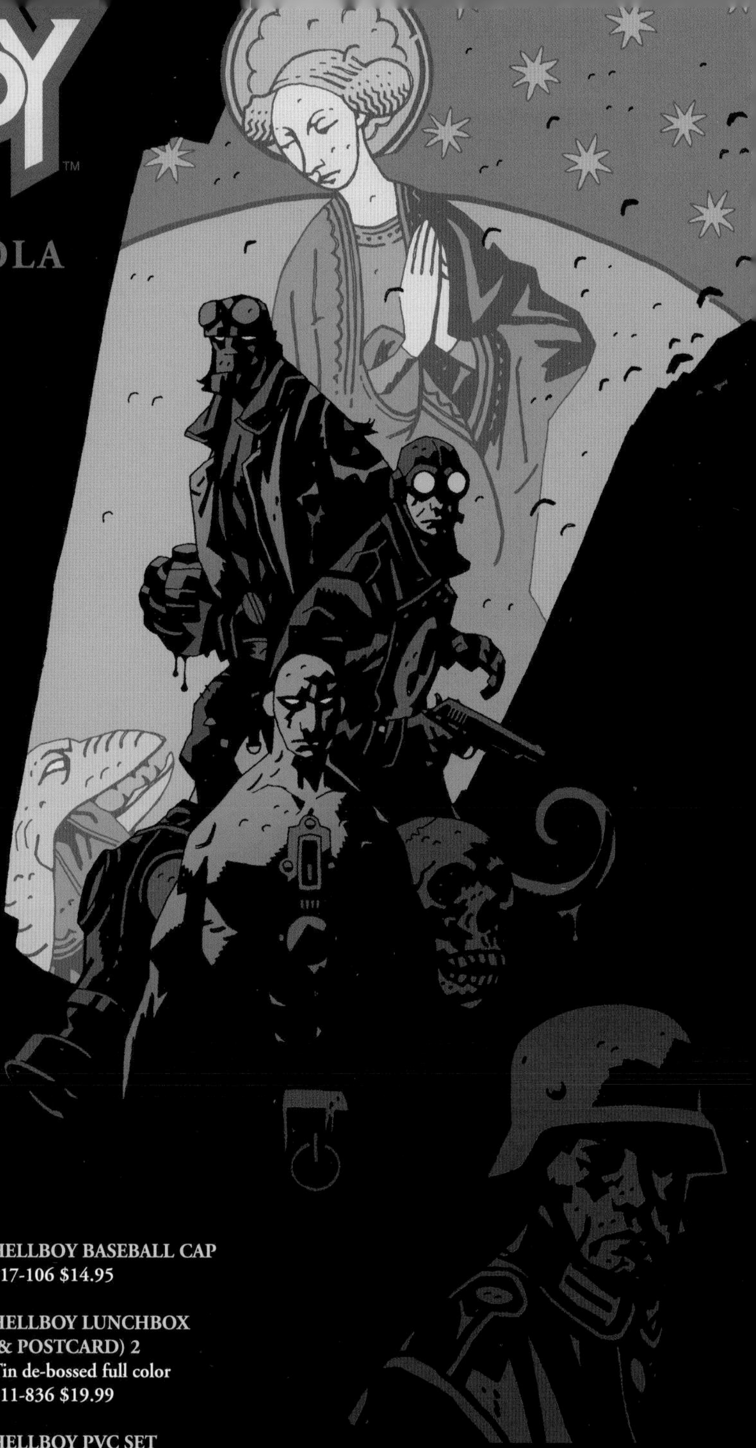

EED OF DESTRUCTION
vith John Byrne
SBN: 1-59307-094-2 $17.95

VAKE THE DEVIL
SBN: 1-59307-095-0 $17.95

'HE CHAINED COFFIN
AND OTHERS
SBN: 1-59307-091-8 $17.95

THE RIGHT HAND OF DOOM
SBN: 1-59307-093-4 $17.95

CONQUEROR WORM
SBN: 1-59307-092-6 $17.95

'HE ART OF HELLBOY
SBN: 1-59307-089-6 $29.95

HELLBOY WEIRD TALES
Volume 1
By John Cassaday, Jason Pearson,
Eric Powell, Alex Maleev,
Bob Fingerman and others
SBN: 1-56971-622-6 $17.95

HELLBOY WEIRD TALES
Volume 2
By John Cassaday, JH Williams III,
P. Craig Russell, Jim Starlin,
Frank Cho, Evan Dorkin and others
SBN: 1-56971-953-5 $17.95

B.P.R.D. HOLLOW EARTH
AND OTHERS
By Mike Mignola, Chris Golden,
Ryan Sook and others
SBN: 1-56971-862-8 $17.95

B.P.R.D. THE SOUL OF VENICE
AND OTHERS
By Mike Oeming, Guy Davis,
Scott Kolins, Geoff Johns and others
SBN: 1-59307-132-9 $17.95

ODD JOBS
Short stories by Mike Mignola,
Poppy Z. Brite, Chris Golden and others
Illustrations by Mike Mignola
SBN: 1-56971-440-1 $14.95

ODDER JOBS
Short stories by Frank Darabont,
Guillermo del Toro and others
Illustrations by Mike Mignola
SBN: 1-59307-226-0 $14.95

HELLBOY BASEBALL CAP
#17-106 $14.95

HELLBOY LUNCHBOX
(& POSTCARD) 2
Tin de-bossed full color
#11-836 $19.99

HELLBOY PVC SET
#10-666 $39.99

HELLBOY JOURNAL
#12-309 $9.99

HELLBOY TALKING BOARD
Pressed paper playing board with
wooden planchette
#10-248 $24.99

HELLBOY ZIPPO LIGHTER
#17-101 $29.95

HELLBOY BOOKS AND MERCHANDISE
CAN BE VIEWED AT www.darkhorse.com

To find a comics shop in your area, call 1-888-266-4226
For more information or to order direct:
•On the web: www.darkhorse.com
•E-mail: mailorder@darkhorse.com
•Phone: 1-800-862-0052 or (503) 652-9701
Mon.-Sat. 9 A.M. to 5 P.M. Pacific Time

DARK HORSE COMICS™ drawing on your nightmares